VIOLENCE, IMAGE AND VICTIM IN BATAILLE, AGAMBEN AND GIRARD

VIOLENCE, IMAGE AND VICTIM IN BATAILLE, AGAMBEN AND GIRARD

John Lechte

EDINBURGH
University Press

Edinburgh University Press is one of the leading university presses in the UK. We publish academic books and journals in our selected subject areas across the humanities and social sciences, combining cutting-edge scholarship with high editorial and production values to produce academic works of lasting importance. For more information visit our website: edinburghuniversitypress.com

© John Lechte, 2023, 2024

Edinburgh University Press Ltd
13 Infirmary Street,
Edinburgh, EH1 1LT

Typeset in 10/13 Warnock Pro by
IDSUK (DataConnection) Ltd

A CIP record for this book is available from the British Library

ISBN 978 1 3995 1977 9 (hardback)
ISBN 978 1 3995 1978 6 (paperback)
ISBN 978 1 3995 1979 3 (webready PDF)
ISBN 978 1 3995 1980 9 (epub)

The right of John Lechte to be identified as the author of this work has been asserted in accordance with the Copyright, Designs and Patents Act 1988, and the Copyright and Related Rights Regulations 2003 (SI No. 2498).

Contents

Preface	vi
Acknowledgements	x
Note	xi
INTRODUCTION	1
1. VICTIM AND VIOLENCE: BATAILLE VERSUS NIETZSCHE	20
2. BATAILLE: IMAGE AND VICTIM	50
3. RETHINKING AGAMBEN ON VIOLENCE	78
4. RETHINKING AGAMBEN ON THE IMAGE	108
5. GIRARD ON VIOLENCE AND THE VICTIM	133
6. IMAGE, VIOLENCE, VICTIM AND THE CRUCIFIXION: GIRARD'S VERSION	163
CONCLUSION: UNDERSTANDING VIOLENCE, IMAGE AND VICTIM	183
References	207
Index	223

Preface

To begin, let us look briefly at the bigger picture within which the following study is situated. In this regard, the world today is riven by violence and flooded with images. But what is this thing called violence and what exactly is an image? Perhaps some will say that a formal definition of violence and the image is unnecessary because when these terms are invoked in everyday discourse the context makes it clear as to what is meant. However, if it is a matter of who is a victim of violence, or of the deleterious effects of images on the psyche or of the sense in which an image is a medium, then something approaching a definition of the terms in question would seem to be indispensable. When victims of violence, especially in a domestic situation, claim – as is often the case – that the violence against them is symbolic or psychological and not just physical, is this truly violence? Can words be made into vehicles of violence? We need to know the answer to these questions. The dilemma is that once the significance of symbolic violence is fully appreciated, the way is opened for almost any form of human action to become violent under certain circumstances. And if the rights of victims are to be protected, violence – despite the difficulties involved – needs to be precisely defined.

Similarly, understanding the effects of the image in society – including the image as it occurs in a religious context – presupposes that it is possible to define an image exactly. And yet, if one thinks about it, it seems that almost any entity can, in equal measure, be a thing and an image. To think of a chair, for example, is to have an image of a chair in mind.

That the definition of an image is not straightforward is captured by the French philosopher, Henri Bergson, when he writes: 'by "image" we mean a certain existence which is more than that which an idealist calls a *representation*, but less than a materialist calls a *thing*' (2004: vii). And for his part, Gilles Deleuze has a chapter in his well-known masterpiece, *Difference and Repetition* (1994) called, 'The Image of Thought' (129–167), by which he means common sense notions that denude thought of its originality. Similarly, would an image of violence thereby denude violence of what is unique to it? How broad indeed is the notion of image!

An influential – if not the most influential – paradigm of the last fifty or so years has been the idea of 'medium specificity', an idea that first saw the light of day with Marshall McLuhan's slogan, 'the medium is the message'. It is a paradigm that appeared in conjunction with the equally long-standing 'social construction of reality' thesis, a thesis explicitly formulated in 1966 with Berger and Luckmann's book, *The Social Construction of Reality* (1966). In *Genealogy and Ontology of the Western Image and its Digital Future* (2012), I have effectively argued against the image being understood in terms of medium specificity, where, for example, a photograph would provide a photographic view of the world. I take this approach to the image in the following study, especially in Chapter 2 on Bataille and the image.

It is precisely because rigorous, general definitions of violence and the image are extremely elusive that it becomes illuminating to examine the way violence and the image operate in the works of key thinkers for whom these two concepts are central to their philosophical and scientific orientation.

Consequently, the aim of this book is to examine the way in which violence, image and victim figure in the work of (to adhere to the order of presentation on the chapters below) Georges Bataille, Giorgio Agamben, and René Girard. What brings the thinkers into proximity with each other with regard to violence is that, for all three, a real or potential victim is in focus. For Bataille, this is the sacrificial victim; for Agamben, this is, ostensibly, *homo sacer* as bare life and the ultimate victim; for Girard, it is the victim as scapegoat. That said, we would like to know just how, for each thinker, the victim comes to be central to violence. As will become evident, the significance of the victim is different in each case. Bataille, for instance approaches the victim not only in order to understand the sacred, but primarily as an experience of the death of the other. A key point in Agamben's take on the victim is that *homo sacer* cannot be sacrificed (which raises the question of whether *homo sacer can* truly be a victim), while Girard is keen to claim that Christ showed that sacrifice in sacrificial societies depends on the killing of a scapegoat, something repressed and hidden in the societies in question.

At play, when it comes in each case to the image as such, will be whether the image is understood to be opaque (the image as object and as 'media specific'), or whether it is understood to be transparent. In this regard, it will become clear that Agamben treats the image as opaque (as a 'pure means', as an object), while the transparency of the image – as will be shown in Chapter 2 – is important for Bataille. Girard also implicitly subscribes to a version of the image as transparent. Of course, to report on the image in the work of the three thinkers in this way does not at all exhaust what is at stake here. For it is the approach to the image as it is differently articulated in the writing of the three thinkers that is central. Consequently, it will be less a matter of how the image is theorised in the corpus at issue, and more a matter of showing the mode of significance that the image assumes in each individual oeuvre.

Closely linked to the latter point is the relationship between violence and the image, not just as this is consciously theorised (if indeed it is at all) by each of the thinkers but also as it emerges in their work. For example, without being the basis of a theorisation, the relation between violence and the image emerges in Girard's treatment of the Crucifixion and the question of Christ's divinity. Christ Himself is the image to the extent that He is divine.

In its broadest terms, then, the study will have been a success if the reader acquires a deeper and broader understanding of violence and the image – not only in general but as these terms work to give a more profound appreciation of the work of Bataille, Agamben and Girard.

No doubt it is worth noting – as a further justification of my focus – that each of the thinkers under investigation has thrown out a challenge as to how Western culture and politics operate. Agamben, for instance, has famously argued that the sovereign power in the West originates with the killing of the one who is outside of all law and moral action and as such is nothing but bare life – a killing that is neither a murder nor a sacrifice. Agamben has also proposed that the acclamation of power in the 'society of the spectacle' is essential to way sovereignty functions. And Bataille has located sacrifice in the general economy, an economy of pure expenditure that runs in parallel with the restricted economy that we are all familiar with – the economy of economic management where expenditure is supposed to be controlled. Bataille's thesis is that all religious experience occurs within the general economy. To speak of the general economy means that the notion of economy cannot be reduced solely to the restricted economy of conventional economic management.

Girard's claim that the scapegoat is at the origin of Western legal institutions entails that the real purpose of law is to curtail violence. But this curtailment will only be truly successful if it activates the main principle of Christianity, namely, the refusal to engage in violence against one's enemies. Girard's interpretation of the Crucifixion, and Christ as image, serves to reinforce this point. The Crucifixion, it could be argued, shows the truly mystical foundation of the image. For the image is both object and medium – a vehicle of pure facilitation – just as Christ is both human (object) and divine (medium). Present and past understandings of the image have endeavoured (unsuccessfully, in my view) to deny the mystical aspect of the image as medium.

Finally, it should be understood that the approach adopted in what follows is as much descriptive (it seeks to lay bare the contexts in which violence, image and victim figure in the work of the thinkers) as it is analytical, or argumentative. In other words, the wager is that it is just as important to show where and how the three aspects (whether separately or together) operate in the corpus in question, as it is to draw conclusions regarding the philosophical or theoretical significance of each of the terms concerned.

Acknowledgements

A shorter version of Chapter 2 appeared as 'Bataille: Image and Victim' in 2021 in *Theory, Culture and Society*, 38 (4), 3–22. I thank the editors of the journal for permission to publish this version of the article.

I would also like to thank the reviewers of the manuscript of this book, one of whom in particular offered meticulous advice that enabled me to make significant improvements to the text.

Note

Unless otherwise stated, all translations from the original French texts are my own.

Introduction

THE KEY TERMS OF this study are 'violence', 'victim' and 'image'. Each may be interpreted as they occur in the context specified. Broadly speaking, for the inflection Agamben wishes to place on them – largely in light of the thought of Walter Benjamin – the most important aspect of both violence and the image is covered by the term, 'mediality', which can rendered as 'pure means' in relation to violence, and as 'acclamation' in Agamben's study of government based on Guy Debord's notion of the 'society of the spectacle' (Debord 2006), where social relations are said to be mediated by images. As will become evident, it is the place and status of the victim that, with Agamben, remains ambiguous. '*Homo sacer*' – the one who can be killed without this being homicide or a sacrifice – is never referred to by Agamben as a victim. Moreover, the precise motivation for the *homo sacer*'s death is difficult to discern, other than to clarify the nature of the absolute power of sovereignty.

If Nietzsche's philosophy – supposedly so influential for Bataille – links the status of the victim to morality in general and to Christianity in particular, this is in order to show, it will be argued, that 'saving' the victim from the persecutor is, for Nietzsche, to rally against life – understood in the fullest sense as the biological, cultural and social being of the human. With Bataille, by contrast, the victim looms large. Indeed, Bataille's thought is consumed by the being of the victim. Bataille is thus to this extent against Nietzsche.

In the work of Bataille and Girard, by contrast with Agamben, violence becomes manifest because it has an object: the victim of violence.

Violence and victim are thus inextricably bound together – in sacrifice and torture, in the case of Bataille, and in relation to the scapegoat, in the case of Girard. We could almost (note the nuance) say that with Bataille and Girard, there is a valorisation of the victim.

With Bataille, image and victim are not connected in a systematic and general way, but in an incidental and more or less contingent way: in the caves of Lascaux, for example, and in the paintings of Edouard Manet. It behoves us therefore to provide an analysis of these themes that is as illuminating as possible. From this analysis, it will be concluded that, quite unlike Agamben, Bataille in no sense takes the image as an object, but rather implicitly assumes it to be a pure transparency. In brief, the image is essentially what is imaged. In one particular situation the image (photos of Chinese death by a thousand cuts) is evidence that, for Bataille, his being and that of the victim begin to coincide. Overall, Bataille's question is: how can one experience the being of the victim – a being that is ultimately confirmed in death?

Girard, too, adopts a contingent approach to the image, which is also assumed to be transparent and therefore not to be an object. However, unlike Bataille, where images seem to feature accidently, Girard's thought, as already mentioned, not only has the status of Christ in the Crucifixion as its basis (the Crucifixion being the 'proof' that Christ is the Son of God, and as such divine), but, at the same time, the status of the image of the Crucifixion is the focal point. For, once the event of the Crucifixion has taken place, Christ's status (divine or human) turns on whether or not He is, or can be encapsulated in, an image.

Problems Implicit in Undertaking a Study of Violence, Victim and the Image

Philosophically, Jean-Luc Nancy ostensibly offers a point of departure for our deliberations with his theory of the inseparability of both the image and violence, and the image and the sacred: 'The image is always sacred' (2005: 1) and, moreover: 'the distinction of the image' resembles sacrifice, although it is not strictly speaking sacrificial (3). Nancy thus evokes the theme of our study in his reflection on the image. In this vein, he goes on to speak of 'what can link, in a particular way, the image of violence to the violence of the image' (15). And he adds: 'Violence always makes an image of itself' (20). And again: 'Violence, as we have begun to see, always completes itself in an image' (20). To the extent that one can follow Nancy's argument, violence is irrevocably attached to the image because violence, to be what it is, makes a mark. A mark, however, is an instance of the 'shadow' (index) of the thing, not the image as such. By making much of the exemplary value for grasping the nature of the image of the Catholic ostensorium, or 'monstrance' as the vehicle-displaying Host (Christ's corporeal presence) (21–22), Nancy comes closer to my understanding of the image, to the extent that the ostensorium would be transparent in the interest of an unimpeded view of the reliquary contained in it. But, to complicate matters, Nancy also says that: 'The image is a thing that is not the thing: it distinguishes itself from it essentially' (2). For this study, the problem is the image as a thing because, precisely, it is theorised as not being a thing.

The body of Agamben's *homo sacer* (Agamben 1998) could be equivalent to a monstrance – to an ostensorium – to the extent that it is a 'showing' of violence. If it is present at all, this body is so only by virtue of violence that forever evokes sovereign power. In short, if one agrees to accept the reality of *homo sacer* the latter puts us directly in touch with power as violence. It may well become an image of violence. This is what I shall develop further. The key here is that the image, as transparent, is the presence of the thing in its absence, as I have argued after Sartre (see Lechte 2012).

The ambiguity of Nancy's postulation lies in the difficulty of deciding whether the image is in the monstrance, or in the wafer (Host), or reliquary, displayed by the same monstrance. Theologically, the wafer is Christ's body – which might give weight to the notion that, as transparent, the monstrance enables Christ's body to be present. On another level, however (that of a secular interpretation), it is the wafer that gives rise to the body of Christ as present. As such, it is the wafer that becomes Host and is the presence of Christ in his absence. Whether taking a philosophical, a quasi-theological or a secular approach to the image, the latter will always be understood in what follows to be transparent, which means that it is not an object.[1] This position can be held because this is how (even for Agamben[2]) the image implicitly works for each of the thinkers in this study, none of whom offers anything like a detailed phenomenological or analytical account of the image, despite its determining role in their engagement with violence and the sacred.[3]

But can violence be treated philosophically, that is, theoretically? Is language capable of addressing violence? According to Georges

Bataille, language is the voice of civilisation and therefore the opposite of violence, which is silent (Bataille 1987: 185). Barbarity, the opposite of civilisation is silent; it is the silence of the inarticulate. Given that I aim in part to engage in a meditation on violence, we are clearly entering the realm of paradox if Bataille's judgement is correct. On the other hand, it is surely possible to write insightfully *about* violence (does Bataille not do this himself?) without being obliged to *show* violence – even if 'hate speech' might come close to blurring the difference in question.[4]

What Bataille has to say about Sade's writing heightens the paradox relating to the claim that violence is opposed to language, that it is silent. For surely Sade writes violence! Bataille, indeed, recognises this paradox (185–188). To understand Bataille's explicit position (which can differ from what is implicit), it is important to note that in no way is he an admirer of Sade, even if he, at the same time, appreciates him for what he is: a depraved provocateur and the presenter or what is entirely outrageous. As Bataille writes: 'I would like to speak of him only with those who are revolted by him and from their point of view' (179). It is thus not a matter of being shown the truth (however awful) about humanity so that, finally, the veil of hypocrisy might be lifted. Just the opposite. Sade reveals the domain that must always be 'repressed', or at least controlled, if society is to exist at all. For all this, Sade does reveal an undeniable aspect of human life – but only an aspect, not human life as such. He shows the aspect that must be controlled and never allowed to have free reign.

But how is Sade able to do this if violence is mute? How can the victim have a voice? How can suffering have a voice? How can Sade be so shocking if violence is silent and unavailable to consciousness? These are questions to be addressed in Chapter 1, where the victim and violence in Bataille's work are at issue, and again in the Conclusion.

*

Jean-Luc Nancy (to turn to him again) gives what he claims to be an illustration of violence: the extraction of a screw with a pair of pliers rather than a screwdriver. How are we to understand violence from this example? Using pliers is not the *proper* way to extract a screw. It is the *wrong* way – the disorderly way – to do it. The screw is extracted, the goal is achieved, but the means are violent. Immediately, two issues arise: the first is that this is only one among countless possible examples of actual, or literal violence. Secondly, rather than thinking violence, it is an illustration of what is *called* violence. Even interpretation can be called violent.[5]

Perhaps Nancy would not be in error by responding to the question of violence with an example rather than attempting an exhaustive definition. Perhaps violence as such might be unthinkable – that philosophising about violence might well do violence to philosophy! When confronting violence – when attempting to think violence – philosophy, more often than not (and perhaps for good reason), is forced to give up the quest by pointing to literal violence, to what is called violence. However, Nancy, as if endeavouring to keep a philosophical approach alive, but at the same time recognising the difficulty it poses, says in part that, 'violence does not participate in any order of reasons, nor any set of forces oriented towards results. It denatures, wrecks, and massacres that which it assaults. Violence does not transform what it assaults; rather, it takes away its form and meaning' (2005: 16). If the latter is the case, how can violence operate effectively in the ritual of human sacrifice and thus in relation to the sacred? Whether it does act effectively will also be discussed in Chapter 1 in relation to the famous study of sacrifice by Henri Hubert and Marcel Mauss (1981), the study that introduces the victim, the entity, as will be shown, so important to Bataille. The victim is not only fundamental in Bataille's thought but is also the central figure – as *homo sacer* – in Giorgio Agamben's political philosophy In fact, this aspect – *homo sacer* as essentially a victim – has hardly been given its due in the voluminous literature on this theme.[6]

Violence and the image are linked in Agamben to the extent that both entities – in light of Walter Benjamin's and Guy Debord's thinking – constitute an extant 'mediality'. Here mediality is the appearance of the medium (or means) as such independently of any end. It is neither a means to an end, nor an end in itself. Walter Benjamin's 'divine violence' (see W. Benjamin 1986) is, according to Agamben, the appearance of pure means. Language is the appearance of pure means, especially in relation to politics, as will be confirmed in Chapter 4.[7] For its part, gesture confirms the idea of 'pure means',[8] and the image is a pure means for Agamben, as mentioned, in the 'society of the spectacle'. It remains, then, to investigate what to many would seem to be the paradox the appearing of the medium – the medium being that which, *qua* medium, does not appear.[9]

Pure violence, as pure means, constitutes a break from the law where violence is always the means to an end and never a means as such. Pure violence, then, is violence appearing *qua* violence and thus as pure means. Whether or not it is possible to agree with Agamben, for him, pure violence opens the way to a new form of revolutionary politics that is no longer connected to the history of the formation of the state and the legal system that gives it currency. Once the state has been 'deactivated' – as Agamben would say – the way is open for the emergence of the human as sabbatical animal – a form of the human not determined by work or a project but by play, by doing for the sake of doing, all in the interest of pure mediality. In this light, the 'society of the spectacle' (where images are rampant) gives rise to the media acclamation that power needs in order to maintain itself. 'Acclamation' is the term Agamben uses to characterise modern-day political life. Political theology shows that the term *oikonomia* is evocative of acclamation and can only be validly interpreted in light of the history of Western theology, where it assumes a meaning that is not related to utility – utility being the basis of so much of modern political theory, most notably as exemplified by the *oikos* in the thought of Hannah Arendt (see Arendt 1958).

Despite the emphasis on the appearing of mediality, Agamben, in a number of texts, also seems to accept that the 'taking place of language' is equivalent to language's disappearance (the disappearance of language as medium) into what it expresses. Thus: 'Language is very weak, in the sense that it cannot but disappear in the thing it names' (2018b: 9–10). Why is it that language, unlike the image, cannot become an explicit mediality here – even if it could be argued that an *explicit* mediality is, by definition, problematic? What distinguishes language as such from the image as such is that, like language, the imaged could not appear if the image appeared as such (i.e., if it were an object in its own right). Seen this way, there does not seem to be any reason to treat the image differently from language. However, as we will see later, there is a difference between language and violence and the image and violence. For while there can be an image of violence, Bataille's insight, as we have seen, is that there can be no language of violence.

*

As I have already emphasised, the image is treated in this study as distinct from the explicit mediality, as Agamben proposes, or from 'media specificity', as many current media commentators propose. Indeed, were the ultimate objectives not different, the image as understood here could well evoke what Jacques Derrida in *Of Grammatology* (2016) calls 'trace'. Even though the imaged might be thought to be equivalent to a sensible plenitude and thus at variance with what the deconstructionist would accept, the image, like the trace (but surely like all media), is not (*pace* Agamben) a sensible plenitude, that is, what is present. Thus: 'The graphic sign is not seen; and the acoustic image is not heard' (70). In my more prosaic language, this means that the image can never be an object or a thing. Again, Derrida confirms that trace is 'that which does not let itself be summed up in the simplicity of a present' (72). The notion of trace is of fundamental importance in Derrida's deconstructive philosophy. In this regard, it contributes to a critique of Saussure's notion of the sign (cf. Agamben 2016: 76–79) as well as to the dethroning of the dominance of presence in Western metaphysics. The trace as such is not present; were there to 'be' presence, the trace would be its condition of possibility. In terms of time, if the trace is the origin of presence, this implies that, as has now become well-known, an origin that is not present, or a non-origin at the origin.

I do not wish to claim that the notion of trace fully comprehends what I intend by image. Indeed, it is likely that what I refer to, after Sartre, as the image as the presence of the thing in its absence, Derrida would say is also implied in the notion of trace. Or as the deconstructionist says, referring to the sign: 'The signified face, to the extent that it is still originarily distinguished from the signifying face, is not considered a trace; by rights, it has no need of the signifier to be what it is' (2016: 79). Thus I say that the imaged has no need of the image to be what it is. The imaged does not derive from the image. By contrast, Derrida argues that the signified face is ultimately trace: 'the signified is originarily and essentially [. . .] trace, that it is *always already in the position of the signifier*' (79).

As I do not wish to follow Derrida any further on this theme,[10] let me summarise that Agamben's claim that 'mediality' can appear as such implies that the medium can be present, that the medium (image, voice, sign) is in the end a mode of presence. The medium as trace, on the other hand, implies that the medium is not present, even if it might give rise to what is present. Whether – and if so how – the notion of the imaged might fall into the category of 'a present' is, as will be seen, an abiding source of debate in relation to René Girard's work.

*

What, however, is the link between image and violence in Girard's thought? Certainly, Girard works with what we commonly think of as images *of* violence, such as the head of John the Baptist and other representations. The head of John the Baptist is indeed an *index* of violence rather than the presentation of violence as such – as an image. It may well be that violence never appears as such. Nevertheless, in an attempt to reveal what is in play here, the study investigates the Crucifixion, which Girard says is not the sacrifice of a scapegoat, but the revelation of the deep injustice of sacrificing the scapegoat. The Crucifixion is about Christ having violence done to Him and in the process 'turning the other cheek' – exhorting people everywhere to love their enemies, to forgive unreservedly. The Crucifixion can be understood either as sacrifice (of a scapegoat) – which is the interpretation that perpetuates violence – *or* as the non-sacrificial, non-violent interpretation, which deifies death. Girard says: 'Christ and the Word of God are [. . .] one and the same thing' (Girard 1987b: 206). If the 'word becomes flesh', it is plausible to say that 'flesh' is also the realm of the image as the presence of God as such. There is not, however, a perfect fit between violence and the image; the link might be only partial. Only after a thorough investigation of the theme in question will it be possible to reach anything like a conclusion on this issue.

So, with Girard's valorisation of the Crucifixion, we want to know whether, theologically speaking, Christ's divinity entails that He is an image and whether, more prosaically, Christ as image can be circumscribed in an image. Also, just how is Christ, as Girard maintains, the medium of the communication of the end of the murder of the scapegoat? This will be the focus of the discussion in Chapter 6. Does Girard imply through his interpretation of the Crucifixion that violence can be eliminated from the world? Political philosophers who follow Nietzsche say assuredly it cannot. And, certainly, the claim that humanity is essentially a violent species founded in conflict has for many an undeniable plausibility. In this study, though, the version of Christ's death as presented by Girard, augers in, as has been foreshadowed, the potential end of violence – violence in the first instance perpetrated on victims. Christ is the first victim to show the possible end of victimage. Violence and therefore victims constitute, for Girard, the origin of humanity, much as the primal horde does for Freud. Furthermore, in reading myths carefully Girard proposes that there was an actual, original act of violence (a murder) that was the result of the first sacrificial crisis, a crisis that began the cycle of vengeance and the killing (murder) of scapegoat victims – killing that supposedly brought a (temporary) halt to violence (Girard 1972, 1986). The truth of this, Girard thinks, was only revealed by Christ on the Cross. Here, Girard does not claim to be a theologian, but a researcher who takes seriously what the text of the Bible refers to. In effect, he claims to take a scientific approach to reading the Bible. Others, as we shall see, are sceptical and sense that Girard's conclusions may be the product of his Christian faith. I will suggest that while some critics may have misunderstood Girard on this point, it is a huge leap on Girard's part to link the Crucifixion to the emergence of an entire culture (Western culture) based in judicial institutions. A more subtle approach is thus called for when it comes to interpreting the role of the Crucifixion in the evolution of law in Western culture, and, similarly, greater subtlety is called for with regard to Girard's approach to hominisation. The main criticism of the latter, as will be seen in Chapter 5, is that Girard ignores the basic findings of prehistorians on the evolution of the human.

The image of Christ on the Cross is thus an image of the end of the sacrificial crises that brought about the deaths of so many scapegoats. But is it correct to speak about the 'image' of the Cross? As we shall see, the theological and philosophical arguments are complex, turning as they do around definitions of the difference(s) between 'icon', 'idol', 'image', 'symbol', 'type' and 'token'. Most of all, perhaps, one would want to know whether, and if so how, Christ's divinity can be ascertained (circumscribed) by way of the image of the Crucifixion – the image, for Girard, of the end of (a certain form of) violence. But can there be an image of the Crucifixion without the Bible – that is, without a theological contextualisation? Or again – to cite Hans Belting – can that be an icon/image for which the prototype is the Crucifixion itself? (Belting 1996: 263).[11] Girard is silent on such questions. Is this appropriate, given the centrality of the Cross in his argument about the ending of violence?

Girard's claims, then, remain to be examined in detail along with the nature of the relation between *homo sacer* and power in the work of Giorgio Agamben. How is it that *homo sacer* can be subjected to unmitigated violence? Is it possible that *homo sacer* as a scapegoat (victim) can offer, in being killed – in being the object of violence – a way of bringing a halt to violence? As noted (see note 6), Depootere is the commentator who has looked at Agamben's figure in these terms. However, the victim as such is rarely thematised in Agamben's thinking, possibly because the theorist of *homo sacer* has little time for conventional anthropological notions of the sacred and sacrifice – notions founded on ambivalence. Instead, the one whose killing can be neither murder nor sacrifice is the basis of sovereignty and thus the basis of the modern political order.

While Girard is an unflinching opponent of violence, Agamben may well be – as I say in Chapter 3 – 'its unrepentant apologist'. For his part, Bataille, glued as he is to death and the violence of sacrifice, engages with violence uniquely with respect to the death of the victim. Violence is inevitable, Bataille says in his reading of Sade, yet we must fight against it.

*

As already intimated, for Bataille, 'victim' has a special meaning and significance. Perhaps the victim is marked above all by a certain passivity – but there are grounds for saying that this is also an active passivity, a passivity that marks itself out as such and thus marks out the victim as victim in relation to violence. Nietzsche, by contrast, puts the opposite case: everything evocative of the victim is disparaged in the interest of the 'persecutor' (to use Girard's term) – the one not afraid to become the exception that he is, the exception as warrior.[12] By endeavouring to occupy the place of the victim of violence Bataille, in stark contrast to Nietzsche's contempt for victims (equivalent to 'the weak' of Christianity), lends a new visibility to this theme, a visibility linked to images, especially in the realm of art.

For Nietzsche's thought after *The Birth of Tragedy*, where the Apollonian principle seems to evoke the image, images become idols in ideals (whether these be moral or political or the ideas of idealist philosophy from Plato to Hegel). Such ideals are against 'life' as the 'will to power'. As idols they need to be hit hard with a hammer, so that the sound of their hollowness reverberates everywhere. Again, for Nietzsche, images are passive, static and eternal, not dynamic and historical, like the will to power. It is also very likely that Nietzsche sensed the theological aspect of an experience of the image, which would be sufficient for him to reject it as a mode of access to a prototype or to reality.

For Nietzsche, the victim resembles an image, in as far as to be a victim is stamped into a milieu from which there is no escape. Even more pertinently, the preservation of victims is against the dynamism of life. Bataille's position, it will be shown, is opposed to Nietzsche's here – whether wittingly or not. Bataille is opposed to Nietzsche because Nietzsche valorises the violence of the strong, of the exception, of the persecutor. Life, says the philosopher, throws up so many instances of violence that it puts the relationship of the weak and life to the test. Here Socrates is the first of the weak, as life for him was a form of sickness. With his death, Socrates, the exemplar of the corruption of the Apollonian principle, becomes the West's first exemplary victim.[13] While Nietzsche commentators are prepared to mention that violence and cruelty do figure in the iconoclast's oeuvre, they are not prepared to concede that in fact violence and cruelty, together with the attack on Christianity, are central to his thought. Least of all is this the case for Heidegger in his four-volume exegesis (Heidegger 1991a, 1991b).[14]

Bataille's valorisation of the victim becomes strikingly obvious when compared to Nietzsche's heralding of the qualities of the warrior-persecutor. Many of Bataille's readers have, however, assumed that an affinity exists between Bataille and Nietzsche, not a diremption. The latter needs to be highlighted. Because it has been assumed that Nietzsche was a positive influence on Bataille, the difference between him and Nietzsche has hardly been remarked upon.

As might have already been gathered, gravitation towards the victim (as opposed to the persecutor) does not mean that victimage is necessarily an explicit theme in Bataille's writing. Sometimes, the contrary is true, as for example when the thinker shows his fascination with the Sadian monster, Gilles de Rais (1404–1440),[15] or with notorious murderers, such as Erzsébet Báthory[16] and Dr Marcel Petiot.[17] The figure of Gilles de Rais is no doubt a cross-over point for an understanding of Bataille and the victim. Initially, Bataille's interest in his introduction to the trial of the mass murderer seems to be in violence itself – in the violence of de Rais the persecutor, engaged, like the Germanic, *Berserkir* ('bear skin'), in the most extreme, uninhibited violence, a violence that revealed a childlike relation to prohibitions.[18] In the end, though, Bataille finds de Rais to be a tragic figure – indeed, one of Shakespearean proportions, and someone who suffered enormously before and during his trial because of his great fear of being excommunicated. But is this enough to justify Bataille's apparent refusal to condemn de Rais's actions out of hand? This is the question that calls for a response.

Nevertheless, by far the greater part of Bataille's trajectory concerns pain and death from the victim's perspective – that of death as communication and the continuity of being, meaning that death is faced full on without mitigation, without the 'discontinuity' characteristic of life as the individuality of beings. Death, Bataille explains in his study of eroticism, overcomes the separation of beings: 'death, being the destruction of a discontinuous being, does not at all touch the continuity of being, which generally exists outside of us' (Bataille 1987: 27). Although he claims that, in considering sacrifice, his point of departure is that of 'French sociology' (Durkheim, Mauss), it is the victim in sacrifice that holds Bataille's attention. To speak of a victim here means that the one chosen to be executed does not deserve to die as it also entails for Bataille the arousal of extreme anguish in an observer/witness. Anguish gives rise to a 'continuity': it is a communication that arises unannounced and is entirely involuntary – like laughter, which is the equivalent of the lifting of anguish. Bataille acknowledges the work of French sociology, but rather than the stages of the sacrificial ritual as set out by Hubert and Mauss, he is absorbed in the fate of the victim. This will be highlighted in detail in Chapter 2. It is, then, death as the sacrifice of a victim that is the clearest instance of the continuity of being. The sacred is where 'a victim is put to death' (Bataille 1987: 29) and where the victim reveals the continuity of being, the equivalent of a loss of self in the other. Bataille's endeavour is thus centred on revealing an experience of the victim as the vehicle of death as communication and the continuity that overcomes the abyss separating discontinuous beings. Here discontinuity refers to the individuality and 'presence' of the self. Through its connection to prohibition and transgression the sacred can also give birth to monster persecutors. But persecutors as discontinuous beings are only of interest to Bataille because their victims evoke death and continuity.

Bataille, in a revelatory reading of Sade and the victim, shows that the 'normal man' (by comparison with the 'sovereign' persecutor) does not evolve into anything abnormal. Rather, normality, we shall see, is part of being human. The normal person is situated in the restricted economy of work and production. Violence, eroticism, intoxication and death are, by comparison, the other side of the moon. It is never possible to normalise violence, nor should one attempt to do so, for fear of ruining everything that is essentially human. To normalise Sade, to admire Sade, as the Surrealists tried to do, is to fail to understand what his writing really signifies.

The question that now arises is whether Nietzsche's much despised herd individual is the equivalent of Bataille's 'normal man'. Certainly, for Nietzsche the herd evokes utility in morality as well as the notion of socialism, which presumably stands for the valorisation of work, or labour, and therefore, utility. Herd individuals cannot cease being what they are; it is in their nature. Whereas the 'normal man' has a foot in both camps: normality can turn into the exceptional, as the phenomenon of carnival (where, compared to what is 'normal', things can be turned on their head) amply demonstrates.

*

As concerns the photograph of *lingchi* (Chinese 'death by a thousand cuts' torture and execution[19]), Bataille's relation to the victim is played out – a relation as we shall see that has been subjected to some intense scrutiny. What is the nature of Bataille's actual relation to these images of torture? Is it in any way of a sado-masochistic, scopophilic, fetishistic, voyeuristic or, indeed, 'mystical' nature? Such propositions are wide of the mark; for it is not (and a full appreciation of inner experience confirms this) about Bataille as ego/subject before the tortured victim, but about Bataille's capacity to experience the victim's suffering. This should not lead us to assume that Bataille is the victim's *advocate* – at least not in the first instance. Rather, just as eroticism in Bataille's depiction is about inducing a dissolution of the borders between discontinuous beings, so an experience of the victim's experience implies the self becoming victim. This is very different from engaging in a battle to end victimage, even if this could, ultimately, be the possible outcome of Bataille's engagement with the pain and death of the victim.

Like the *lingchi* photographs, the image in Bataille's writing on Manet and the Lascaux Caves is not to be understood in terms of 'media specificity', but as a pure transparency that gives access to the real. The images of animals in the caves have magical qualities and are a reminder of the inferiority, compared to animals, felt by Magdalenian humans of prehistory. Moreover, to kill the animal effigy is to enhance the success of the hunt in the sense that the animal will be induced to allow itself to be killed. On one level, the animal could be taken to be the quintessential victim; humans as victims thus resemble animals. But, Bataille suggests, the hunted animal was never a victim in the way that certain humans have been victims of murder and torture throughout the ages. The equality evoked by the animal images is thus something contemporary humanity can learn from.

As will become evident in Chapter 2, Bataille's study of Manet reveals that the image is tied to a certain (scandalous) realism (the figure of Olympia, indeed, is not god-like); nudes are of everyday life (neither idealised nor purified). The victim, as far as Manet is concerned – as with Bataille's encounter with the figure of the child murderer, Gilles de Rais – is inseparable from the issue of Manet *as* victim, a victimage, Bataille says, deriving from Manet's lack of recognition. That is to say, a victim in Manet's paintings is not easy to discern – although such an entity is far from absent. The context in which victimage does play a key part, however, is in relation to Manet's life as a painter. This, then, will be examined in some detail.

Taken as a whole, art cannot be separated from play, Bataille says in his study of Lascaux, and this means that through art there is a link to the festival, to the sacred, and thus to violence. There are examples in Manet's oeuvre that evoke the sacred, violence and death. In every instance of violence, there is a victim. Art, therefore, is – whether directly or indirectly – about victims. As such, Manet's paintings are in keeping with the destiny of art itself, as are the works of Picasso a generation later (cf. *Guernica*).

Origin and Interpretation as Violence and the Image

As mentioned earlier, debate has occurred regarding Girard's claim that the victim of violence is at the origin of society, and this has been compared to Derrida's critique of origin as being fully present, identical with itself – an origin that is undone due to the necessity for a supplement that, like the trace as discussed earlier, would enable the origin to be what it is. Derrida illustrates this philosophical point in his writing on Rousseau, and particularly in a reading of Rousseau's *Essay on the Origin of Languages* (see Derrida 2016: 179–292). Thus every time Rousseau wants to claim the rigour of an origin – e.g., poetry as the origin of language, melody as the origin of music – the logic of the supplement appears. Harmony appears within melody; the chromatic scale of semi-tones (as dealt with by Rousseau in his *Complete Dictionary of Music* (1779)) appears as the necessary supplement of the diatonic scale, so that 'the chromatic scale [*gamme*], is to the origin of art what writing is to speech' (Derrida 2016: 232). Moreover, colour appears as the necessary supplement to the art of design (233). What Rousseau shows, says Derrida, without wanting to show it, is that 'writing [what is thought to be secondary] precedes and follows speech, it comprehends it' (259). And: 'writing had to appear even before there was a question of speech and its passional origin' (259).

As will be shown in Chapter 5 of this study, for Girard, the victim of violence is also the image of violence in as far as the victim – or the object – is the mode of the appearing of violence. The victim becomes the supplement, as it were, of violence. Here, a decision will be needed on to whether Girard's argument, which promotes the empirical origin of society, is in fact susceptible to the philosophy of the supplement, given that Girard's origin *is* violence.

*

In our investigation centred on the work of Bataille, Agamben and Girard, a separate chapter is devoted to the theme of violence in each of the thinkers concerned, and, similarly, a separate chapter is devoted to the image. The following questions serve as the guiding thread of our deliberations: what must violence be if there is a victim? By victim is meant that being who does not deserve to be the object of violence. Again: what is the significance of treating the image as object, as is the case with Agamben, and in treating it as transparent, as is the case with Bataille? How do violence and the image come together in the crucifixion as Girard interprets it?

The uniqueness of Bataille's approach on violence, as Chapter 1 will show, is in the fact that the victim is the one in the throes of death. This is a victim who causes the separateness of individuality (of discontinuity) to become inoperative as it is taken over by an anguished being, one who, as anguished, comes into the place of the victim in an experience of the continuity of being. The response to the victim who is dying, we will see, is not a willed response, but one that overcomes reason and reflection.

As will be shown in Chapter 3, the implications of Agamben's take on violence derive from the nature of the target of violence, which is, in the first instance, *homo sacer*. Are we not dealing here with killing for the sake of killing? Whatever *homo sacer*'s crime, being killed without anyone being responsible for the death assuredly makes this being a unique victim.

By comparison to Agamben's approach Girard argues that the killing of the scapegoat is the killing of a victim, and that this is an inexorable rationale. Although, from the perspective of a society organised in accordance with judicial institutions, the death of a scapegoat is now considered to be the height of injustice, the scapegoat's death functioned to stem the contagion of violence.

Bataille – as will be seen in Chapter 2 – reveals an approach to the image that does not reduce it to 'media specificity'. The photographic image, for example, is not just a photographic view of reality. More broadly, what the image reveals is more than the character of the medium that contributed to its production.

Chapter 4 will be concerned with the way that Agamben privileges mediality in his take on the image. The appearing of mediality raises the question of how a medium *qua* medium can *appear*.

Chapter 6 deals with Girard's unthematised approach to the image as the Crucifixion. At issue is what pertains if the divinity of Christ is assumed. As such, Christ becomes more than the 'historical Jesus' and fulfils His destiny as the image of God.

A key issue to be addressed in the Conclusion to this work is the status of law. For if the law is crucial in the prevention of the scapegoat principle re-emerging, it is necessary to know what it is precisely about the law that can fulfil this mission. In an effort to clarify this, aspects of the history of the law as it has emerged in Western-style societies will be examined. Agamben's negative assessment of the law will be evaluated and the relationship between law and justice will be considered, especially in light of Derrida's oration, 'Force of Law' (1990).

Notes

1. In Chapter 1, which examines the image and violence in Bataille's work, I expand in detail on what is signified by the 'transparency' of the image

and what is meant by its opposite, 'opacity', also understood in terms of 'media specificity'.
2. Although, when following Debord on the image and Benjamin on violence, Agamben treats the image and violence as objects (as opaque) quite separate from their content, when it comes to incidental engagement with the image, as with the image of nudity in his book, *Nudities* (Agamben 2011b: 55–90), Agamben, too, treats the image as transparent – as that which enables something to be seen.
3. Nancy also defines the image more broadly as 'the distinct' (2005: 1–14), by which, as I see it, he intends to evoke the image as an entity in its own right, an evocation that seems to fly in the face of the image as monstrance. Moreover, by saying that this image is sacred, our author is in effect saying that it is an object: this is reiterated when Nancy says that: 'every image declares itself or indicates itself as an "image" in some way' (2). And again: 'Portraits are the image of the image in general' (4). Furthermore: 'Every image is in some way a "portrait"' (4). My approach, by contrast, is to say that the image is the passage to the sacred – that the portrait is the passage to what is imaged in general.
4. The difficulty of giving a philosophical account of violence thus justifies treating violence as it emerges in the work of particular thinkers, such as the three who are the focus of this study.
5. Just how interpretation is violent is elaborated in Heidegger's reading of Sophocles's *Antigone* in his *Introduction to Metaphysics* (Heidegger 2014).
6. Frederiek Depoortere (2012), is one of the very few to have opened up the issue of the victim here. He questions Agamben's interpretation of the Roman sources relating to *homo sacer* and raises the possibility that Girard's conception of the sacred and the victim might well do more justice to the figure that Agamben has claimed is at the origin of modern politics. A critique of Agamben's figure of *homo sacer* and its relation to 'the camp' is also developed in Mesnard (2004).
7. Agamben thus writes in *Means Without End: Notes on Politics* (2000): 'What is in question in political experience is not a higher end but being-into-language itself as pure mediality, being-into-a-mean as an irreducible condition of human beings. *Politics is the exhibition of a mediality: it is the act of making a means visible as such*' (116–117).
8. Cf.: '*Gesture is the display of mediation, the making visible of a means as such*' (Agamben 2007: 155).
9. For a scholarly study of this theme, see Krämer (2015).
10. To engage in a critique of the Derridian notion of trace would take us too far afield. Suffice it to say that with the notion of erasure, or effacement as an essential aspect of the trace (the trace erases itself), the latter seems to risk becoming an entity cut off from that of which it is the trace. The

trace in the 'metaphysical text' is 'so unthinkable' that 'it is necessary to describe it as an erasure of the trace itself. The trace produces itself there as its own erasure' (Derrida 1972: 76). This might open up the possibility of the trace as (a kind of) presence, even if Derrida also claims that 'The trace is neither perceptible nor imperceptible' (76).

11. When discussing a 'new style of icon' in the eleventh and twelfth centuries, Belting refers to the writing of the Byzantine monk, Michael Psellus, who said that the Crucifixion image had 'no existence of its own, nor any independent authority interposed between God and man' (Belting 1996: 263).

12. In *On the Genealogy of Morality* (1996) Nietzsche claims that the origin of the Latin *bonus*, meaning 'good', and the German *gut*, also meaning good, can be traced back to 'the warrior'. Thus, the 'good' man was a warrior (I 5, p. 16).

13. Cf. 'The Problem of Socrates' in Nietzsche (1974b: 29–34). Although, in an essay on Bataille and sacrifice, Nancy singles out Socrates and Christ as exemplary for understanding the 'West's initial relation to sacrifice', the notion of victim as being integral to sacrifice is not thematised (see Nancy 1991: 21–22).

14. As Laurence Lampert writes: 'only selected parts of Nietzsche's thought are discussed by Heidegger. Omitted are such insistent concerns of Nietzsche as the genealogy of morals and the attack on Christianity' (Lampert 1974: 356). But maybe Heidegger could be let off the hook by saying that Nietzsche's life-affirming (thus violence-affirming) position is not part of his deeper thought. That is, one could hold to the necessity of violence from a political or, at a pinch, even a moral perspective, but not from the perspective of thought. But if it is agreed that 'will to power' is a central component of Nietzschean thought – which Heidegger concedes – it is impossible not to include violence in this. Moreover, with such a redefinition of thought, one would have to admit that Socrates's deep adherence to reason, which results in a judgement that life 'is worthless' – is a sickness – would have to be excluded from the philosopher's thought proper, which would make no sense.

15. Fifteenth-century child murderer and model for Blue Beard.

16. Erzsébet Báthory was a seventeenth-century Hungarian noblewoman who is reputed to have tortured and murdered over 650 victims.

17. Dr Marcel Petiot, a French serial killer during World War II. The remains of twenty-three people were found in the basement of his home in Paris. Reputedly, from a concealed position he watched his victims die agonising deaths.

18. There is disagreement in the literature as to the origin of *Berserkir*. It is possibly a product of Icelandic saga or ancient Norwegian poetry that

refers back to an earlier Germanic culture. The point, though, is that whether mythical or not the *Berserkir* (or Berserker) is attributed with qualities of the most extreme trance-like fury and cruelty. See, for a discussion, Jakobsson (2011).

19. *Lingchi*: Chinese 'death by a thousand cuts', death by dismemberment or 'lingering death', a form of torture and execution which existed in China from AD 900 until 1905, when it was banned. The punishment was, in principle, reserved for the worst types of crimes.

1 Victim and Violence: Bataille versus Nietzsche

'the one who sacrifices is himself affected by the blow which he strikes – he succumbs and loses himself with his victim'.

'In [the victim] I was able to perceive myself destroyed by the rage to destroy'.

Bataille, *Inner Experience*

Introduction

THIS CHAPTER AIMS TO determine the nature of the victim and the role of violence in the thought of Georges Bataille. We will see that for Bataille, violence is inextricably linked to a victim. Consequently, access to Bataille's notion of violence occurs primarily through the travails of the victim – the victim in sacrifice, for example.

According to Giorgio Agamben, however, Bataille does not recognise that it is in fact 'bare life' (i.e., *homo sacer*) that is at the heart of sacrifice (see Agamben 1998: 112–113). The reason for this, Agamben says, is that Bataille, by invoking the prohibition against killing, can only interpret killing as a transgression of the law, whereas, as we shall see in the discussion of Agamben in Chapter 3, the killing of *homo sacer* occurs outside the province of the law, in a space where the law ceases to have any effect. Thus, *homo sacer* cannot be sacrificed. And Agamben is quite tranquil about this. Transgression, on the other hand, presupposes a return to the law as the centre of prohibition. Transgression could not be realised without the law.

A different interpretation of Bataille would propose, then, that Agamben does not recognise the victim at that heart of violence. For in terms of its etymology, 'victim' derives from the Latin, *victima*, which means 'sacrificial offering'. *Homo sacer* cannot be sacrificed and therefore cannot be a victim. If there is no victim, there is no executioner. Consequently, it would make no sense to fight on behalf of *homo sacer*. Bataille's approach to the victim, which respects its sacrificial origins, thus intimates that the term, 'victim', can be understood to be a secularised version of a religious term. As such, Bataille makes a contribution to political theology and, therefore, it can be argued that his insight into this theme is more profound than Agamben's.

However, Agamben is correct on one point: Bataille does follow the 'anthropology of his day' (112) in accepting the division between sacred and profane. Indeed, the latter opposition is central – as Hollier (1990: 131) first observed – to Bataille's dualistic materialism. Sacrifice thus occurs in the domain of the sacred (also the domain of Bataille's 'general economy'). Agamben, on the other hand, sees *homo sacer* as being prior to the division of sacred and profane.[1]

Nietzsche has always been thought to be a key influence on Bataille, even when the philosopher is not explicitly mentioned in Bataille's text. Indeed, as has been remarked, Nietzsche's position on the victim and violence will be shown to be the very opposite of Bataille's. However fascinated Bataille might have been by the figure of Nietzsche, he is at odds with the philosopher of the will to power when it comes to the victim. For Nietzsche, we will see, the victim is the founding moment of every morality and the latter is opposed to 'life', which Nietzsche glorifies without limit.

Bataille's deep concern for the victim of violence brings him clearly within the province of René Girard's research on the victim as scapegoat and Christ's Crucifixion as revelatory of the victim's innocence. In a manner that is even more explicit than that of Bataille, Girard becomes a powerful advocate of the victim's case. And this will be examined in detail in Chapter 5.

Having said that the victim is central in Bataille's thought, it is also necessary to recognise that Bataille's response to the historical figure of Gilles de Rais along with the theorist's treatment of 'childhood' in *Littérature et le mal* might well place Bataille on the side of the persecutor. A fully rounded appreciation of the notion of victim in Bataille's thought thus requires a consideration of the figure of Gilles de Rais as persecutor and as victim. This consideration is the theme of the final section of this chapter.

Approaching the Victim

It is possible to speak *about* the victim, or victims, but can the victim speak? Or, perhaps we should we ask: can the victim be heard and understood? Here, one is reminded of Gayatri Spivak's question, 'Can the Subaltern Speak?'[2] – or of Michel Foucault's project to write a history of infamous men: historical characters without a voice of their own.[3] So even though Girard is decidedly on the side of the victim, the latter exists in his work as a category rather than as an entity with a voice that speaks to us. Is this also true for Georges Bataille's engagement with the victim?

In what follows, I shall, firstly, show that Bataille is drawn to the act of violence that results in the death of the victim – and the victim above all. What he is attracted to in the work of Hubert and Mauss on sacrifice is the status of the victim.

Secondly, as already indicated, I aim to show that Bataille's position *vis-à-vis* the victim and violence is opposed to Nietzsche's, so while Nietzsche defends what I will designate after Direk (2004) as transcendent violence (the violence of the persecutor), Bataille's interest is in immanent violence (violence suffered by the victim). Nietzsche is the reference point not only because Bataille wrote a diary during World War II published as, *On Nietzsche* (1992), but also – despite the view of many commentators – because Bataille's approach to violence and the victim can more clearly be revealed through its difference to that of Nietzsche. Showing the position of Bataille on violence and the victim clarifies the role of violence and the victim in Agamben and Girard. Moreover, just as violence for Agamben will be seen to be linked to the image via the notion of mediality, so in the next chapter it will become clear that the image is linked to violence in Bataille through the art of Lascaux and the paintings of Édouard Manet. But, more dramatically, violence and the image will be seen to be linked through Bataille's encounter with the infamous photographs of death by 'a thousand cuts' – death by dismemberment in the process of Chinese *lingchi*.

Jeremy Biles's insightful interpretation shows Bataille to be a thinker who was opposed to cruelty, unlike Nietzsche who applauds it as a key aspect of 'life'. As Biles states: 'His [Bataille's] ethical vision was dedicated not to inflicting cruelty upon others, but to risking a dissolution of oneself through erotic and other forms of communication' (2011: 134n5). Again, although Bataille's work bears the mark of Nietzsche, Bataille, argues Biles, 'diverges from Nietzsche in crucial respects' (2007: 37). Here we have confirmation that with regard to the victim (and therefore to violence), Nietzsche and Bataille are diametrically opposed. By demonstrating how this is the case, not only can a deeper insight regarding the victim and violence be forged, but a key aspect of the thought of both Bataille and Nietzsche can be made explicit. This is not to deny that in a number of respects Bataille was impressed by Nietzsche, especially with regard to the figure of Dionysus and the notion of the 'Death of God'. But Bataille does not follow Nietzsche down the path of 'life come what may' where victims simply have to take their chances along with everyone else in life as the eternal return of the same – an eternal return that is *willed* by the 'overman'.

Sacrifice

Despite it being a point of reference, Bataille's approach to the victim in sacrifice cannot be entirely assimilated to that of French anthropology. Support for this claim can be found by examining the famous text on sacrifice by Henri Hubert and Marcel Mauss (1981), a text that emphasises the religious framework within which sacrifice takes place. Furthermore, the focus of the French anthropologists is the perspective of the sacrificer and those who orchestrate the sacrifice. Sacrifice for Hubert and Mauss does not necessarily entail violence. Food can be sacrificed. Thus: 'In these conditions we must designate as sacrifice any oblation, even of vegetable matter, whenever the offering or part of it is destroyed, although usage seems to limit the word sacrifice to designate only sacrifices where blood is shed. To restrict the meaning in this way is arbitrary' (12; translation modified). Here, I ask: to what extent is Bataille really concerned with sacrifice rather than violence? Sacrifice is at issue because it entails contact with the victim of violence. Is it not this that really engages Bataille's thinking? Again, emphasising the religious aspect of sacrifice, Hubert and Mauss write: '*Sacrifice is a religious act which, through consecration of a victim, modifies the condition of the moral person who accomplishes it or that of certain objects with which he is concerned*' (15). The authors repeat that sacrifice is, 'a religious act that can only be accomplished in a religious milieu by means of essentially religious agents' (19; translation modified).

The aspects of sacrifice outlined by Hubert and Mauss include:

1. The Sacrifier (*Sacrifiant*). The sacrifier is the person or group that arranges the sacrifice and ensures that all due protocols are adhered to. In effect, the sacrifier is the entity in whose name the sacrifice is made.
2. The Sacrificer. The sacrificer is the one (usually a priest) who performs the sacrifice on the victim at the behest of the sacrifier. The priest, being fully versed in the sacred (the world of the gods) can also ensure that the proper protocols are adhered to and inadvertent violations are avoided.
3. The Place of Sacrifice. The place of sacrifice is consecrated ground where the sacrifice is permitted to be enacted. Outside the sacred place, killing becomes murder.
4. The Victim. The victim is in fact the most important element in the proceedings – not only because without a sacrificial object there could be no sacrifice, but also because the position of the victim (a position that, de facto, entails silence) as presented by Hubert and Mauss, indirectly throws light on Bataille's relation to victimage. The victim (or an object) is sacrificed to a divinity. Through the victim, the sacrifier aims to please the gods and thus to receive the benefits of the gods' good will. In this situation the victim becomes the means of the sacrifier's becoming sacred or holy, but only after (at least with the Brahmins) the victim has become sacred or holy. Sacrifice, as is known, changes the moral status of the one who accomplishes it. Sacrifice is not, then, about the victim *per se*. Furthermore: 'In Mexico and at Rhodes the victim was made drunk. This drunkenness was a sign of possession. The divine spirit was already pervading the victim' (Hubert and Mauss 1981: 30). The character of the victim must be sacred in order to please the divinity. Again, the victim in sacrifice is never there for its own sake, but only to appease the god in the interests of the sacrifier. However, the very sacredness of the victim is also potentially dangerous:

There is in the victim a spirit which it is the very aim of sacrifice to liberate. This spirit must therefore be conciliated, for otherwise it might become dangerous when freed; hence the flattery and preliminary apologies.

Then the victim is bound to a stake. At that moment the sacred character it is in the act of acquiring is already so great that the Brahmin can no longer touch it with his hands, and the sacrifier himself hesitates to approach it. (30–31)

After the victim is sacrificed (killed), there is the problem of getting rid of the remains. Frequently, these are eaten by the sacrifier. In any case, nothing should remain.

Sacrifice aims, then, 'to affect the religious state of the sacrifier or the object of sacrifice' (51). But the following in relation to the victim as divine should be particularly noted:

This singular value of the victim clearly appears in one of the most perfected forms of the historical evolution of the sacrificial system: the sacrifice of the god. Indeed, it is in the sacrifice of a divine personage that the idea of sacrifice attains its highest expression. (77)

Again: 'the victim has always something divine within it which is released by sacrifice' (77–78).

The god 'descends' to the position of victim: 'In order that a god may thus descend to the role of a victim, there must be some affinity between his nature and that of his victims' (77). Because the victim, like the god, is sacred, the victim becomes indistinguishable from a god; however, a 'divine victim' is not a 'victim-god' (78). In short, the god as such is not a victim, even if the victim begins to take on the traits of a god. In the end, sacrifice 'takes place in certain given circumstances and with a view to certain determined ends' (95). The latter relate to what participants want to achieve in the profane world, so that victims become a material means to an end. And so, 'the victim does not come to the sacrifice with a religious nature already perfected and clearly defined: it is sacrifice itself that confers this upon it' (97). The victim is a *means* for realising the end of sacrifice (pleasing the god), not an end in itself. Thus: 'sacrifice is carried out by the profane. The action that it exerts upon people and things is destined to enable them to fulfil their role in temporal life' (99).

Even though the diverse forms of sacrifice would seem to make it difficult to specify its unity, Hubert and Mauss do so by focusing on the victims as means:

> [I]f sacrifice is so complex, whence comes its unity? It is because, fundamentally, beneath the diverse forms it takes, it always consists in one same procedure, which may be used for the most widely differing purposes. *This procedure consists in establishing a means of communication between the sacred and profane worlds through the mediation of a victim, that is, of a thing that in the course of the ceremony is destroyed.* (97)

The system, then, is driven by the 'sacralisation of the victim' (95). There can be no sacred entity prior to the procedures of sacralisation. Even though such procedures can render the (human or animal) victim divine, the initial purpose of sacralisation is to serve the needs and interests of the sacrifier or the sacrificer – key figures in the profane world. Indeed, sacrifice could be called that system whereby a victim is engaged in order to achieve certain ends in the profane world by way of the sacred world. Hubert and Mauss – along with other scholars, such as Robertson-Smith – are above all concerned to document, from the perspective of those other than the victim, the diverse procedures of sacralisation. In short, it is not at all in the victim's interest to become sacred. As presented by Hubert and Mauss, sacralisation is something over which the victim – *qua* victim – has absolutely no control or agency. For the anthropologists, then, the victim is but one element in the whole process of the sacrificial system, not the luminous focal point. And, no doubt, an understanding of sacrifice as an institution warrants such an approach.

*

Bataille's perspective differs from the one just elaborated. His question – even if he cannot answer it – is: what is it like being a victim? It is well known that Aztec human sacrifice is the main empirical example discussed by Bataille. The procedures of sacralisation are described, as are the methods of sacrifice (cf. the priest's obsidian knife used to remove the victim's pulsating heart in order to present it to the sun). Concerning the one chosen to die, Bataille writes:

'Once chosen, he is the *accursed share*, destined for violent consumption. But the curse tears him away from the *order of things*; it gives him a recognizable figure, which now radiates intimacy, anguish, the profundity of living beings' (1988a: 59). In other words, the victim is becoming an entity in his own right, so that Bataille is led to wonder 'to what extent the victims of Mexico accepted their fate' (60) And he continues by speculating that: 'It may be that in a sense certain of them "considered it an honor" to be offered to the gods.' However, one thing for Bataille is certain: 'their immolation was not voluntary' (60). Precisely in light of this stipulation, sacrifice becomes a source of terrible anguish for those in the profane world. While Hubert and Mauss are at pains to specify the logic and complexity of the sacrificial system so that how it works for those who choose a victim, initiate sacralisation procedures and then end the victim's life can be understood, Bataille is driven to focus on the victim as such. To do so entails coming to grips with the victim's death while ensconced in today's profane world. That is, Bataille breaks with understanding sacrifice in terms of its internal logic (cf. Weber's *verstehen*) and rather attempts to open the way to an experience of the victim's pain and suffering – an experience of, in a word, the victim's death. The latter experience becomes the basis of communication in the realm of what Bataille calls 'continuity'.[4]

The noted Bataille scholar, Elisabeth Arnould, has remarked that: 'sacrifice is not simply, for Bataille, a theoretical object [. . .] it marks rather a limit to conceptualization and constitutes a stumbling block to thought' (1996: 87). Perceptive as this statement is, sacrifice is not sheeted home to the victim, while it can be, *inter alia*, 'the sacrifice of the profane world, of women's bodies, or of words' (87).

A key concern for Jean-Luc Nancy in his much-read, 'The Unsacrificeable' (1991), is that, in isolating the victim, Bataille is tempted by the bloody aspect of sacrifice, notably as this is captured by the *lingchi* photographs:[5] 'In his desire to put an end to dialectical process as comedy, Bataille wanted blood to spurt. He wanted to weigh in the balance the horribly lacerated body and the look – distraught or ecstatic? – of a young Chinese being tortured' (27). This interpretation does not accord with the victim as the one in relation to whom Bataille would experience death as such. Bataille wants to *be* that other at the moment of death. This, at any rate, will be the thesis presented in what follows. Moreover, Nancy's claim that Bataille does not realise that 'existence cannot be sacrificed' does not seem plausible when considered in conjunction with Bataille's claim in *Inner Experience* that Hegel reduced existence to the realm of the project, that is, to profane existence. Hegel neglected sacred existence, or the realm of non-knowledge, anguish, ecstasy, communication (see Bataille 1988c: 81). On this basis, the sacrifice of existence would entail the sacrifice of sacrifice, which Bataille does not accept.

Christ – or perhaps more accurately, Jesus – for Bataille, we can justly argue, is not the Christ of theology or Christology – not the one who would be the incarnation of a divine essence, thus not Christ of the image who would be both God and Man but, ironically, a more profane being whose god has forsaken him: '*lamma sabachtani*' [*sic*] (47). Certainly, like Nietzsche, Bataille tends to see Christ as the 'historical Jesus', rather than as the one who is both the Son and the Father, Man and God, divine and human.[6] Jesus, like other sacrificial victims, thus becomes one who suffers and whose death opens the way to communication as a non-discursive experience.

Not Sacrificing in the Present for the Future: The Instant

The victim of sacrifice dies in an instant – how is it possible to experience this? Does not the instant separate irrevocably the other from the victim?

That Bataille does not take a strictly anthropological approach to the sacred or to sacrifice finds further confirmation in his notion of the instant.[7] The instant[8] is crucial because concentrated in it is sovereignty, intimacy, continuity, communication, death (but not Heidegger's 'being-for-death', which is futural) – but also, most crucially, the sacred and sacrifice. Sacrifice, therefore, would be exemplary of the instant. The instant as the present blots out the future. Work always has the future in view and is therefore servile. Work is in history, in time; sacrifice as the instant is outside of time and is, for this reason, sovereign. To be sure, Bataille is interested in the anthropological discourse on the sacred and the profane (Durkheim, Mauss), and frequently uses its terminology. But at a more complex level, he leaves this discourse behind and interprets the sacred and sacrifice in his own terms and in his own way, a way that includes the theory of the general economy. Thus, compared to Mauss's notion of the gift, which always entails a *quid pro quo* (exchange) – however disguised this may be – Bataille proposes a form of expenditure without return:

an expenditure of the instant, of the moment, without reference to the future. To be aware of the general economy in relation to the sacred is not to enter into the logic of the system, as do Hubert and Mauss, where those in the profane world perform rituals of sacralisation and sacrifice in order to obtain a given end – an end, by definition, in the future. Just the opposite is Bataille's *modus operandi*, so that sacrifice comes to be understood in and of itself and not as the means to an end, not as something useful for future existence. Bataille thus writes of the Aztecs that 'all their important undertakings were *useless*' (1988a: 46; emphasis added).

In a particularly rich discussion of Gabriel Marcel's existential philosophy, Bataille brings death and the instant together, even though Marcel seems to have a view of sacrifice as a gift (1988b: 121) in the manner of anthropological discourse. Does the pretext for sacrifice as an end realisable in the future (e.g., ensuring an abundant harvest) change its relation to the instant? The answer is no, because every pretext (utility) is misleading in that it takes us away from what is essential, namely, that 'what I feel intensely, passionately, only has value in the instant' (123). The instant has no pretext because it has no goal – no future. It does not entail any form of exchange (no gift). So, if sacrifice and the sacred are other names for the instant, every pretext is a subterfuge. Indeed, Bataille introduces the notion of '*being in the instant*' where, 'sensitivity and the intensity of feelings essentially intervene negatively by suppressing or, more rigorously, by attenuating, care about the time to come' (124). The notion of the '*last instant*' brings out Bataille's point particularly strongly: it is sovereignty (125). And the sovereignty of the instant would dominate utility, as Bataille says in a discussion of Hiroshima (185). In the same article, Bataille refers to that 'man of the instant' whom, he claims (perhaps unwisely), is also the 'man of the atom', because, according to Aristotle and Saint Paul, 'the word atom designates *instant*' (183 note). The dropping of the atom bomb on Hiroshima and Nagasaki thus literally becomes the atom (instant) of death.[9]

Ultimately, to apprehend the instant requires a new discipline (233), or, at least, a different approach, given how easy it is to end up in paradox when the instant becomes an object of thought. Indeed, to speak of the instant, or to represent it in any manner whatever, is to freeze it, to objectify it, to 'save' it for the future. All of which goes against the instant as pure loss.

In the contemporary world, there is, we often suppose, the instant of death – when, for example, life ceases to be maintained by a machine – or, more pointedly, in the enactment of capital punishment, where is it necessary to pinpoint the moment of death. In both these cases, it is impossible to *capture* the instant. An attempt to do so soon collapses in paradox, just as does time as a succession of 'nows'. The latter has been addressed in the history of number, the problem being to know the status of the *point* in time and how – as Zeno's paradox showed – it is possible to move from one now point to another. Is such a trajectory infinitely divisible? If it is, it implies that, as the mathematician, Robert Tubbs, puts it: 'there can be no end to the possible positions between any two positions' (2009: 65). In short, to follow Zeno entails that we can never get from point A to point B.

If Bergson showed how analysis fails to do justice to duration, Bataille shows the same thing with regard to the instant. Bataille's instant does not exist in a series. As present, it has no past and no future. Even in Maurice Blanchot's evocative short story, *The Instant of my Death* (2000), the instant recalls a past and a future.[10] More broadly, the general economy has no history. How is the victim linked to the instant for Bataille? – that is our question.

To appreciate the full significance of Bataille's approach to the instant as intimate experience, one must assume the role of participant rather than observer when it comes to the fate of the victim. Or at least, one should acknowledge the specificity and therefore limitedness of the observer's position. How is this possible? Part of the answer involves recognising that discursivity needs to be displaced as the centre of knowing, so that it comes to give way to 'non-knowledge' as anguish and ecstasy.[11] In fact: discursivity, as linked to epistemological strategies (and thus to science) as well as to ontology, becomes sidelined. Where does discursivity stand in relation to the instant? Can an *experience* of non-knowledge be conveyed in philosophy? As already mentioned, apropos of this question, Bataille says that Hegel reduced the world to the world of work and to the project, thus to the profane world.

Although he does not refer to Husserl, who famously said that a perception of duration turns on the duration of perception,[12] Bataille is sensitive to the aporia that a thinker can fall into on this issue. The instant, here, is non-knowledge, which can be experienced, but not objectified. This differentiates Bataille from Husserl who accesses the experience of time through a 'temporal Object', such as melody, where time is experienced as duration and not as a series of nows (Husserl 1981: 278).[13]

Melody, or any temporal object, is equivalent to the objectification of time. The latter cannot, Bataille realised, give a sense of death, or a sense of the instant as he intended it.[14]

The instant, then, is not equivalent to 'now', for it does not exist in a series and it cannot be constituted as a temporal object because it does not exist as duration. The instant, too, as Bataille conceives it, has only a tenuous relation to memory; for memory of all phenomena has to do with past and future, whereas death cuts everything off from past and present, which means that death as such is above all the death of memory.

The point has now been reached where an anthropological and even a philosophical interpretation (cf. Nancy 1991) of Bataille on sacrifice, violence and the victim can be seen to have missed the key point. This is because Bataille's approach brings into view the unthinkable and non-knowledge. In short, Bataille wants to *be* death, even if those outside this purview might well be sceptical.[15]

*

If 'sacrifice has always occupied a central place in Bataille's thought' (Arnould 1996: 87), the question is: what is the *nature* of this central place? If Socrates and Christ are exemplary victims (= exemplary scapegoats?), as Nancy proposes (1991: 21), would they be so for Bataille? The answer is yes, but under certain conditions. Here, Bataille's significant remark in *The Tears of Eros* (1990) needs to be recalled, the one referring to a voodoo '*sacrificer*' and the victim of Chinese torture: 'The game I am setting up for myself is to represent *what they were living* at the moment the lens fixed their image on the glass or on the film' (185; emphasis added).[16]

Bataille, then, is oriented towards the victim in sacrifice. And it is possible to show that this is his general disposition – his mode of being in the world, as it were. With Nietzsche's thought, it is a very different story. It is oriented towards what in general terms has been called the position of the persecutor and transcendent violence (the violence of war and the warrior, amongst other things), an approach to be found in well-nigh the entirety of Nietzsche's published writing. So, what is the precise relation between Nietzsche and the victim? Nietzsche, who was so important to Bataille as a figure and a thinker, but who, as already stated, Bataille did not follow down the path of life at all costs.

In order to uncover the general orientation of Nietzsche's thought with regard to the victim, it is necessary to take as wide an angle as possible. An engagement is necessary with key texts in Nietzsche oeuvre in order to verify the way that Nietzsche's concept of life proves to be antithetical to victims, otherwise designated as the 'weak' in relation to the 'strong'. In what follows, Nietzsche's opposition to the victim – not just in sacrifice – will be highlighted. As Keenan has shown, if Nietzsche is also concerned with sacrifice it is to the extent that the latter is about the sacrifice of God, which boils down to the 'sacrifice [of] (economical) sacrifice' (Keenan 2003: 168). As will be seen, how Nietzsche valorises 'life' is the key to his anti-victim philosophy, a philosophy that puts the thinker at odds with Bataille.

Nietzsche: Glorious Life and Establishing the Fate of the Victim

The status of the Nietzschean corpus has been questioned by certain scholars, particularly with regard to the extent to which the *Nachlass* (notebooks) should be included in Nietzschean interpretation.[17] Even if one accepts that Nietzsche's oeuvre does include the *Nachlass*, there remains the issue of the meaning of will to power. Bernd Magnus notes that no real consensus on this point exists in Nietzsche commentary and probably even less on the meaning of the eternal return. Despite this, I make my play. For my presentation of things, there is an overall coherence in Nietzsche's published works regarding the notions that most concern this study, namely, life and power.[18] Life and power, I say, are essentially presented by Nietzsche from the perspective of the so-called life-affirming forces, which of course includes the warrior as emblematic of the strong who act according to instinct. By contrast, the victim only appears as the counter to the warrior and as such deserves to perish given that the victim (the weak one) is equivalent to the repression – if not the perversion – of instinct (i.e., of life). I would add that Nietzsche's writing – in all its forcefulness and self-certainty – is entirely affirmative and emphatic, not to say vehement. In short, it also *performs* the will to power that it presents in its statements, which is to say that it is also *a will to violence*.[19] In sum, I agree with Frithjof Bergmann who lucidly observes (without perhaps grasping the full implications!): 'The bifurcation which runs like a spine through the body of Nietzsche's writings is the division between what debilitates and maims *life*, versus everything that strengthens and invigorates it.

He reiterates this again and again with as few circumlocutions and qualifications as one could wish' (1988: 44).

*

In *Thus Spoke Zarathustra*, one encounters a version of the eternal return based implicitly on a theory of time. Specifically: 'all things return eternally and we ourselves with them, and that we have already been here an eternity of times' (Nietzsche 2008: 192). Following current practice, this can be called the 'cosmological version' of the eternal return. The question is: can this statement be understood as anything other than time as reversible – that the same (seasons, actions, death) will recur again and again eternally? Compared to this, irreversible time means that nothing will occur more than once – that contingency and chance are the key elements of time. Newton is often cited as a proponent of time as essentially reversible, while thermodynamics – quintessential lynchpin of nineteenth-century science – would be the incarnation of irreversible time.[20] The further question is: could the notion of time as reversible do justice to Nietzsche's challenge to will the return of cruelty in life? I suggest that Nietzsche (and certain Nietzscheans) are caught in a cleft stick if the main aim is to attribute a reality to the eternal return unless that reality be based in reversible time. In other words, it is not possible to will the most terrible things to recur given that the most terrible things are contingent. Why is this the case? Death, after all, might be said to recur eternally. The issue here, though, is about *how* death occurs, which is essentially a contingent matter. What occurs eternally must be something predictable. Contingent events constituting irreversible time are, by contrast, unpredictable.

The mechanics of the eternal return are, however, less important than the message Nietzsche is intent on conveying, and this is that the strong (including the psychologically and intellectually strong) will be able to accept life in its totality; life – for better or for worse, whether this be life brought to a certain fulfilment by the 'enhancers' of life, as exemplified by great artists, or life as is suffered by the victims of cruelty.[21] The 'improvers' of humanity, on the other hand (Christians, for example), want to change life as it is for life as they think it should be – life changed to encompass the interests of the weak, not the strong, of the crowd or the herd, not the individual, of the pacifist not the warrior, of the slave, not the master. Thus, Nietzsche's philosophy emphasises the pleasure gained from cruelty as part of life as 'will to power'. References to cruelty as a manifestation of the will to power run all through the Nietzschean corpus. Memory in relation to contractual relationships was 'a repository of hard, cruel, painful things' (Nietzsche 1996: II 5, p. 44). Moreover, the beginning of legal obligations, 'all began with a thorough blood letting, like the beginning of all great things on earth. And may we not add that *this world has never really quite lost a certain odour of blood and torture*?' (II 6, p. 45; emphasis added). The imposition of cruelty worked, says Nietzsche, '[t]o the degree that *to make* someone suffer is pleasure in its highest form' (45). He adds: 'not so long ago it was unthinkable to hold a royal wedding or full-scale festival for the people without executions, tortures or perhaps an *auto-da-fé*' (46).[22] Accordingly: 'To see somebody suffer is nice, to make somebody suffer even nicer – that is a hard proposition, but an ancient, powerful human-all-too-human principle' (47).[23] Moreover: 'No cruelty no feast: that is what the oldest and longest period of human history teaches us – and punishment, too, has such very strong *festive* aspects! – ' (67). Note here that to make others suffer (cf. the executioner) is more pleasurable than just watching – just being a spectator. Not being a victim is only part of the story of the life of the executioner! It would not be worth a mention otherwise. This is the exact opposite of Bataille's position. But even the delight of the selfless man 'is tied to cruelty' (88). Cruelty, the key element of the will to power for Nietzsche, is tied to the very nature of human life; that is, to instincts. It cannot be eradicated. Another, earlier, passage from *Daybreak* (1982) (sect 18) recalled in *The Genealogy* (sect 6), says: 'In the act of cruelty the community refreshes itself and for once throws off the gloom of constant fear and caution. *Cruelty is one of the oldest festive joys of mankind*' (Nietzsche 1982: sect 18, 17; emphasis added). Again: 'to practise cruelty is to enjoy the highest gratification of the feeling of power' (17). Cruelty and the will to power are thus inextricably united.

In *The Genealogy* Nietzsche recalls section 229 of *Beyond Good and Evil* (1974a), where he says:

> One should open one's eyes and take a new look at cruelty; one should at last grow impatient, so that the kind of immodest fat errors which have, for example, been fostered about tragedy by ancient and modern philosophers should no longer go stalking virtuously and confidently about. Almost everything we call 'higher culture' is based on the spiritualization and intensification of *cruelty* – this is my

proposition; the 'wild beast' has not been laid to rest at all, it lives, it flourishes, it has merely become – deified. That which constitutes the painful voluptuousness of tragedy is cruelty. (1974a: sect 229, 140)[24]

But, in *Daybreak*, Nietzsche also says that a certain pleasure is gained through inflicting pain *on oneself*. After people are offered the spectacle of cruelty, 'there creeps into the world the idea that *voluntary suffering*, self-chosen torture, is meaningful and valuable' (1982: sect 18, 17). Even more explicitly in *Beyond Good and Evil*, Nietzsche claims that 'there is also an abundant, over-abundant enjoyment of one's own suffering, of making oneself suffer' (1974a: sect 229, 140). Further: 'he is secretly lured and urged on by his cruelty, by the dangerous thrills of cruelty directed *against himself*' (141).

Two things (at least) can be said about this: firstly, that the individual concerned becomes his or her own active torturer, or persecutor. That the object of persecution is the self does not detract at all from the active status of the action. Secondly, the victim (reality and concept) is entirely elided. These two aspects are no doubt what drew Nietzsche's attention to them. They reinforce the idea that it is a matter – in clear contrast to Bataille – of expunging the notion and reality of victimage. The weak, as we know, are supposedly full of *ressentiment*[25] and feelings of vengeance, which they are only too ready to vent against those deemed to be responsible for their plight (the strong). The 'doers' – life's active force – Nietzsche holds, need to be saved from the 'non-doers' – life's reactive force (the force particularly cultivated by Christianity). Nietzsche is opposed to giving sympathy to the weak (victims).[26] As if supporting the weak necessarily would deprive the strong of their strength (whether physical or intellectual)! What possible basis is there for that? What is meant is that sympathy for the weak only occurs in the Occident via Christianity, which makes the strong, the noble – who instinctively want to give vent to their will to power – feel guilty for being who they are, for enhancing life by following their instincts. In short, life without the cruelty of the strong resulting from the manifestation of will to power is an emasculation of life. This is the real message of the eternal return. Significantly, it makes – if one thinks about it in moral terms – the strong innocent and the weak guilty! (More on this below.) For the strong are like the bird of prey that takes the lamb because it is in its nature to do so.[27]

Sade: Violence and the Victim

This active status (of the strong, of the victimiser, of the persecutor) is arguably glorified in Sade, as Hallam proposes.[28] For Bataille, things are not so straightforward. Perhaps they ought to be. Or, again, maybe his argument is more subtle than was first thought. At any rate, in *L'Érotisme*, Sade is viewed, as was noted earlier,[29] as confronting the 'normal' person with violence that rarely, if ever, makes its way into consciousness. Moreover, violence, as profound disorder and as opposed to reason, is mute. Language, as the basis of civilisation, is unable to accommodate violence. Violence, or barbarism – the opposite of civilisation – is silent, entirely inarticulate (Bataille 1987: 184–185). Like work, the normal, orderly person is not to be disparaged. For, indeed, the normal person is in all of us, just as work is necessarily in every extant society; no society can exist without work, or without productive activity of some kind. In a sense, the normal person is the first victim of violence, a violence that is disorder and unmitigated trauma – the abnormal, *par excellence*. Barbarity does not exist in one culture or community and civilisation in another. Rather, all cultures are founded on the civilising force of language and all so-called modern societies possess the potential for barbarity, as lynching (for one thing) in America well demonstrates. Violence can have its day because there is an essential division in the human:

> human life is composed of two heterogeneous parts, which never unite. One part is sensible (*sensée*) and its meaning is given by utilitarian and therefore secondary ends; this part is the one that appears in consciousness. The other is sovereign: it occurs by way of the disruption of the first part; it is obscure, or rather, if it is clear it is blindingly so; it thus hides from consciousness in every way possible. (191)

To be violent is to distance oneself from consciousness (191). In short: violence and consciousness can never be reconciled.

Those admirers of Sade who see in his presentation of violence the truth about what really constitutes 'the heart of man', and who say that, to avoid hypocrisy, violence should be allowed unfettered expression, fail to understand that they are advocating the destruction of all social life. The existence of social life depends on work, order, reason – on normality, in a word. In any case, to make violence fully present to avoid hypocrisy implies normalising it, which is, by definition, impossible. As Bataille explains, a doctrine as strange as Sade's 'could never be generally accepted, or even generally proposed, unless it was blunted, emptied of meaning, reduced to an inconsequential commotion. Who cannot fail to see, that if taken seriously, a society could not accept it for a single instant' (1987: 179). Thus, even though there are two sides to the human – the violent and the normal – this does not mean that the impulse to be violent should not be opposed. Life itself exists in defiance of violence. 'Indeed', says Bataille, 'those who saw in de Sade a scoundrel responded better to his intentions than his modern admirers: de Sade should provoke protestations from those revolted by him, otherwise the *paradox of pleasure* would simply become poetry' (179). No one, moreover, can laud cruelty:

> Short of the paradoxical power of defending the indefensible, no one could claim that the cruelty of the heroes of *Justine* and *Juliette* should not be wholeheartedly abhorred. It is the negation of all the principles on which humanity is founded. We must in whatever way reject that for which the goal would be the ruin of all we have achieved. If instincts drive us to destroy the things that we build, we must condemn these instincts and defend ourselves from them. (182)

Because he has exposed the nature of the general economy, inner experience, sacrifice, eroticism, etc., in relation to which work, for example, is a servile activity, Bataille has been wrongly interpreted as the *advocate* for what he exposes and a critic of life in the restricted economy and of the 'normal' person. At a pinch, he has even been turned into an advocate of violence.[30] Overall, however, if the above statement holds, this is clearly not the case.

The question now is: what are the implications for the notion of victim of Bataille's call to order concerning Sade's imaginary violence? In response, one might point, first of all, to Bataille's reference to the victim in his discussion of Sade. Here, let it be noted that victim and persecutor can be incarnate in the same person: on the one hand, an individual works, looks after family, is kind, loyal and honest; on the other hand, the same person can be responsible for pitiless acts of violence. Indeed, 'the same men pillage, burn, kill, violate and torture. Excess is opposed to reason' (184). It seems obvious that even punishment sanctioned by the law – and capital punishment in particular – tips the scale towards violence and away from the life of normality, even though legal punishment is supposed to protect the latter.

Sade's 'language', says Bataille, 'is that of a victim' (188). How is this so when we might have assumed that it is that of the persecutor? How can the victim speak? If one thinks about it from Bataille's angle, it makes sense. For if the persecutor is inseparable from violence, we know that violence is silent. Or, at any rate, if it 'speaks' in literature, it is only as a 'will to violence' (as imaginary violence), not as violence as such (190).

In addition, though, to be a victim is to be the subject of injustice, which is to be, at the same time, the subject of moral discourse and thus the user of language. As the subject of injustice and moral discourse, the victim always 'speaks' – invokes language – even if this should be understood on occasion as silence speaking. As Heidegger said: one can speak much and say nothing; one can remain silent and 'say a great deal' (Heidegger 1982: 122).

The 'normal man', then is not someone who might one day evolve into a unique individual (perhaps a radical artist), or into a revolutionary, or into a believer of whatever stripe, or, indeed, into a champion of the victim – in other words, into an incarnation that would belie the notion of normality. Or, to put it another way: the unique individual, the revolutionary, etc., never leaves normality behind, but is *also* the 'normal man'. Bataille is thus saying, by way of his engagement with Sade, that normality is essentially part of the human. Violence, eroticism, intoxication and death are, by comparison, the other side of the moon.

In many respects, when Nietzsche refers to 'the herd', he evokes Bataille's 'normal man'. The herd engages in work – indeed, in all things utilitarian; it believes in moral values, such as a concern for others and the preservation of the community for the benefit of all. It is the opposite of the exception, of the individual engaged in violence and cruelty. It opposes the persecutor on moral grounds. And so, while Bataille sees the virtues of the 'normal man' as necessary for the preservation of social life – a life that is *worth* preserving – Nietzsche is opposed to social life because it gives rise to herd existence. Nietzsche and Bataille are thus clearly opposed on this point. Is it the same with regard to *ressentiment*?

Ressentiment and Vengenace

In approaching the notion of *ressentiment* in Nietzsche, it is evident that the victors, the noble, the masters, the strong have a purity of motive and disposition that is lacking in the weak as victims. For whereas the strong simply act affirmatively according to who they are – that is, in a mode of transparency and honesty[31] – the victims act in accordance with the *ressentiment*, cunning and vengefulness of 'slave morality' – a sentiment that leads to deviousness and dishonesty. In other words, if they could, the weak (the slaves) would more than match the strong in their cruelty and violence, but, unable to act, they are limited to 'imaginary revenge', to action as 'reaction' (Nietzsche 1996: 10, 21–22). Thus: '[t]hese bearers of the oppressive, vindictive instincts, the descendants of all European and non-European slavery, in particular of all pre-Aryan population – represent the *decline* of mankind!' (1996: 11, 26). As they are no match for the strong – for the vanquishers – the victims endeavour, through Christianity most of all, to make the strong and noble feel guilty for being who they are – for being the incarnations of life.

The point, from Nietzsche's position, is that the victims[32] are far from having purity of motives and intentions. They even have strength if they band together. That is why the strong need to be protected from the weak. In the end, though, *ressentiment* derives from the fact that the weak (victims) cannot face the fact of life as it is – that it is the key element in their weakness. They rage against life for having dealt them such a bad hand.

But is all this truly plausible? Does *ressentiment* really derive from the difference between weak and strong, victim and vanquisher, noble and base? Does not human *ressentiment* rather occur in situations where the difference between groups or individuals is small, not large – for instance between the high bourgeoisie and the lower aristocracy?[33] What is the significance of *parvenu*, after all? The truly downtrodden – the unambiguous victims of the world – are frequently resigned to accept their lot in life.

Be this as it may, equally telling points are that if Christ is the victim *par excellence*, He is so without a trace of *ressentiment*. Also, though, if the weak are victims, women – in being characterised as weaker than men – will be eternal victims and therefore eternal harbingers of *ressentiment*. Thus: 'Females are vengeful, for instance: this is a constituent part of their weakness, just like their sensitivity to the needs of others' (Nietzsche 1989: sect 7, 82).

Moreover, *isonomia* – ancient Greek term for equality in the *polis* – could produce what would seem to approximate *ressentiment*. As one commentator writes, a major cause of *stasis* or civil discord was the contradiction between the notional egalitarianism of the citizen estate, expressed by the term *isonomia*, and the existence of exceptionally charismatic individuals denied (so they believed) their due portion of status and honour *(timē)*. (Cartledge 2000: 19)

Of course, Nietzsche is less interested in the subtleties of ancient Greek political struggles in the *polis* than he is in pointing to the *ressentiment* supposedly at the heart of Christianity, where the victim – the meek, and the poor – is the explicit *raison d'être*.

With Bataille, the situation is quite different. For him, the victim is anyone who suffers violence through no fault of their own, and particularly anyone who suffers a violent death. Not the text of Christianity – its 'thou shalt not kill' – but the act of violence as such is Bataille's focus. So, it is in no way a matter of Bataille defending Christianity against the Nietzschean attack, but one of revealing the truth of what it is to be a victim in the act of violence that has the victim as object.

But if his position in relation to the victim is opposed to Nietzsche's, how can this be reconciled with Bataille's apparent sympathy for the fifteenth-century child murderer, Gilles de Rais (1404–1440)? This question calls for a response. The answer is that, however implausible if may seem, Bataille treats de Rais as a victim. As such, the encounter with de Rais throws further light on Bataille's notion of victim. It is important to engage with this moment in Bataille's intellectual biography.

Bataille and Gilles de Rais

Gilles de Rais, we are led to believe, killed for pure pleasure in a manner Sade could only imagine. In terms of his military (read: warrior) status and total lack of inhibition in imposing his will through acts of the greatest cruelty, de Rais appears to be the ultimate Nietzschean human of nobility who acted in accordance with his instincts, despite professing to be Christian.

Bataille refers to this knight at arms as a monster, whose 'distinguishing mark is his nobility' (Bataille 1991: 37–38), but he also calls him a tragic figure in the manner of Shakespeare rather than the index of a system that has become totally dysfunctional and corrupt. Or rather, the tragedy of Gilles de Rais, it is claimed, is the tragedy of the whole Feudal system (42).[34] Bataille attributes to de Rais behaviour that could conceivably occur in any human being. Such behaviour is simply an instance of the criminality deriving from the fact that '[c]rime is a fact of the human species, a fact of that species alone' (9). Gilles de Rais is thus a clear possibility of the human species, not a dire aberration that would bring the whole being of the human into question. This is confirmed by the attempt to include the 'ardor of a violence' typical of the German warrior class, or *Berserkir*, in the explanation of de Rais's actions (see 37–38). The *Berserkir* was open to killing and wreaking havoc with a child-like lack of inhibition. No law existed that could keep these warriors in check. De Rais had, then, childlike qualities, Bataille says, 'in the manner of savages' (29). Vestiges of the Germanic past could be observed in that there was a 'tendency to pay no more attention to the life of human beings than that of animals'. The *Berserkir* dreamed of 'terror and butchery' (30). Consequently: 'It is difficult for us to evaluate the distance that then separated the man (magnified by birth and fortune) who did the crushing from the insect crushed between two stones' (37).

While the underprivileged man is reduced to working (38), play best describes the culture of the nobility. The issue arising turns on the significance of the difference between work and loss of dignity, and play, or war – characteristic of the activities of the nobility. 'War itself has the privilege of being a game' (39). War 'most often' is what results from 'an exuberant, explosive impulse' (39). Thus, in Bataille's terms, de Rais disembowels children as an act of play – an abhorrent act of play, but play nonetheless. War, too, is a mode of play (40) for feudal society. This behaviour is still in keeping with the nature of the man as a man, even if it is also extreme and on the edge of what is possible if one is to remain human.

Ruin is one of the aspects of tragedy. Tragedy is confirmed by de Rais's fate (his execution). '*Tragedy is the powerlessness of Reason*' (43). Again: 'The impulse that personifies tragedy can be accounted for by one formula: facing headlong into the impossible' (49). At the point of public execution by hanging, Gilles de Rais, like Joan of Arc, is, in Bataille's view, a victim (58). But: 'Of all the executions of the Middle Ages, as spectacular as they were, that of Gilles de Rais seems to have been theatrically the most moving. Likewise, it appears that, in the beginning, his trial was at least one of the most animated and pathetic of all time' (58–59).

Let us say, after Girard, that, for Bataille, de Rais is used by violence (i.e., is a victim) as much as he uses violence. This is the key to Bataille's interest in the 'monster'. This alone is what makes him tragic; it makes him a tragic figure because he thinks of himself as entirely the subject of violence, whereas, in reality, he is also its object, its plaything.[35]

Nothing of this of course brings us any closer to the victim of violence unless the victim be Gilles de Rais himself in his execution. The monster becomes a victim offered to the crowd in his spectacular execution. All corporal punishments at the time were spectacular: a crowd was always in wrapped attendance, hence the theatrical nature of the execution. Unacceptable as it might be, Bataille paints the torturer and murderer as a victim. It is as though – quite unlike Nietzsche – Bataille were driven to avoid an engagement with the warrior *qua* warrior in lieu of an engagement with the warrior become victim.

In what is no doubt the bitterest of ironies, not only is de Rais characterised as childlike because of his unrestrained barbarity when his very victims are children, but Bataille also says at one point early in his commentary that: 'We cannot deny the monstrosity of childhood. How often children would, if they could be Gilles de Raises!' (20). From this is derived the bizarre logic that de Rais did what he did to children because he himself had not thrown off the mantel of childhood – an estate which, left to itself, is essentially barbarous. In short, the perpetrator commits crimes on his child victims because he is himself essentially a child, like his victims! De Rais is, then, doubly implicated in victimage: initially when he commits his crimes, and then when he becomes the spectacle at his own execution. How unlike Nietzsche's Bataille's view truly is!

Childhood and evil (*le mal*) also come together in another context. This time it is literature (at least the literature that pushes boundaries and refuses to conform). In his Foreword to the French edition of *La Littérature et le mal* (1979: 171–172), Bataille writes that 'Literature is not innocent, and, guilty, it must in the end confess this' (172). Furthermore: 'Literature, I would progressively like to show, is *childhood finally rediscovered*' (172; emphasis added). When interviewed in 1958 on French television about his book, Bataille reiterates the link that he sees between literature, evil and childhood. Only by recognising this can the horrors, the violence, be confronted and maybe overcome.[36] This statement, at least, has an echo of the 'normal man' about it.

But it is difficult to overemphasise the oddness of Bataille's thinking here. For while, as is well-known, childhood, morally speaking, is usually removed from evil and thus assumes a certain innocence, so that children, above all, are potential victims, the author of *La Littérature et le mal* wants to link the human's pre-maturation state to evil – even to the point where children become monsters. Thus, the extent to which Gilles de Rais is evil is also the extent to which he is childlike. Evil thus becomes a return to childhood – which is not a stage of innocence. If the aim were to steer interpretation away from any hint of conventional morality – 'beyond good and evil' – then why invoke 'innocence' and 'guilt' when referring to literature in the Foreword to *La Littérature et le mal*? In doing so, Bataille's thought on this matter seems to be deeply paradoxical. Children, the actual victims of Gilles de Rais, can be compared with children as a generic category and authors of evil, so that children become both victims and persecutors.

As if he intuitively sensed something was amiss, Bataille proposes – again in in the Foreword – the term 'hypermorality' (171). It appears again in the chapter on Emily Brontë's *Wuthering Heights*, where it evokes a moral attitude that recognises that there is an indissoluble relation between prohibition and transgression. In other words, transgression (doing evil) in no way puts morality as such in question, but rather reinforces it, whatever received wisdom might claim. Literature in the truest sense, says Bataille, is essentially a vehicle of evil as transgression – a transgression, he adds in his reading of *Wuthering Heights*, that is based in passion (1979: 186). As transgression, literature is thus implicated in the law.

To say that children are 'guilty' of transgressing the moral law (which will entail their ultimate adherence to it) is very different from saying that they have the potential to be like Gilles de Rais. For while it could be said (à la Nietzsche) that Gilles de Rais is a phenomenon, in his extreme acts of child murder he ceases to be a moral entity. His acts are not just instances of transgression but are 'beyond good and evil' – past the point of no return.

The phenomenon of Gilles de Rais throws us, and Bataille, into disarray. For the dialectic of prohibition and transgression is no longer operable for figures like the former Marshal of France. Thus, to hypothesise, Bataille sees de Rais as a victim in order to be able to cope with de Rais as an appalling historical monster. The risk of course is that this will be found to be entirely unacceptable. More than twenty years ago, for instance, Benjamin Noyes (2000) noted that 'Bataille seems to affirm violence against the weak and helpless, contradicting his earlier claim that "As a child, the notion of torture made life miserable'" (Bataille 1992: 97). What makes this all the more distressing is that Bataille identifies with the torturer rather than the tortured, unlike his meditation on the pain of the Chinese torture victim' (Noyes 2000: 61).

I will examine the image of the Chinese torture victim in the next chapter. But for now, we should accept that although Bataille is left profoundly wanting in his approach[37] to the figure of Gilles de Rais, it is nevertheless his effort to focus on the ordeal of the victim throughout his oeuvre that potentially opens the way to new insights with regard to how victims can be supported.

Notes

1. Cf.: 'The dimension of bare life that constitutes the immediate referent of sovereign violence is more original that the opposition of the sacrificeable and the unsacrificeable' (Agamben 1998: 112–113).
2. See Spivak (1988: 271–313).
3. See Foucault (1979: 76–91).
4. 'Continuity' is part of Bataille's 'general economy' and is the basis of the erasure of borders in communication. For a discussion of Bataille's use of the notions of 'continuity' as a loss of self and 'discontinuity' as identity see Lechte (2018: 104–105).
5. A detailed analysis of Bataille's relation to these photographs will be given in the following chapter.
6. As will be made clear in Chapter 6, it is precisely Girard's Christology (acceptance of Christ's divinity) that separates him from Bataille in relation to the victim.
7. Even in critical texts where sacrifice or the general economy are not at issue, the frequency of references to the instant is striking. For example, in discussing Surrealism and Existentialism, Bataille says: 'If we were truly to break the servitude to which useful activity submits the existence of the instant, the foundation would suddenly reveal itself in us with an unbearable vividness. At least one is led to believe so. The conception of the instant would not differ from ecstasy (reciprocally, ecstasy should be grasped as the instant)' (Bataille 1988b, O.C., XI 81). Again, in discussing Jacques Prévert's poetry, Bataille refers to: 'desires, passions, *jouissances*, angers, and all the other vivid states of feeling, which are all ways of living the instant' (94). Cf. also: 'In the world of the instant, nothing is death, absolutely nothing' (1988b: 103). Bataille also refers to the 'plenitude of the instant' (103, 105).
8. As I will argue below, the instant is not equivalent to the 'now', which only exists in a series, and constitutes the everyday notion of time. Instead, the

instant is absolutely autonomous and able to have an impact in its own right precisely because of this.
9. See also reference to sovereign sensibility as equivalent to the primacy of the instant (Bataille 1988b: 186).
10. The point is that Blanchot's story recounts events and thus evokes past and future. As Derrida notes, the story is presented as a testimony and the latter, to be authentic, is always *after* the event: 'One testifies only when one has lived longer than what has come to pass' (Derrida 2000: 45).
11. As such, non-knowledge is part of the 'general economy'. See Bataille (1988c: 52–53).
12. See Husserl (1981: 278 and *passim*).
13. Of course, Husserl's notion of temporality is not limited to temporal objects and may even be seen to bring into question a naïve view of 'temporal flow' (the series of nows) (see Larrabee 1989). Nevertheless, what is indisputable is that – again, unlike Bataille and the instant – some sort of disposition of past-present-future is at issue for Husserl.
14. Even with Heidegger's 'ecstatic' conception of time that challenges 'the ordinary interpretation' as a stream of nows we know that the future is primary: 'Ecstatico-horizonal temporality temporalizes itself *primarily* in terms of the *future*' (Heidegger 1978: 479). Moreover: 'the future as ecstatically understood [. . .] does not coincide with the ordinary conception of the "future" in the sense of a pure "now"' (479). Ditto for the 'past'. By comparison, the instant in Bataille has no past-present-future disposition.
15. Starting, of course, with Sartre (1947).
16. Of this, he says: 'This photograph had a decisive role in my life. I have never stopped being obsessed by this image of pain, at once ecstatic (?) and intolerable' (206). Bataille's relationship to this photograph will be analysed in the following chapter. His relationship to the victim of torture is one that is empathetic in the strongest possible sense of this term: the sense of an immanent violence that has no voice.
17. The orientation of Nietzschean scholarship has varied according to the era. Studies of the 1960s and 1970s tended to be about whether Nietzsche's text was or was not philosophy in the strict sense (cf. Danto 1965) as well as about its coherence; the 1980s and 1990s began to play up the question of the relation between style and meaning (see Magnus 1991). Overall, though, the predominant component of Nietzschean commentary over the last three decades is characterised by the effort to render interpretation more subtle and complex – to such an extent that it begins to tip over into Nietzschean apologetics.

    Moreover, there is also the question of establishing the Nietzschean text. In the 1980s, in an extremely well-researched and philologically based paper, Bernd Magnus asks about how it might be possible to establish a definitive Nietzschean corpus in light of which the full meaning of putatively key concepts such as 'will to power' and 'eternal return' can be established. Magnus argues that unless one relies on Nietzsche's *Nachlass* – that is, on more than works that the philosopher himself saw to publication – the centrality of will to power fades into the shadows. And yet, to rely on the *Nachlass* (scholars who do, Magnus designates as 'lumpers') is for Magnus highly problematic. But even if the *Nachlass* is given credibility, the book that now bears the title, *The Will to Power*, and which so many interpreters have relied upon to demonstrate the meaning of 'will to power' and 'eternal return' (amongst other terms) was not, the record shows, what Nietzsche himself would have published. Indeed, the evidence that Magnus presents from the *Nachlass* suggests that by September of 1888, Nietzsche had abandoned *'Der Wille zur Macht* as a literary project' (Magnus 1988: 225).

18. In light of Magnus's arguments, I avoid referring to *The Will to Power* as published wherever possible.
19. This aspect of Nietzsche's text, I claim, is far more significant than the metaphoricity or even the hyperbole that has been the focus of so many commentaries (see for an example of this Magnus (1991)). It is interesting that Magnus refers to the 'the litotic voice of Socrates' (1991: 225) – the understated voice that is the diametrical opposite of Nietzsche's; for, as we have seen above, Nancy (1991) proposes that, for the West, Socrates and Christ are iconic victims.
20. According to Magnus (1991: 234), if the same were to recur at a different date, then this is not the return of the same, but the return of the similar. However, this is to have it both ways: for the two different dates (one in the past and one in the present) imply irreversibility, even if the event is the same. Without going into detail, reversible time means the return of time past – time as it was! It is thus not a matter of different dates.
21. On the notion of life as 'life-enhancement' in Nietzsche, see May (1999: 26) and in relation to cruelty (130–134).
22. James Miller, writing on Foucault, Nietzsche and cruelty, cites this passage (see Miller 1990: 475), as does Derrida (2014: 163–164) in a discussion of Nietzsche and the concept of cruelty – *but not the victim* – in relation to capital punishment.

For Miller, cruelty opens up complex questions in relation to law and politics – for example: can cruelty be justified if it is based on legal principles? Following Foucault, Miller asks whether, in the wake of anthropological humanism, humanity has really benefited from abolishing public torture common in the late Middle Ages and the early modern period. For Foucault, Miller says, public torture, with its crowds and its drama in what devolved into a 'carnival' or festival of punishment (cf. Nietzsche), allowed the victims to speak – to curse, to blaspheme – for they had nothing to lose (479). This may be so, but, overall, what is *done* to the victim/criminal is what is at issue. In any case, is a criminal a victim in the same sense that the weak are victims of the strong? I think not. Miller and other commentators fail to acknowledge that Nietzsche links cruelty to life. Cruelty is an ineradicable part of life. Christianity – and possibly every morality – along with idealist philosophy, is against cruelty and the will to power that is manifest in cruelty. Morality, and idealist philosophy are therefore against life. Thus, we read that: 'In every age the wisest have passed the identical judgement on life: *it is worthless* . . . Everywhere and always their mouths have uttered the same sound – a sound full of doubt, full of melancholy, full of weariness with life, full of opposition to life' (Nietzsche 1974c: sect 1, 29).

23. In an article, 'Nietzsche and the Art of Cruelty' (2017), W. Jared Parmer cites this passage and then justifies Nietzsche's position: 'I argue that victims benefit from the severe, prolonged suffering caused by the kind of cruelty Nietzsche has in mind, and that perpetrators benefit from cruel acts as expressions of power' (403). Needless to say, I strongly disagree with this claim. It is not founded on any attention to Nietzsche's clear opposition to Christianity as the advocate for the weak (victims), nor does it attend to the very explicit virility of Nietzsche's philosophical position (cf. the warrior). On the latter point, Parmer's political correctness in always using the feminine pronoun (she) trips him up, so that he says: 'In short, an individual engages in cruelty because *she* has an instinct for it, and *she* has an instinct for it because *she* wills to have power and feel powerful' (407; emphasis added). The author, clearly, has no insight into the philosophical implications of feminising cruelty in relation to Nietzsche's position. No doubt this is but the most obvious example of the folly of Nietzsche apologetics.

24. It is on this basis that Derrida argues that the concept of cruelty has no contrary (2014: 147). It is unclear as to whether Derrida accepts Nietzsche's reasoning, where kindness and pity would also be underpinned by cruelty.

25. There has been debate about the meaning of the term '*ressentiment*' (whether, for example, it simply means resentment) and its significance in Nietzsche's philosophy. The consensus seems to be that it is more the way of those well versed in European high culture (such as Nietzsche) of saying, resentment. However, the sociologists Meltzer and Musolf (2002) argue that *ressentiment*, as Nietzsche employs it, refers to the broad historical feelings of revenge harboured by a group or class, and not just individuals, which is more typical of resentment. For his part, Max Scheler, in 1912 (1994), published a book on *ressentiment* where he attempted to distinguish his approach from Nietzsche's, while at the same time

attempting to define it in Nietzschean terms. In the end, though, Scheler fails to capture the historical specificity of Nietzsche's use of the term.
26. The following passage from *The Anti-Christ* (1974b) is a good summary of Nietzsche's position in his later writings: 'What is good? – All that heightens the feeling of power, the will to power, power itself in man. / What is bad? – All that proceeds from weakness / What is happiness? – The feeling that power *increases* – that resistance is overcome. / *Not* contentment, but more power; *not* peace but war; *not* virtue, but proficiency [...] / The weak and the ill-constituted shall perish: first principles of *our* philanthropy. And one shall help them to do so. / What is more harmful than any vice? – Active sympathy for the ill-constituted and weak – Christianity' (sect 2, 115–116).
27. The argument that Nietzsche's philosophy is anti-victim is also that of René Girard. See, for example, Girard (1999: 221–235).
28. Cf. 'Justine serves as an archetype of the victim, for she receives no respite from the continual torrent of abuse from those around her' (Hallam 2012: 111). Also: 'For Sade, this victimizer/victim scenario occurs throughout nature, in which there is, according to him, a hierarchy of the strong and the weak [...] This natural hierarchy dominates Sade's works' (112).
29. See the Introduction to this study for reference to Sade and the 'normal man'. *L'Érotisme* is collected in Bataille (1987: 7–270).
30. Girard writes, for example, that, 'Bataille is primarily inclined to treat violence in terms of some rare and precious condiment, the only spice still capable of stimulating the jaded appetite of modern man' (Girard 1979: 222).
31. Let us remind ourselves that it is as futile to blame strength for expressing itself as it is to blame the bird of prey from taking a lamb. See Nietzsche (1996: sect 13, 28).
32. Victims include the sick who are a danger to the healthy, especially 'the sick woman' (cf. Nietzsche 1996: III, 14, 94–95, 96. See also III, 13, 15,16, 93–94, 97–101).
33. Mention of 'bourgeoisie' and 'aristocracy' (as opposed, perhaps, to 'noble' and 'base') raises the question of the extent to which Nietzsche is making sociological observations about his era, rather than philosophical claims (e.g., that slave morality, corresponding to Judeo-Christian morality, is a morality of *ressentiment*). With the modern era's push for equality, exceptions are all but entirely eliminated, so that what remains is a kind of *ressentiment in vacuo*, embedded in the system of morality, but lacking an object. For without exceptions, there is only herd mentality. The crossover between philosophical analysis and sociological observation constitutes a continual source of uncertainty – if not confusion – in Nietzsche.

34. The feudal system's demise may well have been tragic; but it could be argued that it largely brought about its own demise. Thus, on this basis, de Rais was in no sense a victim.
35. So, on this basis, is Nietzsche a similarly tragic figure? Quite possibly from a biographical point of view, and thus to the extent that, following a certain definition of tragedy, Nietzsche is caught up in events in a manner of which he unaware. But it is not a matter of Nietzsche's biography but of the coherence of his notion of life and the implications of this for an understanding therein of the victim. As a number of commentators have remarked, there is a stark contrast between Nietzsche's words and his actions.
36. The interview of 21 May 1958 is available on YouTube at: https://www.youtube.com/watch?v=5XCnGuK8CVc (last accessed on 19 July 2022).
37. This is an approach, it might be argued, driven by a misguided Nietzscheanism. For it is Nietzsche, as we saw, who claims that an acceptance of life entails an acceptance of cruelty. An anti-Nietzschean position, while acknowledging the existence of cruelty, then prepares to fight against it, most notably by taking the side of the victim – even when not 'blaming' the persecutor, as Christ does not. That is, one is not automatically impelled by *ressentiment*.

2   Bataille: Image and Victim[1]

THE MAJOR CONCERN OF this chapter – and of this book as a whole – is the relationship in the work of Georges Bataille between the image and violence as manifest in a specific instance of the relationship between and the image and victim. What follows continues an investigation into how the victim in the image does not simply evoke identification. In this regard, the image as transparent emerges for Bataille in relation to the victim of Chinese *lingchi* as portrayed in photographs reproduced in *The Tears of Eros* (Bataille 1990: 204–207). Such transparency contrasts with the notion of the image as 'mediality' – which means that the image can appear in its own right – as proffered by Agamben. The same transparency of the image can also be observed in Bataille's writing on the art of the Lascaux caves (see: Bataille 1979: 7–101) and in his study of Manet's paintings (see Bataille 1979: 103–167). These texts are arguably the most important for understanding Bataille's engagement with the image, an engagement that reveals the intimate relation between image and victim. In this context, the issue of the image in general is raised. The now well-rehearsed argument that the image is media specific, and is thus opaque, will be considered in order to show that, for Bataille, the image is – as has been mentioned – transparent: it provides direct access to the imaged. So that the full implications of Bataille's position can be made clear, recourse to a general theory of the image is necessary.

*

In his introduction to a book on representations of pain, James Elkins writes that the group of scholars giving papers on this theme at the 2005 University College, Cork, conference, 'often had difficulty keeping their attention fixed on the representations' (Elkins 2013: 5). He adds that they were aware of the 'slide from image to subject, from signifier to signified, from medium to historical event, but we were powerless to prevent it' (5). In another essay, Elkins writes that 'The *lingchi* images are painful because they record real events, actual and specific pain, exact forms of violence and cruelty' (Elkins 2004: 13).[2] In other words, an academic – not to say intellectualist – approach to the image, which inevitably treats the image as object, is powerless to prevent the image disappearing into what is imaged. As will become evident, although he rarely thematises the image as such in his writing, Bataille does not take an intellectualist approach to it. The image as 'the presence of the thing in its absence' – a principle first enunciated by Sartre (2004: 23–24) – sums up his approach, so that when the victim appears via an image, as is the case with *lingchi*, the victim as such appears as, for example, in sacrifice.

Against the idea of 'media specific referentiality', the image as such calls to be addressed in order to appreciate the force of the presence of the victim. Reference to Siegfried Kracauer's theory of photography and Herta Wolf's rejection of the image as transparent in favour of media specificity opens the way to a clearer understanding of Bataille and victimage.

On Photography and Media Specificity: Kracauer and Wolf

The image as the presence of the thing in its absence is an approximation. What is really at issue is the imaged in all its multiplicity and diversity. As concerns Bataille, it might be asked whether we are dealing primarily with the photographic image, or the painted image or some other genre of the image. That is, people often ask about the *medium* of the image that is in play, for it is thought that the medium facilitates an understanding of the image as such. In what follows we will see that the image is not media specific – that it is, essentially, united to the *imaged*.

Renowned theorist of the image W. J. T Mitchell also seems to avoid defining the image as being media specific when he says: 'By image I mean any likeness, figure, motif, or form that appears in some medium or other' (Mitchell 2005: xiii). Moreover, like Sartre (and Barthes) Mitchell believes that images have a magical aspect (8). On the other hand, in taking a theoretical approach – prompted by the question: 'What Is an Image?' (Mitchell 1986: 7–46) – Mitchell directs attention away from the imaged and towards a supposed objectification of the medium that brings the imaged into presence.

Perhaps the most significant objection to bringing the imaged to centre stage in an effort to avoid the determinism implicit in the notion of media specificity is found in Kracauer's writing on photography (1995).[3] In an undeniably media-specific gesture, Kracauer endeavours to pinpoint the specificity of photography by comparing it to painting or 'artwork'. An artwork is woven of symbolic traits in a way that a photograph cannot be. In the painting the artist presents things as he or she wants them to be in conformity with socio-psychological imperatives, while the photograph simply presents things as they are, without any personal or symbolic overlay: 'in photography the spatial appearance of an object is its meaning' (52), Thus the nature of the photographic medium determines the nature of the photograph. What Kracauer did not anticipate was that painting would come to imitate photography (cf. super-realism) and photography would come to imitate painting (c.f. works of the American artist, Alexa Meade).

Does Bataille take a naïve position as concerns the photographic image (important when considering his approach to *lingchi*), where, for a contemporary consciousness hypersensitive to a media-specific approach to the image, Bataille appears to be an unreformed realist?

As representative of those who argue for the media specificity of photography, Herta Wolf refers to, 'This barely questioned belief in *iconic evidence*' and asks: 'What causes this blind faith that "a picture says more than a thousand words?"' (Wolf 2007: 67–68). Photographic referentiality would be essentially 'media specific' (68).

For Wolf and others, what is perceived/experienced via a photograph is not the imaged, but 'photography's media-specific referentiality'. Wolf thus opposes Roland Barthes's argument in *Camera Lucida*, where the photographic referent as 'untouched by human hand',[4] and that of Susan Sontag in her book, *Regarding the Pain of Others* (2003), where she clearly accepts that photographs are not simply vehicles of 'media-specific referentiality'.[5]

How, then, should one respond to Wolf when she asks:

Is this evidence not based on photography's *media-specific referentiality*? As the result of a cut in space and time, every photograph always represents precisely the moment captured by this cut, so that any picture is authenticated by the photographic procedure itself: one photograph from Abu Ghraib shows a naked man wearing a hood; another, a stocky (ridiculous, childish, boyish whatever) woman walking a man on a leash; but that is all. (68; emphasis added)

Wolf, following the prevailing trend, is 'convinced that the special impact of photographic images, their power, can only be explained with reference to their media-specificity' (68). What, then, is perceived/experienced via a photograph is not the thing itself, but 'photography's media-specific referentiality'. But Wolf still acknowledges that the photograph '*shows* a naked man wearing a hood' (emphasis added). In other words, it is what is *imaged*, not the abstract entity, image, that is the focus of attention. Wolf, then, does not provide proof of media-specific referentiality. What is referred to is what cannot but be taken to be part of the reality of Abu Ghraib prison.

In addition to its media specificity, the photograph is often deemed, after Peirce (1955), to be an index because it records light reflected from an object onto a light-sensitive surface. It is a sign of the imprint of light – *not* the presence of the thing in its absence (see Doane 2007: 133–135).

However, to treat the photographic image as an index is disingenuous. Although it might be *factually* correct to explain the photograph as an index (as Peirce does), this does not capture how it functions. To explain the photograph as an index is like explaining a table in terms of atoms, which do not have mass in the everyday sense of the term and a true description of which leads into quantum physics and the wave and particle theory of matter. More tellingly, though, to posit the photograph as an index is to commit what I would call the analytical fallacy, which is to assume that any entity is essentially a collection of irreducible individual parts. *Analytically* speaking, the truth of an entity (e.g., a photograph) is in what does not appear as such. The analytical approach is also equivalent to the Cartesian fallacy that Bachelard pointed to – namely, that the essence of things is always reducible to simple elements, whereas in fact essence here is an irreducible complexity (see Bachelard 1995: 143).

Consequently, a photograph, as the imaged, is not an index, especially not when compared to classical instances of indexicality, such as smoke as an index of fire, the footprint in the snow as an index of a foot (or person), the spinning arms of the mill as an index of wind, etc. The visibility – or detectability – of each of these indices contrasts starkly with the situation of the photograph, the indexicality of which is anything but detectable.

Again, it is said that the photograph is an index of the real. And maybe at an intellectual, semiotic and theoretical level it is. But at an experiential level, it is the 'presence of the thing in its absence', with all the immediacy that this entails. In sum, the image as the presence of the thing in its absence goes right against the epoch of McLuhan and the sentiment that, 'the medium is the message'.[6]

The Victim Revisited

For many Bataille readers the thinker's psychological being was at stake in his psychoanalysis with Dr Adrien Borel in 1925. Bataille himself says in *The Tears of Eros* (1990: 205) that it was through Borel that a photograph of *lingchi* came into his possession. According to Michel Surya's biography, Borel was in fact present at the execution of the subject of the photograph, Fu Chou Li, on 10 April 1905 (Surya 2002: 93). Surya, like many observers, calls the *lingchi* a torture. But for the specialist China historian, Timothy Brook, torture implies the extraction of information, and the victim here is being asked for nothing (Brook et al. 2008: 9). While this is true, the infliction of pain without causing immediate death is typical of torture. Therefore, in what follows it will be assumed that *lingchi* is torture. How Bataille relates to the image cannot be separated from how he relates to the photos of the tortured victim. The photographs bring into focus once again Bataille's sense of an *experience* of death. To *experience* death means, of course, being in the place of the victim of violence – he who is at the point of death.

The uniqueness of the position concerned cannot be overestimated. Although, in a sense Bataille – through 'communication' (continuity) – aspires to be in the place of the victim, this is not in order to alleviate the latter's pain, but rather to experience the pain with the victim; it is not a matter, in the first instance, of saving the victim, although in providing a greater awareness of victimage Bataille gives hope for its possible alleviation.[7] Susan Sontag is therefore on the right track when, in speaking of Bataille and *lingchi*, she invokes, 'religious thinking' and 'excruciation' as a kind of 'exultation' (Sontag 2003: 88), similar perhaps to experiencing Christ's suffering on the Cross. However, Sontag overstates the case. For although Bataille is sensitive to the religious aspect, given his interest in the sacred,[8] the real force of his position is contained in his rendering of 'inner experience' and the notions of sovereignty and continuity that are crucial to it. Inner experience signifies that there is a continuity between self and victim. The following words capture well the situation: 'who does not imagine himself to be "dying to die"' (Bataille 1988c: 120). So, in relation to the Chinese man in the photographs, Bataille says that: 'he communicated his pain to me or perhaps the excessive nature of his pain, and *it was precisely that which I was seeking*' (120; emphasis added). As mentioned in the Introduction, essentially, what is stake is the following: 'The game I am setting myself is to represent what they [voodoo sacrifice, and victim of Chinese torture] were living at the moment the lens fixed their image on the glass or on the film' (Bataille 1990: 185). To access this moment is to access the being of the victim via the auspices of the image.

Inner experience never leads Bataille to focus on the perpetrators of torture (the persecutors), or, more generally, on the perpetrators of violence, whereas – as we saw in the previous chapter – Nietzsche does little else. Indeed, for Nietzsche there should be no sympathy – no pity – for victims (the weak) supported as they are in Western culture by Judeo-Christian morality. A large proportion of contemporary manifestations of the imaginary (cinema, literature) demonstrate a profound valorisation of the active (heroic) force, in relation to which a victim is needed, if only to reinforce the idea of the superiority of what is active. The hero substantiates his (or her) active status by 'saving' the victim.

To say, as Elkins does, that the *lingchi* images are painful because they record real events, actual and specific pain, exact forms of violence and cruelty (Elkins 2004: 15) is to propose a fairly conventional interpretation that, while not at all incorrect if one assumes a subject (the one who contemplates the image)-object (the content of the image) approach, is not the same as Bataille's approach; for inner experience cannot be reduced to a subject-object dichotomy. Bataille's way of putting it is to evoke the notion of the 'fusion': 'Experience attains in the end the fusion of subject and object' (1988c: 9).

A rational philosophical understanding (one quite in keeping with Elkin's characterisation of *lingchi*) poses a subject contemplating an object. Inner experience by comparison appears to enter the realm of pure mysticism (Sartre) and to cease, thereby, to have any philosophical credibility. For, the philosopher claims, eliminating the difference between self and other (which, effectively, is what is being proposed) is quite simply impossible. Thus does Sartre interpret 'inner experience', dubbing Bataille *'un nouveau mystique'* ('a new mystic') in the process (Sartre 1947). But, as Derrida points out, inner experience is not about interiority and thus is not about experience in the commonly accepted sense – that is, it is not about the psyche narrowly understood. Were this to be the case, the Bataillian notion of communication would not make any sense. Derrida thus confirms that:

> Bataille above all is not a new mystic. That which *indicates itself* as interior experience is not an experience, because it is related to no presence, to no plenitude, but only to the 'impossible' it 'undergoes' in torture. This experience above all is not interior: and if it seems to be such because it is related to nothing else, to no exterior (except in modes of nonrelation, secrecy and rupture), it is also completely *exposed* – to torture – naked, open to the exterior, with no interior reserve of feelings, profoundly superficial. (Derrida 1978: 272)

This assessment should be kept in mind, for it makes clear that notions of 'communication', 'ecstasy', 'interiority' are not explained by Bataille's psychological state,[9] something no doubt fuelled by references to Dr Borel. As a result, those commentators who have worried about whether Bataille's attitude to torture is sadistic, masochistic, voyeuristic, scopophilic or indeed exploitative and fetishistic in some way have missed the point as far as the victim is concerned.

Again, when interpreting Bataille's relation to the *lingchi* photographs, those who interpret Bataille's work *solely* within or in relation to a theological frame have also missed the point[10] to the extent that Nietzsche's 'death of God' – understood in a secular sense[11] – is an unsurpassable given for Bataille. For their part, the historians of the sources of the *lingchi* images run the risk of fetishising context in their effort to explain the significance of this particular event.[12]

To repeat the question posed earlier: does Bataille take a naïve position as concerns the photographic image? Or does his engagement with the image show that the latter truly is the means of access to the imaged?

*

Theologically, we know that the image cannot capture the Holy without falsifying it: 'either the invisible or the impostor' (Marion 2013: 274) When 'icon' and 'idol' are compared, 'The icon does not represent; it presents ... in the sense of making present the holiness of the Holy One' (280). Unlike the 'media-specific' approach to the image, a theological approach views the image is a vehicle for what is imaged. The iconoclastic position is that the image can never be equivalent to the prototype or to what is imaged (consequently, Agamben, as we shall see, is, theologically speaking, an iconoclast). The effort to make the image equivalent to the prototype can only result in idolatry.

It is, however, important not to confuse the theological and the phenomenological, which would result in theological issues being transferred, holus-bolus, into a secular context. Questions about the status of the image of Christ; questions about iconoclasm; questions about art and the image – such is the terrain Marion's work opens up.[13] These questions are also important for illuminating the role of the image in a secular context to the extent that there is always a mystery – or even magic – surrounding the working of the image. It is this mystery that a media-specific approach to the image denies.

Theologically, then, Christ, for Catholicism, is both human and divine and an image of Christ can capture this humanity and this divinity, whereas for Orthodox Christianity as for Judaism and (to a lesser extent) Protestantism, Christ is at most an exceptional human being who may or may not be able to perform miracles. Seen in this way, images of Christ become perfectly legitimate, to the degree that no claim to capture the divine is being made.

For his part, Bataille follows Barthes and theology (cf. *acheiropoietos* invoked by Barthes in *Camera Lucida* (2010: 82)) rather than those proposing a media-specific approach to the photographic image.[14] The question then is: does Bataille, in his viewing of the *lingchi*, follow Sontag and Barthes, or does he problematise the referentiality of the photographic image? And, any case, is this at all pertinent for interpreting Bataille's privileging the position of the victim? An informed response to these questions requires us to examine Bataille's understanding of the image as this emerges in three key texts: the interpretation of the Lascaux cave images, the study of Manet, and the interpretation of the image in *The Tears of Eros*.

Lascaux: The Animal as Victim

In his interpretation, first published in 1955, Bataille argues that, in the caves of Lascaux where images abound, the 'night' of art can be compared to Greek art as the art of the day – the art of light. Night, it is said, precedes day. Strictly speaking, it is not a matter of art, for this is a modern concept; rather, in a fundamental line of Bataille's thought, the animal as victim is at issue as well as the relation between humanity and animality. As Yue Zhuo (2015) points out in a very astute article that foreshadows part of the trajectory followed here, Lascaux is not, for Bataille, just an event in Paleolithic chronology – an 'emblem of the ages during which the passage from animal to man completes itself' (21). Instead, it 'is above all a fantasized time/space where art, play, and religion join each other in a single backward movement toward the recovery of a lost intimacy with animals and nature' (21). This is not to deny that Bataille seems to avoid going directly to the point that I would wish to highlight. For the 'art' of the caves is, at first blush, viewed less as a celebration of what is imaged – the 'figurations pariétales' (Bataille 1979: 366) – and more as an insight into the evolutionary history of the human in relation to work, religion and art – work being made possible by the invention of tools. Tools (with Neanderthal man) enable work but also the possibility (with *Homo sapiens*) of making art objects, objects that give rise to 'play' (1979: 28).

So, the issue here is about the nature of *Homo sapiens* and the role art played in distinguishing human from animal. Indeed – but: 'At its outset, art was above all and remained a game' (28); that is, it was done for its own sake as much as for what it could signify. In contrast to work (and to art), 'hunting was a prolongation of animal activity' (30); it is not a mark of the human. Individual images engage Bataille as well as the imaged and the nature of art. Art – unlike the tool – distinguishes the human from the animal because the issue is not survival – it is not work, it is not utility; this is why art is in play. In this sense the origin of art becomes the origin of the human as *Homo sapiens*. At the same time, certain images in the Lascaux caves make a particular impression on the observer, most notably the 'Man in the

Well' and animals as victims of the hunt.[15] Indeed, if we step back just a little, what comes across almost immediately in Bataille's text is his reverence for the spectacle of the images on the walls of the caves that he has been fortunate to visit.

What I have exposed thus far about Bataille's writing on Lascaux has been taken up in more detail by others interested in assessing the contribution Bataille makes to prehistory, archaeology and historical anthropology.[16] Through the image as such (not through tools and the products of work), Bataille sees himself in touch with the origin of *Homo sapiens* humanity. This sense comes across in a passage in *The Tears of Eros* referring to the caves:

> We are dealing now with amazing signs, signs that touch our deepest sensibilities: these signs have a force that moves us, and no doubt they *will never cease to trouble us*. These signs are the paintings on the walls of the caves where he [first members of our species] must have celebrated his ceremonies. (Bataille 1990: 29; emphasis added)

Whatever place Bataille's text might have in the scheme of prehistory,[17] Bataille's writing on Lascaux foregrounds images as depictions of victims.[18] This emphasis on the animal as victim distinguishes my interpretation from that of Zhuo, where victimage remains largely implicit. There is no play or art without the sacred – thus without victims, whether animal or human. Transgression, as discussed by Bataille, is religious in nature and linked to an 'ecstatic sensibility' (1979: 40). The latter, in its turn, 'is linked to the festival, where sacrifice is a paroxysmal moment. Antiquity saw in the sacrifice the *crime* of the sacrificer who, in the anguished silence of the assistants, put the victim to death, the crime where the sacrificer, knowingly and himself in a state of anguish, violated the prohibition on murder' (40–41). Now, it is important to note 'that in its essence, and in practice, art expresses this moment of religious transgression, that it alone expresses it with gravity and is its only outcome' (41). This means that art is inextricably linked to the victim of sacrifice: 'Art forms have no other origin than the all-time festival, and the festival, which is religious, is linked to the deployment of all the resources of art. One cannot imagine an art independently of the movement which engenders the festival' (41).

Individual images, then, hold Bataille's attention in his Lascaux study. As Carrie Nolan fruitfully shows in this regard, Bataille breaks with the comparatist approach of French prehistory still popular when he was completing his study (1955) in favour of a focus on *actual* images in the Lascaux cave. The problem with a comparatist approach was that it 'drew attention away from the actual marks on the wall, discouraging analysis of their individual properties and environmental contexts in favor of large overarching theories of social function based on groups that had no direct relation to hunter-gatherers of the Aurignacian times or Cantabrian spaces' (Nolan 2004: 134).

Moreover, in his interpretive analysis, Bataille gives no credence to the idea that the cave images – almost entirely of animals – were, *qua* images, a source of magic used to enhance prospects in hunting. That is, he opposes the claim by certain scholars that the images had a purely utilitarian value, assisting in the struggle for survival. For Bataille, by contrast, the images signify the very opposite of work, project, survival. They are instead – as indicated above – linked to play, festival and the sacred.

But why depict only animals and not humans? The answer given is that when the domain of utility and work is set aside, the life of the animal is the one humans most wanted to emulate. The animal, in short, is the incarnation of non-utilitarian existence; its life is not governed by repetitive work. Great prestige is thus attributed to the animal to the point where the latter becomes the incarnation of the god that the human wanted to be.[19] 'The fact', says Bataille, 'that the animal represented was prey and food does not change the meaning of this humility' (1979: 63). The representation of the human thus seems to merge with certain animal figures. Indeed, the man of the Lascaux caves,

> most often dissimulated his traits behind an animal mask. He showed to the point of virtuosity the possibilities of drawing, but despised his own face; if he acknowledged his human form he, at the same time, hid it; at this moment he presented himself with the head of an animal. It was as if he were ashamed of his own face and that, wanting to sketch it, he was at the same time forced to present himself with the mask of an other. (1979: 63)

The presence of the image of the animal corresponds, therefore, to its prestige, while the absence of images of the human corresponds to an evocation of humility and lowliness. The animal thus seems to attain prestige *qua* victim even if Bataille does not make this absolutely explicit. In sum, according to Bataille's presentation, there are images of animals on the walls of the Lascaux caves (and no doubt elsewhere – cf. Altamira caves in Spain) because animal prestige derives from its status as victim. This point is reinforced by the Russian folktale related by the French anthropologist, Éveline Lot-Falck, of which, Bataille says, '*me semble avoir un intérêt privilégié*' ('seems to me to be of special interest' (1979: 75)). The story illustrates an equality existing between the human hunter and the hunted animal, to the point, indeed, where '"before it can be killed, the animal must have first given its consent"' (Lot-Falck cited by Bataille (75)). The animal is still the victim but is none the less of equal or greater prestige than its vanquisher. Here then is a way of presenting the victim that is not beholden to the wielder of physical power. Such a relation is incomprehensible to modern humanity. Zhuo rightly draws attention to Bataille's conception of human-animal equality, highlighted in particular in passages from 'Le Berceau de l'humanité: La vallée de la vézère' ('The Cradle of Humanity: The Vézère Valley') (Bataille 1979: 353–376), a text written after 'Lascaux' and reproduced as part of the dossier of Bataille's writings on Lascaux and other parietal art. There, we read that as the one who suffers death, the animal at the same time attains a certain transcendence; for it is only through death that one becomes divine. Animals experience death in a way that humans can never do: 'More than man, the animal is close to the world of the gods' (369). Moreover: 'With the killing of the divine animal the hunter overcame the terror of death' (370). The animal has the status of a god and those who kill it, says Bataille, 'feel themselves to be its murderers'. The animal, in short, is victim in the fullest sense – in the sense, perhaps, that Christ appears as victim and, *qua* victim, is divine. Or, as Bataille expresses it: 'One must ask the victim for forgiveness, shed tears for it and honour it like a god' (371). Death thus confirms the animal as victim and as victim it becomes divine. Its death also offers the human a profound intuition of mortality. Through death, humans identify with animals and manifest 'a *religious* sympathy with their victims' (373). Here, it is not a matter of sacrifice, which appeared much later, even if it could be a foretaste (but this is not certain) of a religious orientation. Clearly, whatever the case, the animal figurations offer insights into the victim and it is this that constitutes the foundation of religion.

Seen in this light, Nolan's emphasis, in her interpretation, on the gesture – firstly, on the one that originally produced the Lascaux images, and secondly, on Bataille's gesture of writing in the cave, notebook in hand – seems misplaced (Nolan 2004: 153). For it is not the being of the image makers that is primary, but precisely the status of what was imaged – the animals. Such is the way that, effectively, Nolan privileges the human over the animal (a very modern gesture), whereas Bataille proceeds in exactly the reverse manner. So, *pace* Nolan, it is not the presence of Bataille's body in the cave that should be noted, but rather the presence via images of animal-victims.

Now, in the wake of Lascaux, it is time to ask how, if at all, the victim is present in modern pictures. This is the question raised by Bataille's writing on Manet.

The Image in Manet's Paintings

Caroline Sheaffer-Jones writes that: 'At the heart of Bataille's *Manet* is the way in which a work of art tests the so-called boundaries between life and art, reality and representation, life and death' (Sheaffer-Jones 2015: 234). In other words, for Sheaffer-Jones, it is as much what lies beyond as within the frame that drives Bataille's writing on Manet. While, in a certain sense this is true, it is what Bataille finds *within* the frame that concerns us here.

In his study, *Manet* (first published, like *Lascaux*, in 1955) access to Bataille's concept of the image can be gained from his remarks about various paintings by Édouard Manet (1832–1883). The thinker's interest in the painter's style and personality does not lead uniquely to a media-specific interpretation of the contents of paintings. This is indeed true as regards death and nudity. In effect, Manet paints death,[20] even if his model is Goya's *The Third of May* (1808). Goya, too, 'paints death': 'the scene of the firing squad that we call *The Third of May*, is the *apparition* of death itself' (1979: 132). According to Bataille, Manet saw Goya's painting in Madrid in 1865 and then painted *The Execution of Maximilian* in 1867.

Surely, if Manet takes Goya's work as his model, this is evidence of 'media-specific referentiality'? For how the scene is represented would take precedence over what is represented. Given that some of the artist's most important paintings – such as *Olympia* (1863) and *Le Déjeuner sur l'herbe* (1863) – are clearly modelled on earlier works, how is Bataille able to claim that Manet's paintings give direct access to the referent? Would it be that Bataille exhibits a certain blindness here? The answer is in the style itself, in a matter-of-fact style that communicates (quite unlike Goya) an indifference to the subject matter: 'Manet painted the death of the condemned man with the same indifference as if he had as the object of his work a flower, or a fish' (1979: 132). This indifference, then, gives access to the referent as such. It is what allows Bataille to say later that, 'Manet intentionally represented death' (133–134). And in this regard, he points to the paintings, *L'Enterrement* (The Funeral) (1870) and *Le Suicidé* (The Suicide) (1877) (134).

As to nudity, nothing is more indicative of Manet's approach to realism than his *Olympia* (1863). Such at least is Bataille's claim. Discussing what he believes makes 'Manet's realism' distinctive compared to Zola's is that the latter '*situates* what he describes' (1979: 142), whereas the realism of *Olympia* 'once had the power not be situated *anywhere*, neither in a charmless world that reveals the movement of prosaic language, nor in the convulsive order of fiction' (142). Despite being borrowed from Titian's *Venus of Urbino* (1538), Manet renders the figure in *Olympia* in a 'prosaic' and familiar mode, contrary to Titian's romantic style and its mythological themes. Indeed, Manet's painting is 'realist' in the sense that his figures 'derive from actual forms of life' (1979: 144), which implies that Manet's paintings are not academic. Thus, the figure in *Olympia* appears as a 'young woman and not as a goddess' (145). Consequently, her nudity is real and not metaphorical; it does not evoke the tradition of rules as to how beauty should be portrayed but breaks with such rules in a presentation of the contingency of life. The realism (for want of a better term) at stake is such that in *Olympia*, nudity is not simply a representation; it is nudity as such (144).[21] The same applies to the nudity in *Le Déjeuner sur l'herbe*: its significance is not that it is a 'media-specific referentiality'; rather, it works as an image in giving access to the real. Manet, then, 'introduced the present world' (145) into his paintings even when evoking a model or schema from the past. The present world is the real world, the world or the object as such. Manet's images give us direct access to this. Such is Bataille's central thesis, a thesis that implies the transparency of the image, not its so-called media specificity, or opacity.

But what of the notion of victim? It is difficult to determine the latter given statements like the following: 'Indifference to the subject is not only characteristic of Manet, but of the whole of Impressionism and of modern painting – a few names excepted' (150). And Bataille subsequently notes that, 'what counts in Manet's canvases, is not the subject; what counts is the vibration of light' (157). This is not to be understood in the way usually attributed to Impressionism. It is not really to neglect the subject. Then comes a reference to sacrifice: 'it is not to neglect the subject, but something else: the same goes for sacrifice, which alters, which destroys, which kills, *without neglecting the victim*' (157). Manet's painting thus evokes sacrifice and victim. So, it is less a matter of Manet cancelling the subject in favour of painting as such and more one of a transfiguration of the subject within painting as painting (157). Again, when referring to Manet's *Le Bal masqué à l'opéra* (1873) (night-time scene), and to *Un bar aux Folies-Bergère* (day-time scene) Bataille evokes the festival: 'It is probable that the festival is, in its essence, the suppression of the distinct state of those who live it' (153). And he continues by saying that, 'Manet perhaps better than any other person had the facility to represent it, since he was searching for what could be substituted for the precise element that distinguishes the subject – that which would become lost and hidden' (153–154). Manet, in other words, has the capacity to depict the continuity of communication, which is the other side of existence beyond the profane world, where the boundary between self and other becomes porous. So, too, is this the case with the victim in an exchange of mutual experience. If Manet actively does the depicting, can he really do justice to communication, to victimage? Here, it is instructive to consider the extent that Manet is also a victim in Bataille's account.

Manet never saw clearly what he wanted. In retrospect, what is certain for us regarding Manet's paintings was the source of profound uncertainty for the artist (158). He never 'ceased to search, to doubt, to be fearful of others' judgements' (158). In the 'interminable vagaries of art', Bataille continues, 'the only things that are true are excessive confidence and fatigue' (158). Manet's charm, indeed, derives from his indecision, hesitations and fragility. He is thus a *victim* of fate rather than its master. He is also fragile and tense (159). Nevertheless, the artist's most profound and pointed feelings do appear in his canvases, Bataille asserts, as though the image does, in the end, carry the weight of a certain authenticity, if not of truth (159).

Manet's *Gamin aux cerises* (Boy With Cherries) (circa 1858) evokes the real death by suicide of Manet's painting model. The story is, Bataille notes, the subject of Baudelaire's prose poem, *La corde* (The Rope) (1864), which tells how, after the boy's death, his mother asks to buy the suicide rope in the belief that it would bring good luck. Was Manet in some way responsible for the boy's death, or was he the victim of circumstances? Bataille leans towards the latter conclusion (159).

At the beginning of his account of Manet's life as an artist, Bataille mentions that 'few men had suffered more from the lack of recognition' (118). In other words, Manet is the absolute opposite of Nietzsche's Dionysian artist full of energy whose drive to create can equally include a desire to destroy. On this basis, Bataille's reference to Manet's supposed indifference to the (particular) image in the interest of painting as such does not hold up. On the contrary, it is more plausible to say that Manet was intimately connected to the images he produced, not only because death (such as the model's suicide) brought the image into sharp focus, but because – if the art historians are correct – Manet was concerned to universalise his art through references in his work – especially in the 1860s – to other painters' images – painters such as Rubens, Goya, Velázquez, Delacroix, Watteau, Le Nain, Chardin, Courbet and others.[22] Only a concern for the image as what is imaged, in particular in its content and its form can render such an approach plausible.

The Imaged and Violent Death

> The image, and perhaps to the troubled feeling where a vertiginous horror and drunkenness come together, where the reality of death itself, of the sudden coming of death, holds a meaning heavier than life, heavier – and more glacial.
>
> Bataille, *The Tears of Eros* (1990: 199)

Images are indices of human development. This is a principle of Bataillean prehistory. It is through the image that access to death (death as communication) takes place, the key point here being that communication leads to (an experience of) the living instant of death. In the *lingchi* photographs, reproduced in *The Tears of Eros* (204–206), the one inflicting the torture is to be seen sawing into the victim's left leg. It would be quite possible to identify with the executioner, of course; but Bataille is clear as to where his concern lies: it is with the victim. The image, violence and the place of the victim all come together with the *lingchi* photographs.

Bataille had already referred to the *lingchi* in *Inner Experience* (1988c) (*Expérience intérieur*). There he reveals in intense terms his 'non-discursive' connection with the victim in his recourse to upsetting images:

> I would gaze at the photographic image – or sometimes the memory which I have of it – of a Chinese man who must have been tortured in my lifetime. Of this torture, I had had in the past a series of successive representations. In the end, the patient writhed, his chest flayed, arms and legs cut off at the elbows and knees. His hair standing on end, hideous, haggard, striped with blood, beautiful as a wasp.
>
> I write 'beautiful'! . . . something escapes me, flees from me, fear robs me of myself and, as I had wanted to stare at the sun my eyes rebel. (1988c: 119–120)

A little later, he confirms the intensity of his feeling for the victim:

> The young and seductive Chinese man, left to the work of the executioner – *I loved him with a love in which the sadistic instinct played no part*: he communicated his pain to me or perhaps the excessive nature of his pain, and it was precisely that which I was seeking, not so as to take pleasure in it, but in order to ruin in me that which is opposed to ruin. (120; emphasis added)[23]

Unlike Nietzsche, Bataille – although willing, and even desiring, to meet it head-on – is, perhaps with the exception of the actions of Gille de Rais, appalled by cruelty, whoever the victim might be. Indeed, he says of 'excessive cruelty' that 'it is natural to rebel, to cry out (our hearts fail us): "That can no longer be!"' (121).

With the photographs of the Chinese man (the dress of the executioner, for one thing, signifies 'Chinese'), the 'excessive cruelty' (which, let us not forget, is an excessive violence) is apparent in the image regardless of the context (that is, regardless of whether or not the victim is a criminal[24]). To be appalled at the violence is no doubt to be appalled as someone who has a particular cultural orientation – the orientation (let us say it) of a 'civilised' being, a being able to respond to the notion of universal human rights, a being, moreover, willing to attempt to offer a philosophical as well as a moral objection to capital punishment, an objection that is necessarily uttered from the position of the victim.

In the various passages devoted to sacrifice in *Inner Experience*, the most powerful of them evoke becoming victim. For instance, the sacrificer, when referred to, becomes victim: 'This sacrifice *which we consummate* [Bataille's emphasis] is distinguished from others in this way: the one who sacrifices is himself affected by the blow which he strikes – *he succumbs and loses himself with his victim*' (153; emphasis added). Again, in uniting sacrifice with anguish, Bataille himself becomes the human sacrificial victim: 'the only true sacrifice is human sacrifice. For the victim, whom the sacrificial knife puts into death's power, is there for me. In him, I was able to perceive myself destroyed by the rage to destroy' (194).

A Critique of *The Tears Of Eros*: Victim and Civil Identity

In a scathing critique of *The Tears of Eros*, the authors of *Death by a Thousand Cuts* (Brook et al. 2008) declare: 'Frankly, we find *Les Larmes d'Éros* an obnoxious work executed in bad taste' (228). They go on to decry a tone of 'arid sadism' along with a mixing of genres and the book's poor organisation. But it is, one senses, Bataille's claim that the face of the victim of the *lingchi* might express a certain ecstasy that really constitutes the basis of the negative assessment. The authors suggest that, in terms of their research, there is an absence of any reference to *lingchi* in Bataille's writing before *The Tears of Eros* – apart from the following reference in *Guilty* to

> the young Chinese (a condemned felon) shown in the photos as covered with blood while the executioner tortures him (the blade's already in his knee-bone). I was connected to this unhappy being in ties of horror and friendship. But when I looked at this image to the *point of harmony*, the necessity of being only myself was cancelled. And at the same time this object I chose disintegrated into vastness and, in a storm of pain, was destroyed. (Bataille 1988d: 46)

Questions regarding the authorship of *The Tears of Eros* are raised,[25] and doubt is cast on whether Bataille really did receive a *lingchi* photograph from Adrien Borel in 1925. But, in my view, the most telling issue the authors raise concerns the civil identity of the victims of *lingchi*. Not to be concerned with this, it is said, is to be oblivious of the context of the execution and to treat the victim as 'a suffering body, nothing more' (Brook et al. 2008: 234). Put another way, the victim remains a pure *persona* rather a 'real person' (240). An additional factor is a cultural one: the anonymity of the victim of such mutilation is in keeping with a certain orientalism, in as far as the civil identity of the other has often only mattered when Westerners were victims. The authors of *Death by a Thousand Cuts* say that: 'As historians [. . .] we prefer to know who we are talking about and [in Bataille's case] to understand how the issue of personal identity could be so ignored' (226). There is no doubt, as I have said elsewhere,[26] that to be fully human in a Western sense means transcending 'bare life' and the bestowing of a civil identity in a polity.[27] Even though the authors' aim is to establish the separate identities of 'the actual individuals involved' and 'thereby return them to history' (226–227), the implication is that identity means civil identity (the name on the birth certificate, citizenship), the identity that can be documented. They do not mean what Hannah Arendt called 'natural givenness' and 'mere differentiation' (1968: 182), the sphere prior to civil society that is supposedly not foreign to animals.[28]

We need to ask, now, whether our authors might have overstepped the mark. Certainly, civil identity is an important attribute of the human, but is its absence to be equated with the non-human? If we assume an affirmative response to this question, how can those who lack a civil identity benefit from a struggle for human rights? More pertinently, is it only possible to identify cruelty occurring to a victim with a civil identity? In short, is Bataille wrong in being moved by the photographs of *lingchi*, even though he mis-attributes or fails to attribute a name to the victim? Putting aside for the moment Bataille's questionable (for the authors) interpretation of the victim's facial expression as one of ecstasy, is it not clearly possible to be moved by cruelty (or an ecstatic state) in a photographic image whether or not one is aware of the name and, for that matter, the historical context of the image? If it were not possible to be so moved, how could images of cruelty to animals be experienced and identified? And, I would ask, how would photographic images of concentration camp corpses be deemed horrific if we had to be aware of the actual names and civil identities of the victims?

No. Even though one can conceivably have a different emotional response to the victims in the *lingchi* photographs, it is still a *victim* that implicates us. The question that Bataille's relation to the photographs raises – a question that resounds throughout the Bataillian oeuvre – is: how can we relate to victims? How can we 'be' in the victim's place? Which, of course, can lead to the plea: how can victimage be overcome?

The *Lingchi* and the Issue of Context – Of Being a Victim

With admirable thoroughness, Amy Hollywood, like the historians, also questions Bataille's apparent ignorance of the context of the *lingchi* victim's death (2002: 82), most notably as regards the ethical, political and historical aspects (83). Bataille never asks, she says, why such events occur and how they can be stopped (83). She claims, moreover, that Bataille argues that the other is 'simply a projection of the self' (72), which would bring him close to being the target of Levinas's critique, which, I suggest, is not the case. If it were, Bataille's writing would not have anything original to say about being a victim. His work on the sacred would be insignificant. In fact, though, the notions of continuity and communication entail, if not a potential fusion of beings, at least a logic of fluidity in which the difference between self and other – life and death – is vastly reduced, if not overcome – or, if 'overcome' is too strong a word, is opened up to a unique experience.

Hollywood has much more to say, however, most of it to do with Bataille's approach to suffering as compared to that of mediaeval believers in a crucified Christ. I will leave this to one side the better to focus on Hollywood's engagement with the nature of the photographic image in general and with the *lingchi* photos in particular. To make her point that Bataille's approach to the photograph of the *lingchi* is inadequate (that treating the photos as entirely transparent is inadequate), Hollywood says that Bataille's claim to communicate with the victim 'depends on his bypassing the photographer, the material conditions of the images' production and the other people who appear in the photographs' (89). She then asks a series of apparently searching questions: 'Who took the images? Was the photographer Chinese? European? Were the photographs produced to serve as warnings for other malefactors? As illustrated guides for would-be torturers? As "neutral" anthropological or historical reportage? As images of exotic horror for a Western audience?' (89–90).[29] Far from clarifying the nature of the photographic experience, this series of questions evokes an academic, theoretical or intellectualist approach to the image, one that rather than bringing things to a close provokes still more questions in what is, effectively, a search for truth. We could ask, for instance: what kind of photographic apparatus was available at the time? Were the participants required to remain still for the shot? Did the photographer have any assistants to help organise the shot? Were the images staged in the same manner as in World War I (due to the immobility of the apparatus)?[30] What time of day was the shot taken?, etc. For her part, Hollywood states that if the photographs have an indexical quality, which relates them to the real,

> then we are immediately led back to the questions asked earlier: Who took these pictures? To what end? For what audience? Who speaks through them? – the victim, the seemingly unmoved ring of observers who surround the tortured person and appear to present him to the viewer, the torturers (and Bataille may, at one point, suggest his horrified identification with them [OC V 276–277; G 38–39],[31] or the photographer through whose "eyes" we see? (Hollywood 2002: 92)

Research and questions thus call for more research, which raises more questions. Or, as Derrida said: everything relates to context, but context, if it is not entirely open-ended, 'is never absolutely determinable' (Derrida 1988: 3). So, can it really be claimed that this is how an image – a photographic image in this case – is *experienced*? I think not. What we might be looking for are answers to research questions; what Bataille *encountered* was torture via the image.[32]

Again, it is said that the photograph is an index of the real. And maybe at an intellectual, semiotic and theoretical level it is. But at an experiential level, it is the 'presence of the thing in its absence', with all the immediacy that this entails.

When Roland Barthes, theorist of semiotics, refers, in *Camera Lucida* (2010: 67–71) to a photograph of his mother in the Winter Garden, his relationship to this image is decidedly not of a semiotic nature. For all intents and purposes, the image – at an experiential level – *is* his mother. 'I studied the little girl', Barthes says, 'and at last rediscovered my mother' (69). All the questions that could be asked about this image are not asked. In a way, this is the whole point of Barthes's approach to photography, an approach indebted to Sartre.

In a photo finish, whether at the Olympics or at the racetrack, we are not concerned about asking semiotic-type questions of the photographic image, but only about which entity is the winner (or loser). In short, a variety of contexts exist in which the immediacy of the image is in play. Of course, if I have *posed* for my passport photo then, from a semiotic point of view, this is not the real person, but a persona. However, the passport officer at the airport is not interested in such a possibility, but only in whether or not the photo is a good (or passable) likeness.

In the above quote with the additional questions, Hollywood suggests that Bataille 'may suggest his horrified identification' with the executioners of the *lingchi* photograph. The reference given is the following passage from *Guilty*:

> The Chinese executioner of my photo haunts me: there he is busily cutting off his victim's leg at the knee. The victim is bound to a stake, eyes turned up, head thrown back, and through a grimacing mouth you see teeth.
> The blade is entering the flesh at the knee. Who can accept that a horror of this magnitude would express 'What you are' and lay bare your nature? (Bataille 1988d: 38–39)

Certainly, Bataille describes here what the executioner is doing rather than speculating on the victim's suffering. But to say that this is equivalent to an *identification* with the executioner is, to put it mildly, a huge leap – a leap, indeed, that would begin to undermine Bataille's position as being exclusively that of the victim. The sense the reader gets is that Bataille's words imply an underlying question, namely: how could any human do that to another human?

Stephen Bush writing on Hollywood's interpretation of Bataille remarks that, as Hollywood presents things, '[a] fusion between the self and other occurs' (2011: 303). Certainly, Bataille himself does not shy away from using the term, 'fusion' (see Bataille 1988c: 9–10). But does this adequately portray what, in the end, drives Bataille's thought? As far as the victim is concerned, fusion, clearly, can imply not only that I become the victim but also that the victim becomes me, which can equate to the erasure of victimage: that is, the victim becomes a non-victim. According to Bataille's logic the impossible happens and I take the place of the victim in the victim's suffering.

Whatever the case, I somehow tune into the radical passivity of the other (which includes the woman as object in eroticism) and refuse to glorify the active element – the latter, in Nietzsche's case, being 'the will to power'. The will to power, therefore, is the active principle – transcendent violence – writ large, whereas Bataille suggests something that is at the antipodes of this. It is not an active will to passivity; for this would be too close to mimicking Nietzsche. Rather, it is more like a fundamental recognition of the sanctity of the victim. How one speaks in the victim's name – or, better, how the victim speaks – without blotting out the dire nature of victimage is what is at issue. I am saying, then, that we know what Nietzsche's position is and we know (or so I am arguing) that Bataille does not at all follow Nietzsche here. Life for Bataille – if we read him carefully – can in no way be described as 'will to power'.

Even though a gap to be filled still exists with regard to the status of victim in Bataille's writing, the thinker has led us to the point where we can now only be too aware of the fact that simply identifying with and speaking for the victim, or attempting to enable the victim to speak in his or her own name, or, indeed, to fight on behalf of the victim – that all of these things risk erasing victimage as such. 'And just as well, too', says a voice at the back of the room. In response to that voice I point out that it is not a matter of turning the victim into either a hero or a mystic. Rather than trying to work out how the victim can speak, it is essential to bring into question that force which produces victims – true victims – namely, and for want of a more economical phrase, the will to power.

But is this not to become trapped in Nietzsche's net? Does Nietzsche not argue that, given that the world is made up of a play of forces – of the weak against the strong, the herd against the noble, the warrior against his (respected) enemy (and against Christian morality[33]), etc – so that to have victims opposing the will to power effectively means victims opposing life. To recall: the strong must be protected from the weak, the weak, also being a majority that unite in a 'herd', in a rabble, in a mass, in a community, as opposed to the isolation – the 'pathos of distance' – of the strong and the noble. The weak cannot accept life.[34] But nowhere does Nietzsche say that will to power *creates* the weak (the victims). Rather, the weak are supposedly part of the way life is – just as woman, in all her weakness, is part of the way life is. They (victims) are almost an immanent truth of the world. The strong oppose the weak because it is in their nature to do so. The weak unite and oppose the strong – so the story goes – for the same reason.

With the victim it is different. The victim is essentially opposed to the will to power because it is created by the will to power itself. A definition of the will to power would be that it is: that which creates victims. Who is weak and who is victim is only revealed through the play of forces. Those who strike the other down (spiritually and physically) are the strong; those who are struck down (spiritually and physically) are the weak and are thus victims.

It now remains for this argument about victimage deriving from will to power to be brought into contact with René Girard's work on violence. Before we do this, however, we shall consider the victim and the image in Agamben.

Let us now conclude our remarks on Bataille and the *lingchi* photographs by saying that in contrast to a 'media specific' position, Bataille is in contact – and *we* can be in contact – with the victim in the photograph. This is what the transparency of the photographic image is all about. It presents the victim – makes the victim present. Were this not the case, there would be grave implications for how we relate to the images of death that feature so terribly in both World Wars and in other theatres of atrocity.

Notes

1. A shorter version of this chapter has been published as: 'Bataille: Image and Victim' in *Theory, Culture and Society* (2021), 38 (4), 3–22.
2. Elkins is referring to a series of *lingchi* photographs which has circulated in the West since the early twentieth century.
3. By way of Kracauer's emphasis on detail, or 'non-intentional reality' in photography, Conor Joyce (2003) points to Bataille's article, 'Figure humaine', published in the journal, *Documents* (1929), 4 (see Bataille 1970: 181–185), where Bataille discusses the apparent foreignness for a modern sensibility of the 1905 photograph of a rural wedding. Perhaps this confirms Kracauer's point about detail but see my remarks below. Despite the use of photography in *Documents*, there is, Conor notes, 'no writing on photography as a medium' (69). Ditto for the image in general.
4. On the implications of 'acheiropoietos' for an understanding of the image, see Lechte (2013).
5. For a critique of Sontag on this issue, see Kaplan (2013).
6. On his notion of medium, see McLuhan (2008: 7–23).

7. In light of his reading of Sade, it is clear that, given the nature of sovereignty and continuity in inner experience, a relation to the victim could also be violent. Clearly, Bataille fights against this, but at the same time does so within the province of inner experience. Continuity thus defies reason, but this can happen non-violently.
8. Not to be forgotten is the fact that Bataille's primary interest in religious themes is via the sacred and sacrifice where a victim is involved. To some extent, the position regarding Bataille and victimage being elaborated here is a continuation of Peter Connor's approach, where he writes of 'Bataille's desire to disassociate inner experience from any idea of personhood, to avoid even the suggestion that inner experience originates in or is the expression of a "known personality"' (Connor 2000: 61). Without the strategic reference to Nietzsche, however, Connor still tends at times to become bogged down in explicating the ins and outs of mysticism.
9. On this, see for example, Bush (2011) and Hollywood (2002). While Amy Hollywood defends Bataille against Sartre's designation of him as a 'new mystic', she nevertheless pursues this theme as well as ecstasy and experience in relation to Bataille's writing and invokes Freudian and Lacanian psychoanalytic concepts (cf. masochism, sadism, fetishism, castration, *jouissance*) to partially explain the condition of Bataille's psyche (2002: 51–59 and 90–91). Such an approach cannot but displace emphasis away from the notion of victim and towards something like an ego-subject.
10. See, in particular Heinämäki (2012), who, despite working within a theological frame, develops some interesting insights regarding the dissolution of the self in relation to the other. Also see Hollywood (2002).
11. There is a certain ambivalence here. For, understood within the frame of sacrifice itself, the ultimate sacrifice is of course the killing of the god. As such, the latter would support the sacrificial, or religious, system. Nietzsche's 'death of God', however, supposedly gives rise to the collapse of this system and ushers in nihilism. But, René Girard (1984: 829) draws attention to the passage in *The Gay Science* (1974d), which refers not just to the 'death of God', but to his murderers: '"Whither is God" he cried. "I shall tell you. *We have killed him* – you and I. All of us are his murderers' (1974d: sect 125, 181). Killing the god also confirms the sacredness of the god.
12. See Brook et al. (2008: 222–242). See below for a commentary on this text.
13. Marion's philosophy will be further invoked in relation to the image in Chapter 6, when we come to consider the Crucifixion, the Cross and the image in René Girard's thought.
14. In coining the term, '*athéologique*' to head his works, *Inner Experience, On Nietzsche, Guilty, Halleluiah*, and others, Bataille is presenting a theology

without God, as it were. For themes such as the sacred, sacrifice, evil, morality, faith, life, violence and death remain in focus, as they do in theology proper. As such, the image for Bataille is, in a sense, founded on faith equivalent to a suspension of disbelief.
15. It is the focus on individual images by Bataille that opens up a comparison with the *lingchi* images.
16. As well as Zhuo (2015) already cited, see Gerlac (1996) and Nolan (2004). Also, Steven Ungar, in his illuminating commentary (1990) on Bataille's *Lascaux, or the Birth of Art*, argues that the distinction Bataille makes between animal and human is that the human is constituted in the sacred and transgression and an awareness of death and that it is within the sacred that one should seek the origin of art – that is, seek an origin which is more imaginary than real in a positivist sense.
17. For a detailed and scholarly account of this see Nolan (2004: 125 and *passim*).
18. Bataille's writing on Lascaux has been collected in a dossier prepared by Denis Hollier in Bataille (1979: 317–376).
19. Although it has been suggested (cf. the editors of OC IX (1979: 425)) that the idea of the prestige of the animal compared to the humility of the human is already present in Bataille's article of 1930, 'L'art primitive' (Bataille 1970: 247–254), the latter in fact is exclusively concerned with aesthetic issues.
20. In relation to death and a 'radical "invisibility"' 'beyond the frame', see Sheaffer-Jones (2015: 241–242).
21. Agamben, in his book *Nudities* (2011b), wants to complicate the notion of nudity, so that, by invoking theological notions, nudity ultimately becomes an image in the mind (see 83–84). In any event, nudity cannot be encapsulated in terms of the oppositions, clothed/unclothed, veiled/unveiled. Is Agamben on the same wavelength as Bataille? The answer is: probably not. Nudity, for Bataille, is determined by context. In eroticism, nudity (or the becoming nude) is part of the domain of continuity and communication, the domain of the sacred, otherwise known as the general economy. Bataille thus writes, 'The decisive action [in eroticism] is the becoming nude (*la mise à nu*). Nudity is opposed to the state of closure, that is, to the state of discontinuous existence. This is a state of communication, which reveals a quest for a possible continuity of being beyond a withdrawal into the self' (1987: 23).
22. See Fried (1996: 23, and *passim*).
23. In his intellectual biography of Bataille, Michel Surya (2002: 94) refers to this passage but with a very different orientation from the one pursued here. For Surya, there is no victim as such, only the effect that the victim has on Bataille's psyche. In other words, Surya's approach is Nietzschean.

24. The status of criminal here raises an important issue with regard to being a victim. For it might be conjectured that a criminal's own actions are what led to the punishment inflicted and thus the suffering experienced. Two things can be said in response to this: the first is that Bataille speaks as though the legal status (= context; more on this below) of the one being tortured is of no account in his feeling towards him, so that in the instant of the victim's death he fully assumes the status of victim. But, in addition, to justify Bataille's position, it could be said that any punishment that is, to quote the Eighth Amendment, 'cruel and unusual' (which torture is, by definition) turns the one tortured into a victim, no matter what crime he or she might have committed. In contrast to Nietzsche, however, one is not saying that every criminal is a victim.
25. For instance, the authors ask – in light of a certain 'Italianism' occurring at one point in Bataille's syntax: 'might the entire book have been written by Lo Duca?' (Brook et al. 2008: 235). J. M. Lo Duca, Italian friend of Bataille, helped in the editing of *Les Larmes d'Éros*.
26. Lechte (2018).
27. 'Only the loss of a polity itself expels [Man] from humanity' (Arendt 1968: 177).
28. Cf.: 'they [people of natural givenness] begin to belong to the human race in much the same way as animals belong to a specific animal species' (Arendt 1968: 182).
29. After Hollywood (2002), Herta Wolf (2007), also concerned with the *lingchi* photographs' context, comes to ask similar questions: 'Who took the pictures? Why were these particular acts of violence recorded using a photographic, and thus indexical, medium? To whom are the pictures addressed? To whom are they meant to be shown? Which distribution channels will the pictures enter, and to which secondary uses will they be put?' (Wolf 2007: 80).
30. In fact, according to Wolf (2007: 80), a vérascope (a stereoscopic camera with a dual lens) was used, which would have been quite portable. It was also a French invention, so presumably available to French troops (who may have taken the images) stationed in Beijing where the executions took place. However, stereoscopic cameras were not usually used for portraits, as the spatial aspect was found to be distracting. Given the close-up nature of the *lingchi* shots it thus seems unlikely that a stereoscopic vérascope camera was used.
31. See Bataille (1973); (G = 1988b).
32. In answer to the objection that the position proposed regarding Bataille's relation to the torture victim implies limiting further research, what I am implying is that there are certain limit cases (images of genocide, for example) where a refusal to decide on what is the case can become a

perverse instance of nihilism. Of course, further research should always be considered and the possibility of new interpretations should never be ruled out. However, what also needs to be perfected is the capacity for good judgement as to what conclusion is appropriate in a given context.

33. Cf.: 'the Gospel of the lowly *makes* low' (Nietzsche 1974b: sect 43).
34. Cf.: 'life itself is *essentially* appropriation, injury, overpowering of the strange and weaker, suppression, severity, imposition of one's own forms, incorporation and, at the least and mildest, exploitation' (Nietzsche 1974a: sect 259). Again: every healthy aristocracy 'will have to be the will to power incarnate, it will want to grow, expand, draw to itself, gain ascendancy – not out of any morality or immorality, but because it *lives*, and because life *is* will to power' (sect 259).

3 Rethinking Agamben on Violence

THE NOTION OF, 'DIVINE VIOLENCE' (*Göttliche Gewalt*), as discussed in Walter Benjamin's 'Critique of Violence' (1986), is equated by Agamben with pure means – that is, with pure mediality. With regard to the latter, my thesis would be that a large part, if not all, of Agamben's thinking is organised around the notions of 'means', 'mediality', 'medium' and 'middle' – the latter especially in light of Émile Benveniste's linguistic theory (c.f. 'middle voice'). Of particular interest in this regard is Agamben's development of a philosophy of 'modal ontology', where an entity's being would be understood to be inseparable from its 'mode' of being. That is – to put it another way – where an entity is inseparable from its 'form of life' (see Agamben 2016: 147–175).[1] Here, it is intriguing to see that the *middle* voice (c.f.: '"to walk oneself"'), 'situated in a zone of indetermination' (2016: 28), is invoked as a way of explicating the notion of modal ontology. Thus, in referring to Spinoza on substance and mode, we read that: 'in order to think the substance/modes relationship, it is necessary to have at our disposal an ontology of the *middle voice*, in which the agent (God or substance) in effectuating the modes in reality affects and modifies only itself. Modal ontology can be understood only as a *medial ontology*' (163; emphasis added). The medial is given a broad reach, as the whole idea of 'use' is 'a *medial* process of this kind' (163; emphasis added). All of these terms ('means', 'mediality', medial) raise the question of the appearing of the medium – of the appearing of that which to be what it is normally does not appear.

It is thus through the notion of mediality that violence is brought into proximity with the image, the latter being the subject of the succeeding chapter. Whether or not Benjamin is correctly interpreted here, the notion of violence as pure mediality needs to be rethought when considering violence in Agamben's theory of *homo sacer*. The latter, despite all the commentary on it, remains to be fully illuminated. What follows is an attempt to provide this illumination.

Homo Sacer and Sovereighnty[2] Revisisted

In rethinking the nature of *homo sacer* we recall that the sacred is removed by Agamben from the anthropological and psychoanalytical meaning so often attributed to it in modernity. The '*sacer*' of *homo sacer* is then not to be confused with the anthropological version of sacred as ambivalent. As Frederiek Depoortere (2012) has shown in his commentary on Agamben, rather than explaining the sacred, the term, ambivalence (which Agamben calls a scientific 'mythologeme' (Agamben 1998: 75)) so often applied to the sacred – and its companion term, sacrifice[3] – needs to be explained as a hangover from the nineteenth century. The work of Mary Douglas on the relationship between the sacred and borders ('purity and danger') and its continuation in Julia Kristeva's theorisation of abjection are a manifestation of this. Here, the impure exists on the border; it becomes dangerous because ambivalent. For Agamben, this interpretation lends itself all too readily to a 'psychologisation of religious experience'; instead, he says, it is a matter of seeing the sacred as a 'juridico-political phenomenon' connected to the play of power.[4] What is truly at stake here is how the 'structure of sovereignty and the structure of *sacratio* are connected' (Agamben 1998: 83). It is thus to this relation that we now turn.

At issue is the way that Agamben makes the excluded *homo sacer* (the subject of the ban; the one whose death can be neither homicide nor sacrifice) the basis of the modern political domain. With due acknowledgement to Benjamin, it is shown that the political is inseparable from violence. In fact, a tortuous route is followed in the thinker's explanation of *homo sacer*, one that finally reiterates Benjamin's argument that violence is the basis of both law and sovereignty (see W. Benjamin 1986). If sovereignty produces the *homo sacer* – indeed, if *homo sacer* as bare life[5] is the condition of possibility of sovereignty, then, of course, violence is also the foundation of sovereignty. For Rousseau, by contrast, if not for the Enlightenment as a whole, 'the people' are the basis of sovereignty and of the General Will. And the General Will is incarnate in the law. For the law always encapsulates the 'general'; it does not deal with the 'particular'. Or, as Rousseau puts it, law exists 'when the whole people decrees for the whole people' (Rousseau 1982: 192). To reassert the primacy of law requires that the whole rationale of Agamben's approach be re-evaluated. But law, if one again follows Walter Benjamin, requires violence to inaugurate it and violence to sustain it. Such violence is a means to an end, whereas Agamben – as we shall see in more detail later – in his interpretation of Benjamin, argues for violence as a pure means – as mediality. Once this principle is fully enacted, law will become no more than an archaic, used object, like a child's plaything.[6] Those who valorise the 'rule of law' above all else in politics must face the fact that there can be bad laws. Nazi rule surely furnishes the most extreme example of this.

Sovereignty

At issue, then, is whether, and if so how, *homo sacer* and sovereignty are connected. What is immediately evident is that a potentially symmetrical opposition emerges, one that pits the absolute power of sovereignty against the total impotence of the designated *homo sacer*. As Alison Ross says: 'The picture that emerges from [Agamben's] work is that of a brutalizing tyrant on one side and an innocent, totally passive victim on the other' (2012: 431). More than this, impotence implies a total lack of autonomy, so that the only 'identity' *homo sacer* can assume is the one derived from power itself. In short, to push the logic of this figure to the extreme, *homo sacer* is a nothingness that, as such, can hardly appear on its own account. In Agamben's terms, as we know, it is 'bare life'. It is the life (*zōē*) that was excluded from the *polis* in ancient Greece, but, since Roman times has come to be inscribed within the modern political domain as an inclusive exclusion, such that 'bare life' (life reduced to the managed biological survival – life as the basis of 'bio-power') is now the essential concern of modern politics, especially when seen as the play of sovereignty – or at least when seen in terms of sovereignty as the sovereign decision with regard to the exception, the notion of sovereignty as articulated in the first instance by Carl Schmitt.[7]

What remains unclear, however, is why sovereign power needs *homo sacer* to be what it is, even if sovereignty itself also *produces homo sacer*. As Peter Fitzpatrick has put it in a frequently cited essay, Agamben sees bare life 'as somehow both created by and constituting sovereignty' (Fitzpatrick 2005: 64). Thus, in what seems like pure Hegelianism, it is to all appearances necessary to suppose that, despite the impotence of *homo sacer* and its dependence on sovereignty, to be what it is, sovereignty, in its turn, is dependent on *homo sacer* to be what *it* is. (Is it not the fate of all perfect symmetries to become undone by an inevitable reversal?) Before, however, accepting that there could be something amiss in Agamben's theory of *homo sacer*, let us read some key lines from the eponymous book in detail the better to see exactly what we are dealing with.

My remarks in the first instance will refer to the chapter from *Homo Sacer* called 'Sacred Life' (1998: 75–80). Here, Agamben provides a clear indication of the significance – especially the political significance – of the identity of *homo sacer*.

The Sacred

After rejecting the idea of ambivalence, Agamben also argues against the idea of the reverential, holy or blessed view of the sacred, the view common to various religions.[8] Instead, we are offered a deeply politicised sacred. This form of the sacred appears in the guise of *homo sacer* proposed as the very foundation of the political, which is also to be equated with *homo sacer*'s status as bare life and as the one that can be killed with impunity. *Homo sacer*, as already noted, emerges as the mirror reversal of sovereignty. The rationale for this reversal calls for analysis.

An examination of key points of Agamben's argument regarding *homo sacer* (sacred man) reveals that it is 'not the originary ambivalence of the sacredness that is assumed to belong to him' (Agamben 1998: 82), but rather this figure's exposure to violence, exposure to death.[9] This is a violence that is not to be prevented or punished. As a barely thinkable entity *homo sacer* is a figure existing in good part because it is also a function – an entity that, firstly, points to the foundation of politics as an originary exclusion or 'ban', a ban that is necessary if the notion of inclusion is to be posited; it is an index pointing to those who are the members of a political society (cf. *polis*). Moreover, *homo sacer* allows the sovereign entity to be made manifest and this occurs by making the sovereign the one who decides on the exception. Agamben thus refers to the 'sovereign decision that suspends the law in the state of exception and thus implicates bare life within it' (83). The sovereign decision reveals the truth of *homo sacer* as a reminder of 'the originary exclusion' as much as it reveals the nature of sovereignty itself. This means that sovereignty is not to be confused with the working of the law, but becomes explicit with its suspension, a suspension that opens the way to the enactment of power as the enactment of violence (which seems to imply power as pure force, where the law is in force without significance).

By implication, those who think that the law and violence, or that sovereignty and violence are totally separate from one another are mistaken. Echoing Benjamin, Agamben asserts that in fact violence and the law go hand in hand. Again, as with Benjamin, this violence is 'originary' *vis-à-vis* the law; without violence, there would be no law, just as without *homo sacer* as bare life exposed to death there would be no sovereign and therefore no political realm: 'the production of bare life is the originary activity of sovereignty' (83).

As bare life, *homo sacer* can be killed by anybody with impunity. It follows, then, that when it comes to *homo sacer* 'all men act as sovereigns' (84). Agamben is effectively saying that violence *constitutes* sovereignty. We have thus not just been mistaken in thinking that violence and the law are distinct and separate but also in thinking that sovereignty is not founded on violence. In sum, as Agamben does not fail to repeat, *homo sacer* is 'an object of a violence that exceeds the sphere of both the law and of sacrifice' (86). Rather than ambivalence making *homo sacer* both 'august and accursed' – or, in any event, being constituted by contradictory qualities – it is instead in a 'zone of indistinction between and beyond the profane and the religious' (86). *Homo sacer* is thus beyond ambivalence, beyond contradiction, beyond oppositions. It is not a matter of one or the other simultaneously (as in ambivalence) that defines the zone in question but, instead, it is a matter of *neither* one *nor* the other, *homo sacer* being neither inside nor outside political society. *Homo sacer* is in fact constitutive of both inside and outside as the exclusion that is included in the founding of the political order.

Surely, though, what is indistinct is also open to ambiguity.[10] Shadows, as Rousseau well knew, can give rise to fear because of their indistinct nature, rather like the indistinction of Rorschach images. Again, the notion of indistinction could be pushed further as it might apply to Agamben's own text. Thus, although Agamben's point is that the status of murder does not apply to the violence to which *homo sacer* is exposed, we are nevertheless within our rights to evoke those theories – such as Freud's and Girard's – which refer to a founding murder at the origin of society.[11] While the theory of the founding murder aims to explain how violence, if it is not eliminated, is at least controlled, the theory of *homo sacer* attributes an ongoing role to violence. Only violence, when all is said and done, can make sovereignty explicit. *Homo sacer* as bare life is the basis – as Benjamin had already announced – of the exception which has now become the rule, a point that is reiterated in Agamben's later work, *State of Exception* (2005a), where we read: 'faced with the unstoppable progression of what has been called "global civil war", the state of exception tends increasingly to appear as the dominant paradigm of government in contemporary politics' (2).[12]

The original political relation only involves the law in its suspension. What then is the nature and purpose of the law?[13] Agamben's notion of law is quite conventional, in that the *quaestio iuris* and the *quaestio facti* (cf. 1998: 171) constitute the basis of his analysis of the (bio-) political sphere. Here the point is to know whether the law can allow for its own suspension if certain facts occur that can be construed as constituting a state of emergency – that is, as constituting what is perceived to be a threat to the very existence of the state as constituted power. Agamben clearly says that such a situation would be a *quaestio facti* more than – or at least as much as – a *quaestio iuris*. It is thus with the state of emergency that law and fact become indistinguishable even though they are, analytically speaking, essentially distinct. Sovereignty – and therefore bare life – participates in this blurring of law and fact to the point where, Agamben exorbitantly claims, we have a 'hybrid of law and fact' (170). What is more, 'the camp is the very paradigm of political space at the point at which politics becomes biopolitics and *homo sacer* is virtually confused with the citizen' (171).

Clearly, *homo sacer* is powerless, without rights or any legal protection (although Agamben still implicates this figure, as we shall see, in the 'rights debate'), being virtually bereft of meaningful life even before it is actually deprived of life. In fact, as we know, this entity is only thinkable *vis-à-vis* sovereignty. *Homo sacer* is, to repeat, an index of the absolute power of sovereignty. Sovereignty, then, is nothing but power backed by violence, as *homo sacer* is nothing but the complete absence of both power and a capacity for violence. The question remains, however, as to the *necessity* of *homo sacer* for sovereignty. Does sovereignty really *need* the *homo sacer*? An affirmative response implies, of course, that sovereignty's power is to that extent diminished and that of its counterpart to that extent increased. More paradoxical, no doubt, is the fact that sovereignty cannot even recognise *homo sacer* without – as occurs in the Master-Slave dialectic – undermining the absoluteness of its power – without, that is, ceasing to be sovereign. While Agamben places the sovereign-*homo sacer* relation within a quasi-zero-sum logical frame, the enactment of violence can never be captured by a zero-sum logic. Moreover, it is no doubt characteristic of every symmetry (Agamben's preferred figure) to present two interdependent parts. As the other of power – albeit its mirror-opposite – *homo sacer* shows up a lack in sovereignty.

Interestingly, Agamben actually addresses, as Fitzpatrick indicates (2005: 52), the origin of *homo sacer* by approvingly citing Rudolph Jhering's claim that 'it [*homo sacer*] is a fragment of the primitive life of Indo-European peoples' (Jhering 1886: 282 cited in Agamben 1998: 104).[14] On this basis, *homo sacer*, historically speaking, would be prior to any formal legal system and have its origin in the bandit and the outlaw – or in the werewolf, to the extent that the difference between animal and human is not yet fully accomplished. The werewolf 'is, therefore, in its origin the figure of the man who has been banned from the city' (105). *Homo sacer* as bare life is a kind of prehistoric remnant from an age 'before' the law in the modern sense. It is an age for Girard where violence, giving rise to the scapegoat or surrogate victim, is the main issue to be dealt with by society. The killing of the surrogate victim brings an end to violence and unites the community – for a time!

As encapsulated in the Hobbesian 'mythologeme' (105) of the state of nature, the sovereign, too, we find, is a remnant from a bygone age. The sovereign would not be the entity to whom absolute power is attributed in society, but a remnant of the state of nature and the war of all against all. And so, while the people give up their natural freedom and power, such is not the case for the sovereign, who keeps his. This, to all appearances, implies that the sovereign, like *homo sacer*, is the equivalent of an encrustation of nature within culture. It is thus a matter of the opposition of nature-culture. Lévi-Strauss is, after all, an abiding figure in Agamben's intellectual landscape.

Let us now add to Agamben's penchant for symmetries a penchant for oppositions founded on exorbitant contraries: a juridical order that includes chaos within itself; law that is constituted through violence; the rule/law that can only be confirmed through the exception; language which can only constitute itself in attempting to include the non-linguistic, and of course the inclusive exclusion, characteristic of *homo sacer*. To be noted, too, is that the law 'consists in this capacity [. . .] to maintain itself in relation to an exteriority' (18). In these instances, and in many others, there are no terms that have absolutely no relation to each other – even if this be a relation of non-relation. Thus, we read: '[t]*he rule applies to the exception in no longer applying, in withdrawing from it*' (18.) Or, again, 'the state of exception appears as the legal form of what cannot have legal form' (Agamben 2005a: 1). The invocation of oppositions resulting in paradox has implications for understanding the status of violence. In other words, Agambens's particular way of thinking produces a certain version of violence. We can thus observe a fascination for extreme polarities, prime amongst these being that between sovereign power and *homo sacer*. Unlike Benjamin's linking of violence and law historically, Agamben, by linking life to the state of exception where the law is suspended and violence reigns, thereby posits an essential link between violence/life and law through opposition, so that law being in its broadest most formal sense 'in force without significance' then 'becomes indistinguishable from life' (53) – which means, in effect, 'indistinguishable from violence'. Or, again in the ever-prevalent spirit of paradox, we see that with the state of exception, 'what violates a rule [law] and what conforms to it coincide without remainder' (57). And again, '[t]he violence exercised in the state of exception clearly neither preserves nor simply posits law, but rather conserves it in suspending it' (64).

Mediality and Violence

Mediality is the crossover point between violence and the image. I shall now address mediality principally in relation to violence before considering mediality and the image in the following chapter.

Most pressing here, according to Agamben, is to think beyond every form of law. Only by doing so he claims will it be possible to move 'out of the paradox of sovereignty toward a politics freed from every ban' (2005a: 59). Here the reading of Benjamin's concept of 'divine violence' by Agamben is decisive because he wants to promote a view of the political as pure mediality, where the medium would show itself independently of any end, a 'violence that purely acts and manifests' (62). As is known, this is precisely the definition Benjamin gives of divine, or 'pure' violence.

Instead of violence apparently appearing at the origin of things it now comes at the 'end of history' in a kind of messianic event. But however one interprets the mediality of violence in politics, the point is that violence is now to appear *as such*, in itself, even if this be while serving at another level as a means to an end – for example, as Benjamin says at the beginning of 'Critique of Violence', in its relation to 'law and justice'.

Politics and law as mediality

Mediality is linked to violence because it turns the latter into an end in itself. At the conclusion of his book, *State of Exception* (2005a), Agamben calls politics the action that 'severs the nexus between violence and law' (88). And this action corresponds to 'pure means' (*reine Mittel*). What our theorist apparently has in mind is cutting the link between constituent power as violence and the law (constituent power being the 'violence that makes law' (68)). Constituent power is not as such being privileged, despite Agamben's obvious hostility to constituted power (revealed, for example, in references to the current situation where the state of exception as the rule becomes equivalent to the camp (2000: 39)). Politics 'has been contaminated' – not by violence (which Agamben completely approves of if it is a pure mediality) but by law! Evidently, law, too, is only acceptable if it can become a 'pure' law – law as mediality – that ceases to be used to justify violence – along with language as mediality, action and politics as mediality and, presumably, thought as mediality. What is desirable is 'means without end', as the title of Agamben's book first published in Italy in 1996 would have it. And Peg Birmingham's reading suggests that the figures of the Muselmann and the refugee 'manifest the pure mediality of gesture' (2014: 105). The Muselmann and the refugee, on this reading, are essentially images.

Mediality as the taking place of language and inoperativity

For Agamben, violence as mediality connects with other domains where medialty is at issue, such as language. Even if mediality were only uniquely connected to violence, this concept is clearly crucial. Indeed, as I suggested at the beginning of this chapter, it is possibly the most important concept in the whole of Agamben's theoretical lexicon. With this term, then, one can feel to be on more solid ground as to meaning and significance.[15] One imagines Agamben thinking that while the *doxa* always sees mediality in relation to an end, he is going to insist (following Benjamin) on the idea of *pure* means – of mediality detached from any end whatsoever. This implies that mediality is entirely disconnected from utility or use value and becomes a kind of end in itself. Further instances of mediality in Agamben's writing are seen in relation to: cinema as gesture; the pure experience of language – or the 'taking place of language' (Agamben 1991: 102); the inoperativity and 'strategies of spectacular power' (Agamben 2011a: 216),[16] strategies that come into play with the dominance of the media and the image (also called 'glory') in today's 'society of the spectacle'. All this is in addition to mediality as violence as a pure means. It also signals what 'severs the nexus between violence and law' (Agamben 2005a: 88). In brief, pure violence – violence as mediality – is violence that is absolutely detached from law.

Violence Once Again in Question

Influenced by Benjamin, then, Agamben argues against law making and law preserving violence, as both constitute violence as a means to an end. Similarly, as Daniel McLoughlin has admirably demonstrated (2016), Agamben opposes the Schmittian view of the sovereign decision as still within the orbit of law even in its suspension, as the 'force-of-law' ['law' with cross through it]. Instead, the sovereign decision opens the way to violence pure and simple, which becomes a real problem once the exception has become the rule.[17] The gatekeepers of the law (the image is from Kafka) of course continue to maintain that the law is still in force – that there is no sphere absolutely outside the law. To the extent that there was a real state of exception, as McLoughlin indicates (526), there would be lawlessness. It is lawlessness that the gatekeeper/guardians of the law keep hidden.

So, Agamben claims, the state of exception, as the rule, cannot be separated from a generalised lawlessness. In referring to Benjamin, Agamben says: 'While Schmitt attempts every time to re-inscribe violence within a juridical context, Benjamin responds to this gesture by seeking every time to assure it – as pure violence – an existence outside of the law' (Agamben 2005a: 59).

Elsewhere, at the beginning of the nineties, Agamben had said that:

> *Violence is not something like an originary biological fact that man is forced to assume and regulate in his own praxis through sacrificial institution; rather it is the very ungroundedness of human action (which the sacrificial mythologeme hopes to cure) that constitutes the violent character (that is* contra naturam, *according to the Latin meaning of the word) of sacrifice.* (Agamben 1991: 105)

It is thus action/praxis that occurs essentially *ex nihilo* that, *qua ex nihilo* is violent. This is action prior to the enactment of any law to the extent that law would be the outcome of action-violence: 'the foundation of violence is the violence of foundation' (106). How can we not read this in a Feuerbachian key as man operating in the place of God? Through violence, man has replaced God as the author – if not of all creation, at least of his own destiny.

Paradigm and History

To turn to the notions of 'paradigm' and 'history' in Agamben's theory of *homo sacer* and violence is to come to grips with Agamben's controversial method. Perhaps it is even the case that the issues surrounding Agamben's political philosophy are essentially issues of method.

In contradistinction to Freud or Girard, who view human violence anthropologically and historically hypothesising an actual discoverable, original moment of violence (a murder), Agamben counsels that his theoretical work should be seen as presenting paradigms, rather than as revealing actual historical events – although he also claims that 'figures such as *homo sacer*, the *Muselmann*, the state if exception, and the concentration camp' (2010: 9) are 'all actual historical phenomena' as well as paradigms. A paradigm is an analogical figure of knowledge that relates particular to particular (it is not universal and particular, nor the reverse). It is a set of relations between phenomena that cannot necessarily be proven to have come into existence historically, but which conform to the analogical form of 'as if'. Thus, there may never have been an actual, recorded moment when *homo sacer* became the excluded inclusion produced by sovereign power, but it is *as if* this really had occurred, given the centrality of this figure for an understanding of sovereignty and the state of exception. Or again, it is as if – in Agamben's own words – 'the exception [= *homo sacer*/bare life] is the originary form of law' (1998: 26).[18]

Consequently, the figure of the 'state of nature' is also a paradigm, even though Agamben himself does not want to work with this figure beyond the idea that it is *as if* the 'state of nature survives in the person of the sovereign [. . .] Sovereignty thus presents itself as an incorporation of the state of nature in society' (35). With the state of exception, which defines sovereignty in Schmitt's schema, it is *as if* law and the state of nature merged into one another to the extent that law allows the sovereign to act independently of law, with the result that, 'the sovereign is the point of indistinction between violence and law, the threshold on which violence passes over into law and law passes over into violence' (32). That is, violence is legitimated. Through a reading of Plato on law and nature Agamben is careful to point out that it is not a matter of nature or violence being prior to law and society, but one of 'the coincidence of violence and law constitutive of sovereignty' (34). In this scenario, the Sophists saw nature (*physis*) as being anterior to law (*nomos*) while, for Plato, there is no nature or violence in itself as an origin to be overcome prior to and separate from law, just as there is no law separate from violence; instead, law and violence go together *originarily*. And even though for Hobbes the state of nature is supposed to be prior to society, or the 'commonwealth', in fact, as we have seen, the so-called state of nature, continues – and necessarily so – in the 'person of the sovereign'. Thus, in Agamben's interpretation of Hobbes, it is *as if* a continuity existed between sovereignty and nature, violence and law. Indeed, it is *as if* violence becomes the basis of law but, equally, that law becomes the precondition of violence.

Nevertheless, the relation between 'paradigm' and 'history' in Agamben undeniably leads to confusion. This is because, at certain points, our author wants to assert a certain historical validity for structures such as *homo sacer* and sovereignty. Moreover, as Peter Fitzpatrick has noted (2005: 55), Agamben claims to point to an actual historical moment of the 'first recording of bare life as the new political subject [...] already implicit in the document that is generally placed at the foundation of modern democracy: the 1679 writ of *habeas corpus*' (Agamben 1998: 123). For Fitzpatrick, 'this is close to fanciful' because a 'case using *habeas corpus* in its seemingly modern form can be found in 1214, and from the report of the case it is obvious that the writ was already commonplace' (Fitzpatrick 2005: 55). To say that *homo sacer* is part of the constitution of sovereign power is one thing; to claim that it has a clear historical presence is another. While etymological research – which is Agamben's forte – might be useful for establishing meaning and forming concepts, it is not the same as detailed historical research. Much as Agamben wants to harness Foucault to the cart of paradigm, Foucault is relentlessly the historian. At the level of history, Agamben is decidedly not Foucault's heir – even if he is the aspiring inheritor of the Foucauldian legacy as concerns 'bio-power'.

Of course, Foucault is not a historian in what could be called a conventional, disciplinary sense and for this reason he might seem to be closer to Agamben in approach, making bold theoretical claims apparently divorced from a genuine historical corpus, or archive (for an overview of the issue, see Megill (1987)). In short, Foucault's approach to writing history remains open to debate. The point, however, is that there *is* an identifiable historical corpus in each of the key Foucauldian studies and from which Foucault derives his theses. By comparison, Agamben's etymological strings from which he derives key claims about the present moment (e.g., the camp as the 'nomos of the present') seem to be very meagre indeed. I suggest that very little is learned about the actual being of *homo sacer* in Agamben that is not already available in Benveniste's entry on the sacred in *Le vocabulaire des institutions indo-europeans 2* (1969), specifically, the reference to Festus and the fact that to kill the one designated as '*sacer*' is not a 'homicide' (189).[19]

Lemke supports this reading of Agamben by pointing out that:

> Agamben does not use the figure of *homo sacer* for a historical reconstruction of legal procedures and institutions. Rather, he applies it as a theoretical concept that is supposed to inform political analysis. Consequently, Agamben is less interested in the question whether in antiquity human beings were indeed confronted with this kind of ban; he is more concerned to display the political mechanism of rule and exception, bare life and political existence. (Lemke 2005: 5)

Moreover, for her part, Alison Ross points out (correctly in my view) – no doubt in light of Heidegger – that Agamben's theses on law are essentially ontological (2012: 427–428). By contrast, Foucault's attention is directed towards revealing the underlying rationality pertaining to specific historical practices, as outlined in 'the manuals of modern institutions' (425). These practices are not independent of what people think of them. In this sense, the interpretation of texts is aligned with the focus on practices. Moreover, Ross claims that: 'The speculative style of Agamben's analyses leads him to commit the same fault Foucault ascribed to classical political philosophy: as political theory Agamben's work founders because his core fidelity is not to explain complex events but to defend concepts with dubious explanatory value' (425).[20]

Ironically, just prior to citing the historical significance of the writ of *habeas corpus*, Agamben refers to the camp as the 'hidden *paradigm* of the political space of modernity, whose metamorphoses and disguises we will have to learn to recognize' (1998: 123; emphasis added). In other words, it is *as if* the political sphere in modernity is structured like the German concentration camp (which is historical), so that the latter ceases to be a uniquely historical phenomenon. Here, paradigm rules, not history.

Concerning Agamben's status as historian, as well as the commentators already cited, we also know from the work of Depootere (2012), Gratton and Fitzpatrick, that, especially regarding the historical status of *homo sacer* within Roman law, Agamben's efforts leave a lot to be desired. Peter Gratton concisely summarises the state of play:

> What thus comes to the fore in reading Agamben is both a minimum of evidence and a maximum of conceptual detail. Silences in the record proves [*sic*] only the silence of the record, though as we have noted, Agamben usually reads these silences as obscuring an 'underlying code' that must be brought to light through his paradigmatic method. In this regard, it is striking how much of what is extant must be avoided to make Agamben's description consistent, not least the later distinctions between *ius divinum* and *ius humanum*, and between private law and public law. (Gratton 2011: 609)

In keeping with the distinction between 'paradigm' and 'history', bare life as *zōē* as taken from Aristotle would be a paradigm, while bare life as a biological entity would be the version furnished by history. The confusion about Agamben's notion of bare life largely stems from the uncertainty as to whether we are dealing with history or a paradigm. The fact that Agamben claims that figures like *homo sacer* are both historical and paradigmatic only adds to the confusion.

Signatures

Any effort to plumb the depths of violence in Agamben's thought must address his method, a fact already intimated by the notions of paradigm and modal ontology. In this respect, as interpreted by William Watkin (2014), Agamben is essentially concerned with signatures, and thus his approach is paradigmatic and archaeological rather than historical in any conventional sense. It includes the signature of things. 'Signature' can be defined as that which is distinctive in itself, while the sign is valued for what it refers to, not for what it is. Thus, the signature manifests a certain opacity in contrast to the sign's transparency. In this sense, a proper name is a signature. Moreover, signatures – as Agamben says of photos in Abby Warburg's 'Atlas' – 'have value *in themselves*' (2010: 56). Again, in wanting to equate Foucault's notion of 'statement' in *The Archaeology of Knowledge* (1974: 79–131) with 'signature', Agamben claims that statements become signatures to the extent that their importance lies in their 'sheer fact of existing' (2010: 64). Statements in Foucault's sense have neither a semiotic (pure sign) nor a hermeneutic (pure meaning) status, both domains being relatively transparent, while the signature status of statements renders them relatively opaque – i.e., renders them of value as objects in themselves. 'Archaeology', Agamben further claims, 'is the science of signatures' (64). Moreover, in mobilising once again one of his favourite motives for thinking, Agamben brings statements (significant because they exist) into the orbit of the taking-place of language: 'The statement is the signature that marks language in the pure fact of its existence (*darsi*)' (65). Later, our author confirms: 'language is the place of signatures' (76). And as if to confirm the signature's opaque character, Agamben refers to the 'absolutising of the signature' in the twentieth century, 'that is to say, a doctrine of the constitutive primacy of signatures over signification' (77). Similarly, the theory of the excess of signifier (its 'zero degree') over signified proposed by Lévi-Strauss in his reading of Mauss is designated as another instance of the signature (78).

How is Agamben's own work to be understood if it is true that, in light of Benjamin, the 'historical object is never given neutrally; rather, it is always accompanied by an index or signature' (73). And, moreover, '[a]ll research in the human sciences – *particularly in a historical context* – necessarily has to do with signatures' (76; emphasis added). This statement taken in conjunction with the idea that the existence of the signature is inseparable from its *signator* would imply that there is an 'Agambenesque' approach to history and ideas. Would the index of Agamben's signature not be the presence – as indicated above – of symmetries, oppositions, paradoxes, the latter summed up by 'the state of exception appears as the legal form of what cannot have legal form' (Agamben 2005a: 1). If justice is to be enacted, is it thus not a matter of escaping signatures and aiming for complete transparency? Indeed, the signature might be said to reinforce Agamben's penchant for opacity (of the image, of language, for example) over transparency.

Origin

When elaborating upon the nature of an archaeological study (Agamben 2010: 81–111), it becomes clear that what is at stake overall for Agamben is the question of origin – not in order to resurrect it as a guiding theme, but in order to problematise it without reserve. Historical research using the notion of origin as its guiding thread will always come up against the question of what was before the origin, or the question of whether there was a 'pre-origin', so that a split occurs between the origin and something even more original. With the origin of law, for example (one cited by Agamben) there arises the issue of 'pre-law' when 'law and religion were indiscernible' (90). But there is also a split when the animal is deemed to be the origin of the human, so that 'human' is what is to be distinguished from 'animal' and yet has its origin in animality, so that the *original* human becomes what the human is not. In relation to such aporias generated by the 'before' of an origin, Agamben writes: 'To imagine such a "before" indeed involves, following the logic inherent in the split, presupposing an original condition prior to it that at a certain point divided itself' (99).

Foucault's essay, 'Nietzsche, Genealogy, History' (1984) is a key reference for Agamben in his argument against the privileging of 'origin'. In the piece in question, Foucault sees Nietzsche as the philosopher whose concept of genealogy 'opposes itself to the search for origins' (77). The reason for this opposition is that historical time is not to be understood as a neat and continuous chronology with an original starting point, or with an 'original identity' (78) in relation to which the 'origin always precedes the Fall' (79). Instead, genealogy observes a historical time that is subject to the play of chance, so that rather than being concentrated in a homogenising narrative, historical events are understood to be dispersed and deriving from the 'exteriority of accidents' (81). Historical events, indeed, constitute a moment of arising and emergence (83). In capturing what is at stake, Foucault specifies that: 'If interpretation were the slow exposure of the meaning of a hidden origin, then only metaphysics could interpret the development of humanity' (86). That is, history written with reference to the notion of origin, however empirical and factual its aspiration might be, is inevitably determined by a metaphysical assumption before a word is written. Thus, the assumption that violence and chaos preceded the instauration of human law and order is an entirely metaphysical assumption – that is, an a priori notion that is unavailable to critique. Such is the case whether one proposes history as a science or as an interpretive practice.[21]

Consequently, historical research which claims to avoid the excesses of the theory and philosophy of history runs the risk of leaving unscrutinised metaphysical assumptions of an origin, of continuous narrative and linear time, assumptions that can give rise to a golden age, a state of nature or indeed to Freud's primal hoard that supposedly existed prior to the murder founding the law and society.[22]

While it can be accepted that Agamben's aim is to enact an archaeological philosophy rather than write history in the conventional or even in the Foucauldian sense, so that *homo sacer* must be understood as a paradigm, this seems to run counter to the claim – already noted – that *homo sacer*, like the *Muselmann* or the state of exception or the camp are 'all actual historical phenomena' (Agamben 2010: 9). We have been so busy coming to grips with 'paradigm', 'signature' and 'archaeology' that 'actual' history has been neglected. Although archaeological philosophy might put paid to naïve assumptions about an origin, what is its significance for 'actual' history? If *homo sacer* has a certain explanatory power as a paradigm, the evidence brought to bear thus far suggests that from a historical point of view *homo sacer* works far less well.[23]

On the other hand, historical research, because it uses language, continually produces paradigms or images that are the way collections of facts are organised. To invoke Foucault again, the facts relating to the way schools, hospitals, factories as well as prisons were organised in the nineteenth century can be described in terms of the disciplinary model of the Panopticon. History might well be a history of the particular, but language only allows the particular to be grasped at a certain level of generality. Steven DeCaroli (2001) is thus correct to draw attention to Agamben's entry on 'Example' in *The Coming Community* (2005b). As with a paradigm, a fact used as an example 'transforms singularities into members of a class, whose meaning is defined by a common property' (2005b: 8). Set theory reinforces the paradox of the class (trees) that is also a member of itself. Or, the named individual object (this tree) also names the class (trees) of which it is a member. For its part, an example is a particular that assumes universal significance. As Agamben explains, an example 'is one singularity among others, which, however, stands for each of them and serves for all' (10). An example evokes the paradigm: 'Hence the pregnancy of the Greek term, for example: *para-digma*, that which is shown alongside' (10).

Example and set theory could therefore be added to Agamben's list of items related to method, where the issue concerns the way the particular, unique instance can only be grasped as a certain generality. In *Homo Sacer* (1998) the section at the beginning dealing with set theory now takes on its full significance as a challenge to the basis of conventional history. Referring to the work of Badiou on the event, Agamben discusses the difference in set theory between membership and inclusion in relation to the exception. An event, like the exception, is 'an element of a situation such that its membership in the situation is undecidable from the perspective of the situation' (1998: 25).

Set Theory and Violence

Set theory assumes a certain explanatory power in relation to the state of exception. It links in with Jakobson's notion of shifters and with Benveniste's notion of discourse (act of stating) – an abiding point of reference for all of Agamben's writing. Paul Livingston (2009) has pointed out in relation to Russell's paradox that: 'the problematic possibility of linguistic self-reference is, Russell's analysis itself suggested, already inscribed in everyday speech by its ordinary and scarcely avoidable recourse to deixis – that is, to indexical pronouns such as "this", "I", "here", and "now"' (303). And again, Livingston explicitly refers to Agamben's debt to Jakobson and Benveniste in relation to 'those indexical and demonstrative expressions that Jakobson, drawing on Benveniste's earlier analysis, termed "shifters"' (306). Shifters are bound to context in as far as context relates to utterance. In a note, Livingston summarises the position of the exception in relation to Russell's paradox:

> More rigorously, we can put the paradox this way. Within a specific legal order, consider the set of all normal and exceptional acts; call this O. Then for every subset x of O, let d(x) be the act that decides, of each element of x, whether it is normal or exceptional. (We can think of d(x) as the 'decider' for x, the act of enacting the law or prescription that decides normalcy within x.) Then we have the following consequences:
>
> (1) For any x, d(x) is not an element of x [ARGUMENT: No act can decide its own normalcy].
> (2) For any x, d(x) is an element of O [ARGUMENT: The act that decides normalcy is itself an act]. (2009: 312, note 39)

From the logic of set theory, the moment of the sovereign decision on the exception means that there will no longer be, in Benjamin's terms followed by Agamben, law making or law preserving violence, as the law has suspended itself leaving the way open for violence to become a pure mediality. Or, at least, it is difficult not draw this conclusion. Moreover, would sovereignty in itself be included or excluded from the sovereign decision? In other words, is the sovereign decision exceptional or normal? Unless the law is normally sovereign (which would appear difficult to sustain here), the sovereign decision comes across as being the normal activity for a truly sovereign agency. In short, the essence of sovereignty becomes the capacity to decide on the exception. Schmitt, according to Agamben, wants the sovereign to be legitimated by law. But for Agamben, this is of no moment because once anointed the sovereign becomes independent of law and free to use violence as the situation demands. For example, thinking in set theory terms leads one to ask whether the sovereign would be subject to the curfew he or she imposed. If the sovereign is not subject to the curfew, the sovereign becomes an exception in relation to which the law/command does not apply. If the opposite is the case, doubt is raised as to whether the sovereign *is* truly sovereign.

To sum up the key point being outlined here: for all his interest in paradox, Agamben fails to address the point as to whether the sovereign is also subject to the implementation of the state of emergency. In other words, the question we are left with is: how absolute is sovereignty in relation to the violence perpetrated in the state of emergency?

The Paradigm of the Camp as the '"Nomos" of the Modern'

A key instance of Agamben's method in action in relation to violence turns around the notion of the camp as the underlying 'law' of politics in modernity. This is, of all Agamben's theses, his most controversial. As a reminder of what is at stake, let us quote again Agamben's claim regarding the camp: 'the camp is the very *paradigm* of political space at the point at which politics becomes biopolitics and *homo sacer* is virtually confused with the citizen' (1998: 171; emphasis added). Just as the city (*polis*) was the enduring paradigm of politics prior to the modern era (let us say, prior to the twentieth century), the camp replaces the city and *homo sacer* replaces the citizen as the normal political actor. The situation depicted is to be explained by the fact that sovereign power entails that the exception has become the rule. Another way of putting it is to say that with the camp becoming the rule, the camp is in fact no longer exceptional. It is no longer an 'a-nomaly'.

The exception has become the rule because law is now continuous with life. Contingency begins to take on a 'juridico-political structure' (166).[24] On this basis, instead of the camp being totally removed from law, Agamben endeavours to show, via the notion of the exception, that what transpired there has a juridical status.[25] Thus: 'what is first taken into the juridical order is the state of exception itself. In so far as the state of exception is "willed", it inaugurates a new juridico-political paradigm in which the norm becomes indistinguishable from the exception. The camp is thus the structure in which the state of exception – the possibility of deciding on which founds sovereign power – is realized *normally*' (170). Crucially: '*The camp is a hybrid of law and fact in which the two terms become indistinguishable*' (170). Thus when 'fact and law become completely confused' (170), so that '[w]however entered the camp moved in a zone of indistinction between outside and inside, exception and rule, licit and illicit, in which the very concepts of subjective right and juridical protection no longer made any sense' (170).

The theme of the indistinguishable nature of law and fact is reinforced at the end of *Homo Sacer* under the title of 'Threshold'. There, Agamben endeavours to equate the *fact* – 'bare life' – with the functioning of the law. The most significant and telling example given is that of Hitler's word becoming law (= fact becoming law); the Führer's physical body (here called, '*zōē*') becomes indistinguishable from his political body (called *bios*) (184). Here, then, is 'a life that is absolutely indistinguishable from law' (185). In the end, just as the Führer's word is immediately translated into violence against the Jews, so law as such becomes indistinguishable from what occurs in the camp.

In *State of Exception* (2005a), Agamben returns to Benjamin's 'Critique of Violence' and the notion of 'pure' or 'divine' violence (*reine Gewalt*) – violence as a 'pure' means. This is something quite distinct from the violence that supports the law. The problem now is not that of finding ways to separate law from violence, but of showing that '[t]he only true political action [is one] which severs the nexus between violence and law' (88). Already, in *Homo Sacer*, this task was attributed to 'divine violence'.[26] And a statement in the *State of Exception* confirms that a key marker of *reine Gewalt*, in its very autonomy, as it were, is that it becomes a 'pure medium':

> Here appears the topic – which flashes up in the text only for an instant, but *is nonetheless sufficient to illuminate the entire piece* – of violence as 'pure medium', that is, as the figure of a paradoxical 'mediality without ends' – a means that, through remaining such, is considered independently of the ends that it pursues. (61–62; emphasis added)[27]

Earlier, Agamben had said that while the notion of 'purity' needs to be understood in a 'relational rather than a substantial' sense, 'pure violence is never simply a means – whether legitimate or illegitimate – to an end' (61). It is, then, the fact of being a means that Agamben claims is crucial to a correct understanding of 'pure violence'. Such violence is seen as equivalent for Benjamin to both 'divine' and 'revolutionary' violence (53).

Benjamin's controversial and much commented upon essay on violence[28] forms a guiding thread in both *Homo Sacer* and *State of Exception*. Agamben's gloss on Benjamin's 'divine violence' (*Göttliche Gewalt*) as pure mediality[29] highlights the centrality of both violence and mediality, or medium, in Agamben's conception of politics. Agamben's reduction of pure violence to pure or divine violence is in keeping with the postulates of Fenves, who equates violence as a pure means with the notion of 'medium' and 'middle' (1998: 48), and of Werner Hamacher who similarly equates 'divine violence' with 'pure mediality'. For Hamacher, because 'divine' or pure violence is also a pure means, it is ultimately nonviolent. Hamacher's claim that violence as a 'pure means' (*reine Mittel*) is exemplified by Sorel's 'proletarian general strike' (1994: 120) would seem to be confirmed by Walter Benjamin in the following passage from the 'Critique of Violence': 'While the first form of interruption of work [the political strike] is violent since it causes only an external modification of labor conditions, the second as a pure means, is nonviolent' (1986: 291). Although Ross, for one, argues against both Fenves and Hamacher (and, by extension, Agamben), in their privileging of 'pure means' in Benjamin's essay,[30] Agamben – as we will see in more detail the next chapter – makes both pure violence and Debord's cinema image incarnations of pure mediality, and this results in a mediality that stands on its own account and not in relation to an end. It is thus not – in the linguistic sense – transparent. While Agamben notes that this is 'paradoxical', Fenves explains the paradox: 'Means can be defined as such only if they are means to certain ends, and means are even more dependent on the ends they serve than ends are on the means through which they are accomplished' (1998: 46). Agamben runs with the paradox. Thus, with regard to violence as a pure means, the influence of (a certain version of) Benjamin's essay[31] is particularly marked. Indeed, we are led to ask how Agamben's view of violence that is separate from law can be distinguished from Benjamin's. Whatever answer might be given to this question, the concern of this study is to analyse the implications of treating pure means as an object in its own right. The argument to be advanced is that treating pure means as an object finds a parallel in treating the image as an object – or, again, in treating the medium as an object – and that such a treatment fails to do justice to the essential 'disappearance' of the medium.

Conclusion

We have referred above to the way that the exception becomes integral to the juridical structure to the extent that law and fact become indistinguishable. Agamben actually goes further than this by arguing (with reference to Pompeius Festus) that violence is 'a primordial juridical fact' in that it allows vengeance and that 'in this sense, the exception is the originary form of law' (1998: 26). This is also equivalent to the capture of life in law. One would have to be forgiven for thinking that, following Benjamin, law, far from acting as a bulwark against violence, is in fact derived from an originary violence that continues to be on display in the sovereign exception. Thus: 'The "sovereign" structure of law, its peculiar and original "force", has the form of a state of exception in which fact and law are indistinguishable' (Agamben 1998: 27).

Although Agamben wants to argue – again after Benjamin – that violence as a pure means is in principle *discernable*, the question arises as to the relation of violence to the camp in Agamben's theory. Given the preponderance of paradox and the resultant focus on the *appearance* of mediality, it is more than likely that the camp becomes the zone of the appearance of violence as such, a violence thus separated from any victim. In any event, one thing is certain: once violence as pure means appears, the victim as such fails to appear.

If Agamben's 1970 essay, 'On the Limits of Violence' (Agamben 2015a), can be taken as a guide to his later view of violence as a pure means (which, I propose, is entirely plausible), the glorification of the very Greek mythical violence, violence that Girard and others oppose, is indeed promoted by Agamben. It cannot be otherwise when violence is internal to itself. Thus, as an example of pure violence, Agamben points to the violence of the sacred of 'primitive peoples' (235) and to the violence in Euripides's play *The Bacchae* (cf. 236), where, it will be recalled, Dionysus was torn to pieces.[32] Such violence, 'that deliberately refrains from enforcing the law, and instead breaks apart the continuity of time to found a new era is not as inconceivable as it initially seems' (235). The whole tenor of Agamben's 1970 reflection here is to argue that violence can appear *as such* with the most profound example being revolutionary violence that '*negates the self as it negates the other; it awakens a consciousness of the death of the self even as it visits death on the other*' (236). Violence 'when it becomes self-negation, belongs neither to its agent nor its victim; it becomes elation and dispossession of the self – as the Greeks understood in their figure of the mad god' (237). In reading these lines, there can be little doubt that pure violence appears and that it is indeed violent (not nonviolence, or the suspension of violence). The following would be nothing but a confirmation of this: 'At the dawn of every new temporal order [...] it shall be written: "In the beginning there was violence"' (237).

In contrast to what has just been confirmed, William Watkin in his characteristically rigorous defence of Agamben on violence (Watkin 2015) raises the prospect of reinterpreting Agamben's appropriation of Benjamin's notion of divine or pure violence by claiming, amongst other things, that divine violence undermines the myth that the state must use violence to avoid regressing back to the original violence upon which it was founded (2015: 150). 'Violence' as a term, Watkins says, is a signature in Agamben's sense, implying that it is a sign without meaning, open to various semantic contents depending on the context (151). Divine violence problematises the very meaning of violence and might indeed be bloodless, or, as Watkin writes: 'For Agamben, divine violence suspends violence rather than violently deciding on violence' (142). This is to say that: 'The problem with pure violence is that it does not exist as such' (150). Although these points are, to be sure, contained within a complex argument about the nature of sovereignty, law and the state in Agamben's thinking, Watkin hardly addresses what I have taken to be a key element of Agamben's thought – namely, the appearing of violence as 'mediality' and the signature as opacity – as the mark of *signator*. Violence as a pure means *entirely detached from law* is what is at issue in Agamben's thinking. Just as language is pure means as poetry or as *énonciation* in Benveniste's sense, or just as the image in cinema is pure mediality as gesture, so violence is pure mediality. Agamben's book, *Means without End* (2000) is thus of prime significance. There, it is said emphatically that, '*Politics is the sphere of pure means, that is, of the absolute and complete gesturality of human beings*' (60). Apart from joining politics to the cinema image, this is to say that politics is about action done for its own sake, just as there is no getting around the fact that violence, likewise, is action done for its own sake. In a manner totally in keeping with the 1970 essay on violence, Agamben repeats in *State of Exception* (2005a) that 'revolutionary violence' – a violence of pure means – 'is the name for the highest manifestation of *pure violence* by man' (53; emphasis added).

Just how Agamben engages with mediality in relation to the image and how the image and violence might be linked is the theme of the next chapter.

Notes

1. With respect to form of life, or 'form-of-life', where life as such would be inseparable from its form, it is worth noting Ian Hunter's argument (see Hunter 2017) that the approach here is not at all historical because the essential thrust of the theorising involved derives from Agamben's debt to Heidegger's philosophy of the inseparability of Being and existence – that, in keeping with a modal ontology, existence is the becoming manifest of Dasein and the latter is the becoming manifest of Being. The plausibility of this claim would seem to be reinforced by the following passage from the final page of the first *Homo Sacer* study, a passage quoted by Hunter: 'Today *bios* lies in *zoē* exactly as essence, in the Heideggerian definition of Dasein, lies (*liegt*) in existence' (Agamben 1998: 188). Let it be said that for this relation to work as indicated, both *bios* and *zoē* would have to be absolutely bereft of any historical specificity, which I would suggest is not the case, whether Agamben intends this or not. Also, the figure of *homo sacer* – the incarnation of bare life – does not seem to fit into this relation.
2. Due to its continued reliance on the notion of sovereignty and the juridical framework through which it operates, Foucault claims that political theory is based on a redundant concept of power: 'the king's head', as everyone is fond of quoting, 'has not been cut-off'. Although this claim may well have some purchase, it is notable that the bio-politics of population upon which it is based implicitly brings to the fore *zōē* as bare life – that is, as I propose, life as pure survival, not as a mode or way of life. This is also the basis of *homo sacer*, thereby making it worthy of our interest. As Foucault presents it, life in the new paradigm of 'bio-power' and 'bio-politics' refers to things like, 'birthrate, longevity, public health, housing, and migration' (Foucault 1979: 140). Also: 'For the first time *in history*, no doubt, biological existence was reflected in political existence' (142; emphasis added). Note that this historical approach differs from Agamben's paradigmatic approach, which will be addressed on more detail below. Now, because wars are fought between populations, combatants become pure canon-fodder in the interest of the physical – that is, biological – survival of the population. Again, in the new paradigm, 'what was demanded and what served as an objective was life, understood *as the basic needs*, man's concrete essence' (145; emphasis added). In short, the human essence is presented as being equivalent to biological survival as the survival of a population – or nation (cf. the German nation) – as opposed to the survival of an opposing population. The potentially racist basis of survival here should not be missed.
3. John Milbank has argued that there are, 'four great "stories of sacrifice" which we have inherited from the nineteenth century, and which assume

the status of veritable "meta-histories": those of Wellhausen, Robertson Smith, Frazer and Hubert with Mauss' (1995: 17).
4. Despite Agamben recoiling from an anthropological explanation of *homo sacer*, and although he never mentions the term, there is a strong echo of the 'scapegoat' here, and as we will see (cf. Chapter 5, below, on Girard and violence) the scapegoat is the negative foundation of society. The main difference between *homo sacer* and the scapegoat is that unlike the latter, *homo sacer* does not become transformed into the hero/god – or victim – at the origin.
5. In a previous study (Lechte 2018), I have examined bare life as it is conceived in contemporary thought as the pure survival of the biological being – the animal conceived as the ultimate origin of the human. This is contrasted with the human as ensconced in 'ways of life' (*bios*), a syntagma that echoes Agamben's 'form of life'. Although mindful of Agamben's insistence that 'bare life' is not natural life (for a reiteration of this, see Agamben (2016: 263)) – for 'bare life' in a human context takes on a form – at the level of what is commonly presupposed about the origin of the human, bare life (Benjamin's 'mere life') is assumed to be 'natural life'. What is at stake in the current discussion, however, are the issues bare life raises in Agamben's theory of power and sovereignty.

As a number of Agamben scholars have pointed out (see Salzani (2016), Robert (2013)), the Italian original, '*la nuda vita*', when translated as 'naked' or 'nude' life can lead in a totally different direction to that of life as pure survival, or as mere biological existence. Naked life would be life revealed not in terms of its appearance or as veiled, but life in its essence, life as it really is. It is a direction that Agamben partially pursues in his essay, 'Nudity' in the book, *Nudities* (2011b). I make this point in order to show the potential instability of the term, '*la nuda vita*'. The translation of *la nuda vita* as 'bare life' would seem to be an excellent way of ensuring that the term has the political focus that Agamben intends.
6. Cf. the much quoted: 'One day humanity will play with law just as children play with disused objects, not in order to restore them to their canonical use but to free them from it for good' (Agamben 2005a: 64). Does this mean that 'divine violence' will eventually replace law?
7. Where it is said and endlessly quoted that 'Sovereign is he who decides on the exception' (Schmitt 2005: 5).
8. However, in his 1970 article on violence, Agamben does subscribe to the regenerative nature of sacred violence in 'primitive' cultures: cf. 'it was precisely and only through the sudden irruption of the sacred and the interruption of profane time that primitive humans could fully engage with the cosmos, asserting power through the extreme act of spilling their own blood' (2015a: 235–236).

9. William Watkin's point that 'violence, as a signature contains no stable semantic content' (Watkin 2015: 151) alludes to the difficulty of defining violence addressed in the Introduction to this study. In other words, for Watkin, violence cannot be definitively defined. The result is that literal or empirical violence is frequently pointed to as a substitute for a definition. However, if Bataille's point holds and violence is the other of language, then the value of any definition is drastically reduced.
10. In this respect, it is interesting (if not ironical) to note Alison Ross's argument that Benjamin is most opposed, in his 'Critique of Violence' essay and other early works, to ambiguity. The law, for example is problematic for Benjamin, Ross claims, because it is ambiguous. See Ross (2015).
11. In his early piece, Agamben seems to accept the idea of violence as the origin if it has to do with revolutionary violence – that is, violence that inaugurates a new era (cf. Agamben 2015b [1970]: 237), whereas, later, as we shall see, he seems to be opposed to the very idea of origin (cf. Agamben 2010: 90).
12. Agamben does not examine in any detail the possible historical context of Benjamin's Eighth Thesis of the Philosophy of History, where it is said that the 'state of emergency' has become the rule rather the exception (Benjamin 1979: 259. This is cited by Agamben (2005a: 57).). Suffice it to add here that Article 48 of the Weimar Constitution made it very easy for governments to call a 'state of emergency'. For example, Article 48 was invoked 135 times in 1924, and sixty times in 1932. The Weimar Republic (1919–1933) was notoriously unstable, with twenty different governments, none remaining in power for more than two years. Benjamin is, moreover, cited as saying that his 'Theses on the Philosophy of History' were 'motivated by the experience of his generation in the years leading up to Hitler's war' (see Eiland and Jennings 2014: 659) – that is, the years leading up to 1933, the year Benjamin left Berlin for Paris. Thus, while Benjamin's thesis is almost literally true, to be able to propose the same thesis today Agamben has to claim that the contemporary dominance of the executive government over the legislature is equivalent to the exception having become the 'paradigm' or technique' of government (cf. 2005a: 6–7, 18). The question is: does the dominance of executive government entail the 'state of emergency' becoming the rule? Perhaps a case could be made for this, but Agamben does not make it.
13. For her part, Hannah Arendt sees the origin of law in its capacity to set the boundary between the private and public spheres as well as between the city and what lay outside it (cf. Arendt 1958: 63 and 198), even though the 'boundlessness of action' (191) – the essential characteristic of the *polis* – is likely to upset all existing boundaries. Does this mean that action upsets the law? Arendt does not say.

14. This reference points to a confusion between history and paradigm in Agamben's thinking on violence.
15. By contrast, Agamben has been criticised for the way he has appropriated the Greek term, *zōē* without adequate elaboration (see Derrida 2008: 433–434; Debreuil 2006; Finlayson 2010). Also, Peter Gratton (2011) has said that there is a strong hyperbolic element running through much of Agamben's writing to the detriment of precision. I am arguing that mediality is not open to these criticisms, even if its implications with regard to violence turn out to be unacceptable.
16. With 'inoperativity' means break the equivalence between life and work or production, so that the essence of human life becomes its 'sabbatical' character: cf. 'Man has dedicated himself to production and labor [*lavoro*], because in his essence he is the Sabbatical animal par excellence' (Agamben 2011a: 246). Also: 'This inoperativity is the political substance of the Occident, the glorious nutrient of all power' (246). Moreover, 'inoperativity' has a double inflection in relation to Agamben's notion of means: on the one hand it evokes the Bataillian 'theme of *désoeuvrement*' (Agamben 1998: 61) (idleness as an active passivity, or of the human whose destiny is not a project, as it was for Hegel). This is Agamben's human as 'sabbatical animal'. Inoperativity can also be associated with rendering all 'purposiveness', or ends, inoperative, thus revealing 'pure means' (Agamben 2018a: 82). This idea will be elaborated upon in the following chapter.
17. Support for this can be found in *State of Exception*, where Agamben claims that there is only violence outside the law, which is also Benjamin's position in relation to Schmitt. Thus: 'What now takes its place are civil war and revolutionary violence, that is human action that has shed [*deposto*] every relation to law' (2005a: 59).
18. With the 'as if', Agamben's thought remains within the social contract tradition, where it is not a matter of proving that there was, historically, a real state of nature, but that it is 'as if' a state of nature preceded the emergence of political society. This also implies a continued attachment to the tradition of political theory, which valorises the law, the tradition (as opposed to 'bio-politics'), from which Agamben is attempting to free himself.
19. For an appreciation of Foucault as historian, see Veyne (1997).
20. Here, it is appropriate to recall Hunter's argument noted above regarding Agamben's debt to Heidegger, the result being that history is marginalised in favour of ontology. As Hunter indicates, Agamben's theoretical practice is a 'sophisticated form of allegory in which historical phenomena (such as monasticism) are treated as symbols or "paradigms" for hidden metaphysical or ontological philosophemes (such as the relation between life and form)' (Hunter 2017: 136). Again, the historical aspect is clouded

because: 'For Agamben [...] historical events are allegorical or symbolic by nature; that is, by virtue of being the taking-place of transcendent Being' (139) – read: by virtue of Agamben's modal ontology.
21. Girard's notion of origin, as we shall see in Chapter 5, would seem to be in question here.
22. Some, like Robert A. Paul (2010), have argued that, following Freud in *Totem and Taboo*, the 'primal crime' did in fact take place. Certainly, this is also René Girard's position (see Girard 1989).
23. Even though Agamben claims that Foucault's history is based on paradigms, such as the Panopticon, it is to be noted that Foucault at the same time treats Bentham's architectural plan as a historical document, one that is reproduced together with other documents as the thirty illustrations at the beginning of Foucault (1975).
24. As our author says early on in *Homo Sacer*: 'All law is "situational law"' (Agamben 1998: 16).
25. As Ross points out, for Agamben 'the camp situation cannot be located outside the juridical order; it is, on the contrary, an ever-present possibility of law, the possibility of the state of exception' (2012: 427).
26. Cf.: 'insofar as divine violence is not one kind of violence among others, but only the dissolution of the link between violence and law' (Agamben 1998: 65).
27. In his most recent formulation, Agamben repeats the point: 'At the center of the study on violence stands the concept of "pure means"' (2018a: 80).
28. As a reminder of the controversial nature of the "Critique of Violence" ("Zur Kritik der Gewalt"), see the following: Fenves (1998), who suggests that the notion of 'means', or 'mediality' (cf. 'pure means' (*reine Mittel*)) evokes 'medium' and 'middle' (46); Ross (2014), who claims that, generally, 'the meanings attributed to the essay are often arbitrary and artificial' (99); Hamacher (1994), who, like Agamben (as we will see), argues that 'divine' violence should be equated with 'pure mediality' and that this is 'nonviolent'; Derrida (1990), who is wary of the possible implication that 'divine' violence might foreshadow the 'Final Solution'; and Andrew Benjamin (2013, 2015), who refuses to equate the German, '*Gewalt*', uniquely with the English word, violence, but rather proposes 'operability', as a possible translation, the aim being, as with Hamacher, to bring 'divine violence' (*Göttliche Gewalt*) within the purview of 'nonviolence'.
29. First of all, Agamben equates 'pure violence' ('*reine Gewalt*') with 'divine' violence (2005a: 53), then he equates the latter with pure mediality (62). On the valorisation of pure violence as mediality, Agamben is preceded by both Fenves (1998) and Hamacher (1994).
30. Thus Ross writes: 'Such accounts of Benjamin aim to defend the idea that his politics is the "politics of pure means." One of the key problems

with the idea that Benjamin advocates a politics of pure means is that in Benjamin's essay on violence the notion of "pure means" has no necessary connection to politics and no connection at all to the category of divine violence. It is simply intended to mark those social relations and institutions that have no relation to the law, and it includes such politically innocuous categories as "conversation"' (2014: 157n5).

31. A problem for the argument that, with Benjamin, divine violence as mediality can appear as such would seem to be contained in the following statement from the essay: 'only mythical violence, not divine, will be recognizable as such with certainty, unless it be in incomparable effects, because the expiatory power of violence is not visible to men' (W. Benjamin 1986: 300).

32. Throughout his work, as I shall show in Chapter 5, René Girard points to *The Bacchae* as an illustration of how Dionysus and violence are inseparable.

4 Rethinking Agamben on the Image

IN THE PREVIOUS CHAPTER, the key term in relation to violence was Benjamin's violence as a 'pure means' or – in Agamben's terms – as a pure mediality, or, again, as a recent text reiterates, as a '"politics of pure means"' (2018a: 80). Mediality would supposedly evoke the appearance as such of the medium. The latter approach is – unlike Bataille's – opaque, not transparent. It can be an object to be thought about and reflected upon.[1] As was indicated in the Introduction, violence as mediality is a violence without an object – without a victim. This differentiates Agamben on violence from Bataille and Girard, for whom violence and victim are inseparable. In a formulation that has relevance for understanding the status of the image in Agamben's political theory, it is said that 'mediality without end is in some way active because in it *the means shows itself as such*' (82; emphasis added). Thus, the image in the Agamben universe, *shows itself as such*. Like violence, it, too, is a 'pure means'. What, precisely, might be the consequences of this?

In response, we investigate Agamben's thesis in *The Kingdom and the Glory* (2011a) that the human has evolved as the 'Sabbatical animal' (as inoperativity)[2] within the milieu of 'acclamation', the milieu of the mediatisation of public opinion in a 'society of the spectacle' – or, equally, of the image. Media and public opinion (acclamation) are inextricably bound together in the articulation of glory. The undoubtedly political implications of this are only given indirectly. At the forefront of Agamben's deliberations is theology and the concept of 'economy' as contained the notion of *oikonomia* as 'a government of men' (2011a: xi). These theological roots will be considered in some detail in what follows.[3]

Agamben refers to Guy Debord and the 'Society of the Spectacle' (= society of the image) in a number of places (see Agamben 2005a: 78–83, 1998: 10, 2016: xv–xix, 2000: 73–89), but it is *Kingdom and the Glory* (2011a) and especially its detailed analysis of the Christian Trinity,[4] where Christ glorifies the Father, that is particularly significant for deepening our understanding of Agamben's approach to the image. The analysis of the Trinity leads on to the idea of glory at the 'centre of the political system' (256) and to the image as pure mediality (pure means) that becomes the modern incarnation of glory. In contemporary society images would supposedly become equivalent to the appearance of the medium in the context of the Debord-inspired 'strategies of spectacular power' (256), the latter being driven by a mediatised version of glory. In this chapter, I will argue that the image as glory should not be conflated with a glorious image. For an image, as I define it (as was outlined in Chapter 2), is what makes it possible for the imaged to appear. Sometimes, as we shall see, Agamben's text verges on a similar conclusion, albeit indirectly, a conclusion that would undermine the notion of mediality as the substance of the image. Thus, in Agamben's 'archaeology of glory', Christ does not appear on his own account as is confirmed in the biblical passage from John, quoted by Agamben: 'Now is the Son of man glorified [*edoxasthē*], and God is glorified [*edoxasthē*] in him. If God be glorified in him, God shall also glorify him in himself, and straightaway glorify him' (201–202).

Ultimately, theology will give way to politics – or rather to a thesis explaining why power and sovereignty require praise and acclamation, that is, glorification. Acclamation as public opinion managed by the media – glory as the 'central mystery of government' – profoundly implicates the image as mediality. This explains Agamben's appropriation of Debord's thesis that 'capitalist politics and economy' become – in the now familiar words – 'an immense accumulation of *spectacles*' (Debord 2006: sect 1). The society of the spectacle is the society of social relations mediated by images, where, says Agamben, 'the commodity and capital itself assume the mediatic form of the image' (Agamben 2011a: 255). This alienates individuals from what is real in a violent uprooting of the self from itself. In other words, in Agamben's view, the image in society today produces profoundly negative effects.[5]

What government as glory amounts to in the end is an expanded version of the play of the image; what power amounts to is violence mediated by glory – thus, by the image. Such would the synthesis (albeit brutal) that captures the content of Agamben's *Kingdom and the Glory*.

Agamben then proposes that the commonly accepted understanding of the image is Hegelian, in that the image is supposed to disappear in the expression. Thus, the mediality of the image would disappear into what is imaged. In another context, however, he refers to the idea that the 'taking place of language' is equivalent to language's disappearance into what it expresses: '[l]anguage is very weak, in the sense that it cannot but disappear in the thing it names' (Agamben 2018b: 9–10). This is only the case, however, if language is viewed through the prism of the history of philosophy and linguistics and not in terms of the act – that is, of the taking place of language, where we 'become aware of the pure fact that we speak' (28) As such, language as voice becomes an explicit mediality. For Agamben, the distinction between language and the image as such is thus vastly reduced. The image will become, via Debord, mediality made explicit. By contrast, I suggest that the imaged could not appear if the image as such appeared (i.e., if it could be an object in its own right). If we extend the notion of image to include spectacle – if image and spectacle are inseparable, as Debord claims, then the image in Agamben's work would, in all probability extend to the notion of acclamation, which is dissected in detail in *The Kingdom and the Glory* (2011a: 167–259) in the context of the relation of theology to politics, especially during the Roman era. Indeed, in a single stroke, as it were, not only are violence and the image joined in Agamben's political philosophy by mediality, but they are also joined because politics is the play of power as acclamation and spectacle. This, then, is what I will endeavour to confirm.

Ironically, key aspects of the image as I propose it are evoked by Agamben's treatment of messianic time that emerges in a reading of Paul's 'Letter to the Romans' (Agamben 2005d). In response to the question as to whether time can appear in a representation, Agamben argues that representations of time (e.g., as points on a continuum) tend to it being spatialised (this is Bergson's argument). Spatial representations cannot do justice to time as a lived experience (64). And so, if time is what is aimed at, could an image do it justice? The answer is 'no', if the image is understood as an object in its own right, but the answer could be in the affirmative if the image is understood as the mechanism that allows time to appear as such. What is needed is not an image of time, but an image that facilitates an experience of time, an image (or images) that would be radically transparent. Although he uses the term, 'representation', rather than 'image', Agamben recognises that transparency is crucial when it comes to an image/representation of time. This is why he brings to bear the notion of '"operational time"' forged by the linguist, Gustave Guillaume. 'Operational time' is '*the time the mind takes to realize a time-image*' (66).

The problem, however, is that the form the representation of time takes is given precedence over the presentation of time itself. What is presupposed is that time is intended to be captured *by* the representation, rather than being allowed to appear *through* the representation/image. This is not to deny that a particular representation – most notably a diagrammatic one – might be predisposed to give a false idea of time – e.g., time as a series of static moments. But the supposedly static photographic images of Muybridge or Mery become dynamic once the image is understood as transparent rather than as opaque. A photograph can capture movement; if not, we are forced to conclude that there is no movement and therefore no time because the photo (image) itself is not in movement.[6] Such would be another instance where media specificity is invoked to explain the significance of the image.

Oikonomia as Glory and Acclamation

To gain a fuller appreciation of the image as it operates in *The Kingdom and the Glory*, we turn to the preface of that work where Agamben sets out a key aspect of his investigation into the relation between *oikonomia* and government: 'In opposition to the ingenuous emphasis on productivity and labor that has long prevented modernity from accessing politics as man's most proper dimension, politics is here returned to its central inoperativity, that is, to that operation that amounts to rendering inoperative all human and divine works' (2011a: xiii). Clearly, the intent is to bring into question the dominance of the secularised meaning of *oikonomia* (evoking the Greek, *oikos* or household) as concerned exclusively with ensuring the physical survival of humanity and giving rise in modernity to the term 'economy', the meaning of which evokes the problem of utility and the scarcity of resources. Consequently, political economy would have to do with the contest over the distribution of these resources resulting in relative wealth for some and relative poverty for others. This, as Agamben's work has principally shown,[7] is a very circumscribed view of 'economy', one that interprets it almost exclusively in terms of the Industrial Revolution, where the ultimate destiny of the human was believed to be the overcoming of material poverty. This interpretation has largely, if not exclusively, followed the example of Hannah Arendt who claimed that ancient Greek society was based on an essential division between *oikos* and *polis*, where men's striving for glory in the *polis* was only possible because their material needs were taken care of in the *oikos*. In similar vein, many so called primitive societies, like certain developing nations today, were seen only to have reached subsistence level with regard to the problem of meeting material needs in the battle for physical survival.

We now know, partly in light of Agamben's investigations, that there *were* no, and that there *are* no, exclusively subsistence societies because the basis of the human condition is that of ways – or forms – of life and that there is no human life (whether of the *oikos* or modern-day slum) that can be reduced, outside of every historical, social and cultural context, to a pure struggle for existence (Darwin).[8]

Part of the way of life that constitutes the history of the term *oikonomia* is, Agamben argues, essentially theological and religious. Hence the subtitle to *The Kingdom and the Glory* reads: '*For a Theological Genealogy of Economy and Government*'. Occupying as it does a place in the history of theology *oikonomia* evokes the Western way of life, especially as encapsulated in the Christian Trinity. Like Marie-José Mondzain before him (see Mondzain 1996),[9] but taking a view broader than the Iconoclastic debates of the seventh and eighth centuries AD, Agamben points to the fact that through the Trinity *oikonomia* evokes, firstly, the specific relation or arrangement between the Father, the Son and the Holy Ghost and, secondly, the way that God organises the world through administration. Without *oikonomia*, God's world would have no order; there would instead be chaos. Referring to Aristotle's discussion of order in the *Politics* (1298a) and the *Metaphysics* (1075a), Agamben says that 'order is [. . .] a relation not a substance' (2011a: 82). Similarly, even though God must still be understood as a substance, the Trinity is an ordering or arrangement (*oikonomia*), not a substance (being).

The first half of Agamben's book is devoted to showing that theologically inspired concepts with regard to God's plan, such as providence and fate, transcendence and immanence, order, substance (*ousia*) and praxis (*oikonomia*), all evoke the division between Kingdom and Government, a division that lives on in the politics of modern democracies in the relation between legislature and executive. As Agamben summarily puts it, we are dealing with the Kingdom (providence) as immediate government and Government as mediated government (fate). The mediated level also corresponds, as we shall see, to government as the spectacle and image – as glory and acclamation, power and inoperativity. In essence, just as being (substance, God) cannot 'be' without praxis, transcendence without immanence, providence without fate, God without angels as administrators, so the Kingdom cannot be (is nothing) without Government. In short, the immediate cannot exist in itself; it 'is' only to the extent that the mediate domain allows it to come to fruition. What we learn from theology is that the world needs God, but, equally, God needs the world: He needs glory. On this basis Christ becomes the incarnation of world and God. Christ's being depends on God the Father; but, equally, the being of God depends on His incarnation in Christ. This is the mystery of the Trinity. Moreover, the world needs God, but God needs the Son as glory and praise. There is, most significantly – as Agamben points out – 'reciprocal glorification between Father and Son (and, more generally, between the three persons). The Trinitarian economy is constitutively an economy of glory' (2011a: 201). Agamben then cites the following passage from John's Gospel:

> Father, the hour is come; glorify [*doxason*] thy Son, that thy Son also may glorify [*doxasēi*] thee [. . .] I have glorified thee on the earth: I have finished the work which thou gavest me to do, And now, O Father, glorify thou me with thine own self with the glory which I had with thee before the world was. (John 17:1–5, cited in Agamben 2011a: 201)

The circularity here is noted: while Jesus has glorified the Father with his work on earth, at the same time it is 'the glorification of the son through the work of the father' (202). Ultimately, 'to the glorious economy of the Trinity corresponds the reciprocal glorification of men and god' (202).

Although Agamben refers to the economy of glory expressed in optical terms by Paul in the Second Letter to the Corinthians (203), for the most part, the image is not pivotal in its particularity (it is not a matter of a specific image of Christ) but rather in its generality as medium in relation to immediacy.

In conformity with the notions (already referred to) of being and praxis, providence and fate, or of God and the world of men, 'modern theologians distinguish', Agamben tells us, 'between "economic trinity" (or trinity of revelation) and "immanent trinity" (or trinity of substance)' (207). Economic trinity is equivalent to 'God in his praxis', while immanent trinity corresponds to 'God as he is in himself' (207). All of this presages the point where modern government will also be found to be marked by this division: 'The economic trinity (Government) presupposes the immanent trinity (the Kingdom), which justifies and founds it' (207–208). Glory is the place where the trinities mutually interpenetrate (208).

Agamben's lengthy study of the way that glory and glorification function in the sphere of theology concludes that not only does God demand glorification simply because He is worthy of it, but glorification by humanity allows Him to exist. The secular version of this was proposed by Durkheim who is quoted as saying: 'No doubt, the men could not live without gods, but on the other hand, the gods would die if they were not worshipped' (227). This line of thinking about the *raison d'être* of the glorification of God in Western culture leads to the conclusion that, 'without ritual practices, the divine pleroma loses its strength and decays; the God in other words, needs to be continually restored and repaired by the pity [sic] of men, in the same way that he is weakened by their impiety' (229). The crux of Agamben's argument is that the maintenance of God through glorification has, analogously, been carried over into secular politics: power needs glorification; it needs acclamation as public opinion. Thus, 'profane acclamations are not an ornament of political power but found and justify it' (230).

It is in relation to glory that Agamben ponders the image of the empty throne (*hetomasia*), and he asks whether the latter is, as some commentators have said, a symbol of regality? Agamben answers in the negative and asserts that '*[t]he empty throne is not* [. . .] *a symbol of regality but of glory*'(245). And he continues:

Glory precedes the creation of the world and survives its end. The throne is empty not only because glory, though coinciding with the divine essence is not identified with it, but also because it is in its innermost self-inoperativity and sabbatism. The void is the sovereign figure of glory. (245)

Images of the empty throne are invoked to illustrate not regality – as has been said – but glory. The fifth-century mosaic on the arch of Saint Sixtus III in Santa Maria Maggiore in Rome as well as a mosaic in the church of San Prisco in Capua (north of Naples) both depict the empty throne, as does another mosaic in the Byzantine basilica of Santa Maria Assunta in Torcello (Venice). Finally, Agamben refers to a thirteenth-century fresco in the church of Saint Demetrius (*sic*). Here exhibited is 'an empty throne suspended from the air, draped in purple, and surrounded by six acclaiming angels; just above it, in a crystalline transparent rhombus, there is a book, an amphora, a snow-white bird, and a black bull' (244). And, on the cover of the English translation of *The Kingdom and the Glory* there is the empty throne of the Papal Basilica of San Paolo Fuori le Mura in Rome – a plethora of images, we might say.

    An empty throne could of course be a real entity. However, Agamben's point in referring to Byzantine examples is that the empty throne is Christ's, in which case it cannot be anything but an image. The empty throne is an image – or, rather is what is imaged via the image – but it symbolises glory (not glorification). Glory is the equivalent of God as substance (immanent Trinity) for which there can be no image. However, an ambiguity arises, one that is not noted by Agamben. It is said that the throne is an image of emptiness, of a void. We supposedly see the absence of God/Christ in the emptiness of the throne. But, in fact, we 'see' the emptiness only if a throne is conceptualised as a seat that is normally occupied. What is imaged (the empty throne (cf. Throne Room at Knossos)) evokes an absence. Thus, an image makes present an object: the empty throne. The image is necessary in order that the object can be interpreted as an empty throne – in order that there be a signature: a sign or symbol that is also an object in its own right.

    By way of comparison, when we see van Gogh's painting of a chair in his bedroom at Arles (1888), we do not say that it is empty. For it passes for an image of a chair – not an empty chair. A throne (a seat identified as a throne) is a different matter. As a physical object, it is either occupied or empty. An empty throne presupposes that it could be occupied – that an incumbent is absent, as is the case with God or Christ.[10] The empty throne is thus an image that symbolises glory. In fact, it can be an image of glory because, in Agamben's terms, glory presupposes the absence of the sovereign figure (whether this be God or the monarch). What is interesting, if not significant, here is that Agamben treats the image of the empty throne as being transparent in the sense just elaborated above. That is, he does not treat the image as an object detached from what is imaged, but instead describes the throne as such, not the image: 'the fifth-century mosaic on the arch of Saint Sixtus III in Santa Maria Maggiore in Rome *shows an empty throne* encrusted with multicoloured stones, on which rests a cushion and a cross; next to it one can make out a lion, an eagle, a winged human figure, some fragments of wings, and a crown' (2011a: 244; emphasis added). In short, an image *qua* image brings what is imaged into presence; it cannot – *pace* Agamben – be isolated as a pure means. Thus, if the '*empty throne is not* [. . .] *a symbol of regality but of glory*' (245), it is the image as transparent as just illustrated by Agamben's description, and not as a pure mediality, that enables such an interpretation. Such a conception of the image is in conflict with Agamben's valorisation of the image as pure mediality in Debord's theory of the 'society of the spectacle', which is referred to at the end of the final chapter of *The Kingdom and the Glory*. For whereas we have seen glory as the interpretation of an object (the empty throne) made present via an image, Agamben's reading of Debord turns the image into a manifestation of glory, pure and simple, 'the "becoming-image" of capital', as our author called it in an earlier commentary on Debord (Agamben 2000: 76).

From a Theology of Economy to a Theology of the Image

The discussion of a theology of economy and glory leads us now to discussion of aspects of the theology of the image, something Agamben leaves in abeyance even though the image has played a crucial part in the Father-Son relation in the theology of the Trinity, as Marie-José Mondzain has shown.[11] Also important in this regard is the work of Hans Belting (1996 and 2005) and Jean-Luc Marion (2013).

Mondzain, in her now classic study, argues that the sources of the image in today's secular society are theological, that – to use Schmitt's and Agamben's phrasing – the image in contemporary society is a secularisation of a theological concept. Thus, Mondzain writes that: 'today, there is no alternative system of thought concerning the image capable of competing with the theoretical and political power of the one that the church developed during its first ten centuries' (2005: 173).

Belting also sees that the origin of the image is decidedly theological having to do with the depiction or non-depiction of Christ as the Son of God – as equivalent or not equivalent to the prototype. Unlike Mondzain, however, the historian of art argues that the image in modernity – the secular image – is now specifically aesthetic, valued for its own sake and not for what it can reveal. In discussing the so-called traditional image in his article, 'Image, Medium, Body' (2005), Belting asks, tellingly: 'Is it possible to distinguish images from so-called reality with such ontological naïveté?' (316). I have previously answered 'no' in a general sense to this question (see Lechte 2012). It means that an image makes reality present. Theologically, God can be present in Christ, and Christ can be, artistically, present in an image, and, theologically, present *as* the image. As Mondzain shows in commenting on Byzantine theology, this iconophile argument can be presented with great subtlety. In other words, it is not a matter of mimesis in any simple sense.

The issue is that if one says that an image of Christ can only capture the flesh (because divinity cannot be circumscribed), then to worship/venerate such an image is idolatry. The latter can only be avoided if indeed Christ's spiritual being (the Father) is present in the image. Mondzain shows that the task Patriarch Nicephorus (758–828) took upon himself was to provide a theological basis for the image and the icon that avoided the aporia of an image of a spirit that cannot be circumscribed. Nicephorus said that while the image could never be equivalent to the prototype (or natural image), there was a likeness. In effect, likeness was to be distinguished from identity (see Lechte 2012: 37). On this basis, an image in an icon could evoke the divine without claiming to be divine. Idolatry is thus avoided.

Similarly, Jean-Luc Marion, in his take on the prototype-image relation, refers to the proceedings of the Second Council of Nicaea (787 AD). To avoid it becoming an idol, Marion says, the Council recognised that the icon is a (visible) 'type' that is not equivalent to the (invisible) prototype: 'Icons are thus opposed to idols by two qualifications: first because they alone deserve and can demand the veneration of the faithful; second because they alone keep and maintain a trace of the brilliance of the holiness of the Holy' (275). Maintaining a trace of the Holy without laying claim to being equivalent to the Holy is what is crucial. In Marion's words, with the type 'a prototype is more indicated than shown' (276). On the other hand, an iconoclastic approach turns the image-icon solely into an object, the veneration of which results in idolatry.

Just as Agamben invokes theology to explain that contemporary politics is based on public opinion and acclamation through the media (the society of the spectacle/image as the contemporary form of *oikonomia*), so Mondzain and Marion employ theology to discern the iconoclastic approach to the image in society today. The image has become, the thinkers argue, exclusively an object, and no less so in Debord's society of the spectacle (more of which later). It refers to nothing but itself. In its most radical form of simulacrum, it has become completely detached from reality, whether material or spiritual. For her part, Mondzain's argument (which I reiterate in Lechte 2012: 4, 5–46) is precisely that the debate about the image and the icon inaugurated by Byzantine theology continues in a secular form today, so that there are image sceptics, as it were (iconoclasts: those who say that images are purely conventional and media specific) and image faithful (iconophiles: those who say that images are transparent and do present the imaged entity). Marion adds to this by saying in summary that: 'Being iconoclastic, metaphysics condemns the image to the rank of an idol' (282). And in response to the argument that nihilism brings metaphysics to a close and gives rise to Nietzsche's notion of the image, Marion asks: 'Has not iconoclasm – from Platonism to Hegel – disappeared in the epoch of what Nietzsche defined as the inversion of Platonism and the devaluation of all values?' (282). Marion answers by saying that: 'On the contrary; it is necessary to recognize that the idolatrous status of the image has never attained its ultimate consequences more than with Nietzsche' (282). This is because Nietzsche rules out the possibility that the image (or appearance) could refer to anything but itself. There is, he claims, no original, no in-itself, no prototype, no reality beyond the image – beyond appearance. In telling and well-known statements Nietzsche says that there is no 'true' and 'apparent' world, just as there is no Kantian 'thing-in-self' and appearance (see Nietzsche 1968: sect 553). Nietzsche's epistemological stance implies that there are only images and that the imaged is an interpretation – that is, it is created.[12]

No doubt there is irony in the fact that the title, *Twilight of the Idols* (first published in 1889) signals (with the notion of 'idol') an iconoclastic stance that – if we are to accept Marion's claim – ultimately gives rise to the image as idol, the image referring to nothing but itself – the image becoming object, in short. Nietzsche's trenchant critique of 'idols' thus gives rise to the image as idol. Caution is necessary here. For Nietzsche never thematises the image as such. He does, however, famously refer to grammar and, by extension, to language: 'I fear we are not getting rid of God because we still believe in grammar . . .' (1974c: pt 2, sect 5). In Nietzsche's take on things, the acceptance of, or belief in, the transparency of language is a false belief; therefore, language becomes an idol – albeit, perhaps, one that is not yet fading. Language is an idol because it is deemed to be transparent when it is not. Presumably, the same applies to the image: it would be an idol if one believed in its transparency. As we have seen, though, it is through the elimination of transparency that the image is turned into an object, thus becoming (the equivalent of) an idol.

*

Of course, the antecedents of government and the image can be theological without these antecedents continuing to be influential in modernity, a modernity which so many, like Max Weber with his notion of the disenchantment, have viewed as essentially secular. The point, as Alberto Toscano (2011: 127) has said, is that using a theological paradigm to explain politics today can give the appearance that history is being defined as essentially continuous, while Agamben's mentor, Michel Foucault, argued that history is on the contrary a series of discontinuities. So, not only does Agamben need to validate the idea that king and government, executive and legislature, power and glory, people substance and people communication are, in the end, indivisible (despite appearances from a secularist perspective), but also that theology – as the instance of the past which would give the present its momentum – can, in all rigour, be called upon to validate and verify the thesis that government is founded in glory and acclamation as the secular form of *oikonomia*.

But history is not essentially discontinuous any more than is it essentially continuous. The point is that the History of Ideas (especially in relation to the history of the social sciences), tends to privilege continuities, whereas, at a deeper level (e.g., the level of the *episteme*), history presents a series of discontinuities. Here, we should recall that Foucault came out of the French tradition of epistemology (Bachelard, Canguilhem, Althusser, Lecourt) and this in some ways limited his focus – even in his later work. As such, the ontological level (what is the essential nature of history?) tends to be neglected.

In any case, I suggest that by invoking a theological framework for interpreting *oikonomia*, Agamben counters the dominance of utility as the key term for explaining politics and economy in modernity. By this is meant that *oikonomia*, rather than leading to the modern term 'economy' as the theory of utility, production and scarcity, is at the origin of activities that have no 'use' in the narrowly macroeconomic sense, activities such as acclamation which renders economic utility inoperative. To the extent that inoperativity evokes, as has been said, Bataille's *désoeuvrement* as 'unemployed negativity', *oikonomia* evokes – however faintly – Bataille's 'general economy', where the latter can be defined as 'expenditure without reserve'.[13]

Overall, though, what we shall witness in Agamben's trajectory is the reinterpretation of *oikonomia* as the administration of government where acclamation is primary and the predominance of the mediatised image in the society of the spectacle.

*

We will now see how Agamben's invocation of the image of the empty throne allows us to gain a better grip on the working of the image. A certain transparency clearly governs the presentation of the empty throne in its Byzantine incarnations. Indeed, for this point to have any impact, Nietzsche's refusal of transparency to the image must be rejected, so that the image of the throne becomes equivalent to a real throne and the iconophile (as opposed to an iconoclast) position prevails. Because the image is equivalent to a real throne, Agamben is thus able to evoke, at the level of the symbolic, the notion of glory and, subsequently, the notions of acclamation, sabbatical animal and public opinion. While the latter are distinct from the image, the condition of possibility of their evocation depends on the transparency of the image, of the throne. In other words, the image gives access to the throne as such quite independently of it being a photograph.

But what of the situation with Agamben's appropriation of Debord's theory of the 'society of the spectacle', where representations (images) have replaced 'what was directly lived' (Debord 2006: sect 1). Society has now become an immense array of spectacles underpinned by images. Or rather, the spectacle is 'a social relation among people mediated by images' (sect 4).[14] Agamben treats Debord's theory as *sui generis*: he does not relate it to other (iconoclastic) theories of media – such as those of Baudrillard[15] or McLuhan.

As is known superficially, McLuhan emphasises the active role of 'medium' (over message), so that the content of a medium is another medium.[16] Medium is technology. An electric light is a pure medium. This example highlights the ambivalent aspect of the 'medium is the message' principle. For, firstly, one needs light to see before one can see the light. Similarly, one needs to have acquired language (the alphabet) before one can understand language as language. McLuhan always assumes that media are what can be understood and objectified before being what enables understanding to take place. That is, the transparency of media *qua* media is radically occluded. In addition to this of course, McLuhan takes a purely secular approach: the structure of media in modernity has become entirely detached from any religious antecedent. As media are objects of study before they are what makes the study of them possible, images are objects before being what allows any object to appear. Thus, McLuhan says: 'it is only on those terms, standing aside from any structure or medium, that its principles and lines of force can be discerned' (McLuhan 2008: 16). Here, a medium can remain a medium even in its objectified state, whereas I have argued (Lechte 2012, 2013) that objectification (e.g., the image as object) and medium are irreconcilable.

As key references for the modern version of the iconoclastic position, Debord, Baudrillard and McLuhan signal the thesis emerging in the 1960s of the dominance of the code and the image as object. Debord's *Society of the Spectacle*, first published in French in 1967, can be considered a pioneering, post-war iconoclastic text. Does Agamben remain locked into this version of iconoclasm, or does he take things further with his idea of acclamation and public opinion? Everything hangs on the meaning, significance and function of the notion: 'mediality', and on whether it can appear as such. Is mediality simply reducible to McLuhan's notion of medium, or does it supersede it? When referring to the image in relation to Debord's films, we know that Agamben opposes what he calls the 'Hegelian model' where an image would disappear into its expression. But in his writings of the early 1990s, collected in *Means Without End* (2000), he often refers to 'mediality' in relation to a theory of gesture. Gesture would thus be the appearing of mediality. Cinema is its privileged avatar. What Agamben intends by gesture is summed up in the following: '*The gesture is the exhibition of a mediality: it is the process of making a means visible as such*' (2000: 58). In relation to this, Deleuze's philosophy of cinema reveals that the latter is the attempt through moving images to capture a lost gesturality. Debord's films, for their part, if they are not specifically about gesture, are the revelation of mediality – the revelation of the dimension that is normally hidden. The image is thus implicated in gesture as mediality: '[c]inema leads images back to the homeland of gesture' (56).

The Cinema Image and Politics as Gesture and Mediality

Mediality is linked to divine violence (Benjamin) because the latter is a pure means. As such, it becomes the crossover point for Agamben between the image and violence. Agamben's remarks on cinema and the society of the spectacle bear this out. Indeed, mediality becomes constitutive of politics.

Gestures are fragmentary, always dynamic and never static, always part of a larger whole. As such, they are, as we have seen, pure mediality. Is this not also the exact definition of violence that we have just witnessed in the previous chapter? Confirmation is found in the following statement: '*Politics is the sphere of pure means, that is, of the absolute and complete gesturality of human beings*' (60). In 'Notes on Politics', Agamben reiterates the point:

> *Politics is the exhibition of a mediality: it is the act of making means visible as such.* Politics is the sphere neither of an end in itself nor of means subordinated to an end; rather, it is the sphere of pure mediality without end intended as the field of human action and of human thought. (2000: 116–117)[17]

Also:

> Now, man is an animal who is interested in images when he has recognized them as such. That's why he is interested in painting and why he goes to the cinema. A definition of man from our specific point of view could be that man is a moviegoing animal. He is interested in images after he has recognized that they are not real beings. The other point is that, as Gilles Deleuze has shown, the image in cinema – and not only in cinema, but in modern times generally – is no longer something immobile. It is not an archetype, but nor is it something outside history: rather, it is a cut which itself is mobile, an image-movement, charged as such with a dynamic tension. (Agamben 2002: 314)

In this statement, humans are beings interested in the image *qua* image (unlike animals). In other words, it is the opacity of the image that constitutes the basis of fascination for the human. Debord's films have the capacity to reveal this opacity, as opposed to a supposedly Hegelian notion of expression (which would include the image) that interprets the image as a medium that passes into what is imaged. Through repetition and stoppage Debord's films reveal the image *qua* image.

Debord's films thus constitute the *appearing* of mediality. This gives them their avant-garde quality. To argue against this is to fail to understand what avant-garde means in the world of cinema. It is to fail to grasp the fact that Debord shows us 'the image as such'. Here, things become a tricky, because to show the image as such means to show the image as contentless. To show an image with an imaged content would entail a certain transparency with the image as medium disappearing into what is imaged:

> Since his early films and ever more clearly as he went along, Debord has shown us the image as such, that is to say, according to one of his principles from The Society of the Spectacle, the image as a zone of undecidability between the true and the false. But there are two ways of showing an image. The image exhibited as such is no longer an image of anything; it is itself imageless. The only thing of which one cannot make an image is, if you will, the being-image of the image. The sign can signify anything, except the fact that it is in the process of signifying. What cannot be signified or said in a discourse, what is in a certain way unutterable, can nonetheless be shown in the discourse. There are two ways of showing this 'imagelessness',

two ways of making visible the fact that there is nothing more to be seen. One is pornography and advertising, which act as though there were always something more to be seen, always more images behind the images; while the other way is to exhibit the image as image and thus to allow the appearance of 'imagelessness', which, as Benjamin said, is the refuge of all images. It is here, in this difference, that the ethics and the politics of cinema come into play. (Agamben 2002: 319)

To ask why Debord's cinema image and cinema as the return of gesture are so important for Agamben is of course to raise once again the question of means-ends that we discussed in relation to divine violence. It is a matter of avoiding the cul-de-sac of means-ends logic, where the verification and validation of ends unavoidably runs fowl of metaphysics and ideology: 'the gesture then breaks with the false alternative between ends and means and paralyzes morality and presents instead means that, *as such*, evade the orbit of mediality without becoming, for this reason, ends' (57). In another context, writing about the image and silence, our author asks: 'How are we then to think of a silence that is not merely an impossibility of saying, that doesn't remain separate from language, but that brings language itself into view?' (Agamben 2012: 96). The image would make language itself visible in the very silence of the word. This is language, let it be emphasised, that is not to be understood as achieving any end – least of all communication. This then would be language as pure mediality. These examples show that Agamben is always striving for the original (as he sees it) opacity of media (medium as object), not its transparency. Again, in another essay on the German term, *Stimmung*, brought to light by Heidegger, Agamben says in relation to Hölderlin's poetry:

> That which in *Stimmung* is the possibility for speaking man, of an experience of the birth of his own word, of gathering, that is, the very taking place of that language that constantly anticipates him, throws and destines man outside of himself into a history and a tradition. (Agamben 2014: 501)

Here, 'the very taking place of language' is one of Agamben's key formulas, embracing as it does Benveniste's notion of *énonciation* (as opposed to *énoncé*) (see Agamben 1991: 25). It means that the essence of language can in no way be beholden to its content. It is, like Debord's image, like gesture, like the cinema image, a pure mediality. Perhaps if Agamben had remained faithful to his Heideggerian heritage, as brought to notice by Hunter,[18] then, in keeping with a modal ontology, the image as such would only appear as the imaged (its mode), just as Being only appears in existence.

*

So where does this leave us as far as Agamben's appropriation of Debord in *The Kingdom and the Glory* is concerned? Acclamation and glory, in the modern, secular sense of public opinion, is purveyed by the media. The media is at the heart of 'spectacular power'. 'What was confined to the spheres of liturgy and ceremonials has become concentrated in the media' (2011a: 256). The point is that a different interpretation (also invoking theology) would say of the image as such that it enabled parishioners (certainly after the partial resolution of iconoclastic crisis) to have a certain access to an imaged content, whether visible or invisible.

The appearance of pure mediality can therefore be sheeted home to the appearance of secular modernity, firstly, after Darwin and Saussure in the nineteenth century, then with structuralism after World War II. It is the image as something real.[19] The notion of mediality (or the medium as such) would supposedly break with a theological approach to the image,[20] even if Agamben attempts to bring it on side with his version of political theology, a version that would offer a new take on the nature of politics by making glory central to its articulation. Thus: 'What is the substance [. . .] that allows one to confer on something a properly political character? The answer our investigation suggests is: glory, in its dual aspect, divine and human, ontological and economic, of Father and Son, of the people-substance and the people-communication' (2011a: 259). It is within the dualities enunciated then that the image appears for its own sake as a representation entirely divorced from any reality. The theological significance of this is, as we have seen, that the image becomes an object evocative of an idol. As such, Debord and Agamben would come to join latter-day iconoclasts.

The human, then, is defined as the Sabbatical animal in the sense that work (production) and the institutions within which it is organised (the governmental bureaucracy and the business sector) no longer defines the essential being of the human. This is to say that, ultimately, *homo sacer* no longer defines the human as human. But, if we are to follow Agamben, we must recognise that everything essential is inscribed in dualities. Thus, there is no work as such without play – or, rather, play makes work as such possible. But maybe the reference to dualities is hasty. For, ultimately, Agamben claims that, just as violence leaves law behind as a child's plaything, so play and inoperativity as manifest in the human as sabbatical animal can be realised in the new society in their unique specificity, leaving work behind, as a project of ends. Or, to the extent that work persists, it no longer plays a part in defining the essence of the human.

Because the human *qua* human 'is' inoperativity (it is a plurality of potentialities and impotentiality), the apparatus of glory is bent on 'capturing' the 'inoperativity of human and divine life' (Agamben 2015a: 265). If this summary is correct, it implies that glory subjects human inoperativity to all the wiles of images understood as separated from what is imaged. Indeed: 'This inoperativity is so essential for the machine that it must be captured and maintained at all costs at its center in the form of glory and acclamations that, through the media, never cease to carry out their doxological function even today' (265). And how do images evoke violence? Precisely through the fact that glory as that which appears in the play of the 'mediatic form of the image' (2011a: 255) is in secret solidarity with the power that is glorified, a power that easily turns into a killing machine, as occurred in Germany in the 1930s and during the War.

Power, sovereignty – God – the ultimate backdrop to glory, call to be glorified, to be acclaimed, not because they need to be acclaimed to survive: 'Just as liturgical doxologies produce and strengthen God's glory, so the profane acclamations are not an ornament of political power but found and justify it' (230). Today, as we have seen, the sphere of glorification has shifted to public opinion fuelled by media images and spectacles, which exist in their own right. Agamben does not address the question of what happens in the event of a refusal to participate in the glorification of power, but a response would seem to be implicit in the theory of sovereignty. The result is no doubt manifest in an extreme form in the violence of the Nazi regime. But what of the era of the 'society of the spectacle'? What would Agamben have in mind here? Possibly media campaigns that stigmatise individuals and/ or groups – such as immigrants – that are deemed to have betrayed the nation-state in their action or simply in their very being. In other words, it is quite likely that this is the form of violence that lies behind or within (who can say?) the society of the image/spectacle.

If, as it is said, '[t]he Trinitarian economy is constitutively an economy of glory' (201), and if older forms of glorification, such as hymns of praise and the '*amen*' of the Christian liturgy, have fallen into desuetude, the modern, 'profane' form of the glorification of power becomes the image in its mediatic form of public opinion. In this regard, the spectacle of the 'society of the spectacle' glorifies power and corresponds to the 'Trinitarian economy'.

But to the extent that images constitute the glorification that power needs to exist, they are not opaque – they are not objects, nor pure means, as Debord and after him, Agamben, would like to think. In short, to repeat: images of glory are not glorious images. Agamben's response, we have seen, is that there is a void (cf. the empty throne) at the heart of glory. So the image of glory is the image of a void. Or rather it is the image of the incarnation (symbol) of the void in a given context. To reiterate: there is no glorious image – which implies that there is no mediality (means) that appears as such. Thus expressed is the thesis that underpins the theory of the image presented in this study.

*

In an extremely short chapter of barely more than a page, entitled 'The Six Most Beautiful Minutes in the History of Cinema', Agamben comments on a fragment of Orson Welles's unfinished film, *Don Quixote* (Agamben: 2015b: 93–94).[21] In the Welles's version, Don Quixote and Sancho Panza are in a cinema. Sancho has become separated from his master and is forced to sit next to a young girl who, Agamben speculates, plays Don Quixote's (imaginary) lover and muse, Dulcinea. The scene of interest in the cinematic fragment is the one where Don Quixote, seeing a knight in armour on the screen and a woman in danger, rises from his seat, mounts the stage of the screen, sword drawn, and begins slashing at the white cloth until only the frame remains. For Agamben, The Dark Knight's actions are revelatory of the imagination (Don Quixote obviously has a very vivid one!). However, what is far more significant is the fact that Don Quixote's relation to the images he engages with so ferociously is the exact opposite of the supposedly revealed mediality that Agamben perceives in Debord's films. Indeed, quite clearly, Don Quixote takes the transparency of the image to its extreme point, acting as though reality as such were being played out on the screen.[22] The thing is that, up to a certain point, Don Quixote's approach to cinema images is that of the average film audience when it suspends disbelief. In her interpretation of the scene, film scholar Janet Harbord notes this (2016: 33), but then proceeds to focus on the materiality that Don Quixote exposes in slashing at the screen. It is as though, for Harbord, the truth of cinema *is* its materiality (that is, the apparatuses of cinema) rather than the play of images. She says: 'When the screen is slashed and torn, the exposed structure supporting the projection screen is a shocking void, an absence of an image but also the revelation of cinema's materiality' (33). Given that the suspension of disbelief is equivalent to the 'so-called childish investments we all make in the cinematic image' (33),[23] the implication is that the transparency of the image is childish – but childish in relation to what? – while the intellectual contemplation of the nature of the image is an adult pursuit. Harbord thus seems to reinforce the opposition between childhood as experience (image as transparent) and adulthood (image as opaque), where there is an all-too-knowing suspension of disbelief.

Broadly speaking, however, it is that, for every spectator, what is on the screen is *both* real and at the same time only an image (both/and – not either/or). The Man of La Mancha fails to act in accordance with the latter part of this insight. So, while Agamben would prefer to define the image as a pure mediality, Don Quixote is there to remind us that a zero-sum logic can never apply to the image: it is never a pure mediality that appears (i.e., an object) nor is it identical to reality. It is rather both poles simultaneously.

It is because the image for Don Quixote is entirely transparent that he is induced to slash the screen, which is indeed an act of violence. From Don Quixote's perspective, he is not slashing the screen, he is not slashing the image as object, he is slashing what is imaged – namely, the knight who is putting the woman in danger. As Frances Restuccia also recognises, it is Agamben's view of the image as pure mediality that allows Don Quixote's gesture to evoke Benjamin's 'divine' or 'pure' violence, 'a law-destroying "pure means"' (2012: 237). Thus, if the image is opaque it can appear as such; if violence, similarly, is opaque (a pure means), it, too, can appear as such. If, by contrast, the image is transparent and virtual (but no less real for all that), and not reducible to the material through which it is incarnated, what are the implications for the appearance of divine violence? It would imply that *if* divine violence were to be a pure means, it would not appear as such, but – contra Benjamin – only through the auspices of some kind of end.

Let it be noted that on a number of occasions, Agamben claims that the spectacle as first brought to notice by Guy Debord is violent and destructive (Agamben 2005b: 80). It is violent because it ushers in alienation and expropriation. Because the 'violence of the spectacle is so destructive' it offers, Agamben disingenuously claims, 'a positive possibility that can be used against it' (2005b: 80). This 'positive possibility' supposedly emerges the more that workers – and even whole populations – are divided against themselves. If everything 'that was directly lived' has become an image or a representation, and if this is equivalent to expropriation and alienation, it is also supposed to be the case that the image is powerless to put people in touch with what was/is directly lived – including the possibility of 'a common good' (80). On this basis, the conflation of reality and the image that leads to alienation can supposedly enable alienation to be overcome. Just how this might occur remains entirely unclear.

The overriding point that I wish to emphasise, however, is the following: 'When the real world is transformed into an image and *images become real*, the practical power of humans is separated from itself and presented as a world unto itself' (78; emphasis added). The 'real world' becomes an image because the image is essentially understood (by Debord and by Agamben) as a pure means objectified.

Ironically, from the perspective of the argument on the image presented here, it is only theoretically that the image could become an object – a 'pure mediality' – separated from 'what is directly lived'. From an experiential perspective, an image is transparent and only appears as the imaged, as Don Quixote demonstrates. It was, in all probability, the 'era of '68' (to which, on this issue, at least, Agamben remains attached) that first gave rise to the notion of the image as object, as the product of media specificity, as 'socially constructed', etc.

Now, we know that the 'era of '68' has passed and that it is time to take a fresh approach to the image and to the notion of the violence of the alienation that was thought to be inseparable from it.

Notes

1. In the jottings of Agamben's *The Idea of Prose* (1995), we read that: 'Only man is concerned with images as images: only man knows appearance as appearance' (127). The potentially opaque status of the image is thus confirmed.
   Nevertheless, as noted above in the Introduction, when the image is not explicitly at issue – as it is in relation to the 'Society of the Spectacle' – the image verges on becoming transparent, as in *Nudities* (2011b: 55–90), where reference is made to Helmet Newton's famous photographs of clothed and nude women (78–80). Consider also the image of the *Muselmann* in the *Remnants of Auschwitz* (Agamben 2005c) and the reference in the latter text to the English film shot in Bergen-Belsen, of which Agamben says: '[i]t is difficult to bear the sight of the thousands of naked corpses' (50). Here, the image is entirely transparent.
2. Recall here that the term 'inoperativity' has a double inflection in Agamben's notion of means: it evokes *désoeuvrement* (Agamben 1998: 61) (idleness) and can also be associated with rendering all 'purposiveness', or ends, inoperative, thus revealing 'pure means' (Agamben 2018a: 82).
3. Agamben's invocation of theology to interpret *oikonomia* undermines utilitarian interpretations of this term, such as one finds in Arendt's reading of the ancient Greek *oikos* as the place of the satisfaction of basic needs. The latter also contrasts with Daniel McLoughlin's scholarly analysis of the theological basis of Agamben's position and of Agamben's appropriation of theology (McLoughlin 2015). However, as opposed to my approach, for McLoughlin neither the image nor the issue of utility are of relevance.
4. Cf.: 'The Trinitarian economy is constitutively an economy of glory' (Agamben 2011a: 201).
5. By way of elaboration, our author points out that the image as pure 'mediality' appears as such in Debord's films, albeit in the form of what is 'imageless'. But is it the image or mediality as such that appears? If the latter, there is a link straight to Benjamin's 'divine violence', which is also the appearance of pure means, or mediality. Such, then, would be a direct link between violence and the image.
6. On this see Lechte (2012: 89–96).
7. But see also Sahlins (1974).
8. For an elaboration of this theme, see Lechte (2018).
9. In Mondzain's explication, 'economy' is implicated with the image, especially in relation to Christ in the Trinity: 'Christ is [. . .] par excellence economy in every sense of the term, since he is intrinsically a part of the trinitarian distribution [. . .] He is image, relation and organ' (1996: 51). In Mondzain's commentary on the theology of the image in the debate

between the iconoclasts and the iconophiles, if the image is a medium, its 'essence [...] is not its visibility' (110). Agamben's – and, more broadly, a contemporary – approach to the image is the opposite of this.
10. While, in general, an incumbent could be imagined via a mental image, this is not easy when it is question of God or Christ.
11. See Mondzain (2005). Agamben does in fact refer to Mondzain's work early in his study only to brush it off as being limited to iconoclastic debates (see Agamben 2011a: 2), despite the issue of 'economy' being central to Mondzain's approach to the Byzantine image. Like Agamben, Mondzain notes that economy means arrangement, ordering, disposition. Cf. for example: 'Christ is [...] economy par excellence, in all senses of the term: he intrinsically forms a part of the arrangement of the Trinity' (Mondzain 2005: 34). And again, in a manner similar to Agamben, Mondzain says: 'By means of Christology, the economy becomes the dominant concept of every possible kind of thought concerning similitude; by means of trinitarian doctrine, it remains faithful to thought concerning the organization and management of divine operations throughout the world and history' (34).
12. Cf.: 'if there is anything that is to be worshipped it is *appearance* that must be worshipped' (Nietzsche 1968: sect 1011).
13. For Bataille, the restricted economy is, as mentioned, the economy of utility and scarcity, where expenditure is limited to *necessary* expenditure. By contrast, the general economy is expenditure for the sake of expenditure – an unproductive expenditure of loss. As Bataille explains: 'the accent is placed on a *loss* that must be as great as possible in order for that activity to take on its true meaning' (1986: 118). *Oikonomia* as inoperativity and acclamation would be equivalent to unproductive expenditure on such things as festivals, spectacles and the arts. The big difference between Agamben and Bataille on this front is that Bataille particularly includes sacrifice in the general economy (on this see Agamben 1998: 112–113).
14. By implication, images are not transparent (they are the opposite of what was directly lived); therefore, they do not give direct access to lived experience, whether of the self or of others.
15. Like many of those influenced by structuralism, Baudrillard emphasises the role of the code, or reproduction (over production), the simulacrum and hyperreality (over nature and reality), images as medium (over something imaged) – all aspects, in effect, which lead to the image (to focus on it) being treated as an object in an iconoclastic sense (see Baudrillard (1993: 50–86).
16. See McLuhan (2008 [1964]: 7–23) Ironically – or punningly – perhaps, McLuhan says that, '[t]he instance of the electric light may prove illuminating' (8).

17. As is known, Rousseau inaugurated the tradition of the principle stating that: 'He who wills the end wills the means' (Rousseau 1982: 189). Agamben, I would say, is absolutely opposed to this.
18. See above, Chapter 3, note 1.
19. In referring to Debord in *The Coming Community* (2005b), Agamben states that: 'When the real world is transformed into an image and *images become real*, the practical power of humans is separated from itself and presented as a world unto itself' (79; emphasis added). Moreover, the spectacle is violent. It is the 'extreme form' of Marxian 'expropriation' (80).
20. This would be the image as transparent, or the image the primary task of which would be to put one in touch with what is imaged. In this sense, Christ *is* (the image of) God. As such, the image takes on a quasi-divine – or magical – aspect.
21. Although much scholarly attention has been given to the place of the Don Quixote fragments in Welles's oeuvre, Agamben ignores this. See, for example, Rosenbaum (2007: 296–307) and Müller (2016).
22. Frances Restuccia (2012) opens her study of Agamben's notion of profanation by focusing in the first instance on the role of the imaginary for Agamben, rather than on the image as such. Ultimately, according to Restuccia, 'Quixote's sword destroys the images on the screen, de-creating them in a gesture that nullifies expressivity' (235). Clearly, images and the screen are equated because for Restuccia, as for Agamben, the image is an object, that is, a 'pure mediality'.
23. Harbord argues (2016: 32) that Agamben – in inaugurating a distinction in *Infancy and History* (2007: 15–18), between experience, as incarnate in childhood, and language – or, more broadly, processes of communication – shows that experience has been destroyed – childhood has been destroyed – through the privileging of science, and other intellectual processes. This approach does not, however, prove to be consistent with the idea of the image in Debord as explicit mediality. For the latter is not an experience of the image, but a theoretical account of it.

5 Girard on Violence and the Victim

With our investigations of Bataille and Agamben on violence and the image in the background, the aim of this chapter is to show the connection in René Girard's work between violence, origin and victim. In pursuing this trajectory, what remains to be seen is the extent to which Girard's approach to violence compares with that of Bataille and Agamben. 'Victim' for Girard means 'scapegoat', which in turn means the victim arbitrarily selected, and the injustice that this implies. Unlike Agamben for whom there is effectively no victim at the origin, and rather than being in the victim's place (Bataille), Girard offers a justification for modern society's movement away from the scapegoat mechanism. Although the latter can still make itself felt in various – and maybe unavoidable – ways, this, he maintains, is in no sense to be encouraged. How then does our author arrive at his position of denouncing the scapegoat mechanism?

Girard partly follows the Freudian thesis of a link between violence and the origin (the original event founding society) and the idea that this origin reverberates throughout secular, empirical history.[1] How and why is this connection made?

The Origin of Society: Derrida on the Origin

The origin of human cultural, social and biological life – or life, tout court – is a theme in the research of disciplines such as prehistory, archaeology, biology, physics and astrophysics (cf. origin of the universe). Girard says on numerous occasions that he works within a 'scientific' framework – a framework, Jacques Derrida argues, that is constituted by writing, understood in the broader sense as exteriority. Is he, then, to be denied the legitimacy of a pursuit of origin because, philosophically, this is open to question? As Varela and Dupuy put it in the introduction to the book they edited on origins, Girard's approach 'does not hesitate to confront the question of the origins of the sacred and, through it, the origin of all social and cultural institutions' (Varela and Dupuy 1992: 6). Given that the most influential, if not most important, critique of the notion of origin derives from Derrida's early work, *Of Grammatology* (2016), it is appropriate to return to this text in order to establish whether Girard's theory of society and culture can survive Derrida's deconstruction of 'origin'.[2]

No doubt in light of debates around structural linguistics, Derrida confirms what is for deconstruction the key relationship between the signifier and writing. Thus, as soon as one says 'signifier', one at the same time says 'writing' as exteriority: 'without that exteriority, the very idea of the sign falls into ruins' (15). This should be kept in mind throughout the chapter; for it has implications for Derrida's concept of the text and 'reality'. The following points are also germane:

- There may well be origin myths, but Derrida's position is that there is only the myth of origin. The issue is that of origin as presence, a metaphysical notion. Can Girard overcome this?
- Can Girard really deal, as he claims to do (Girard 1992), with the idea that there is essentially a supplement at the source, so that an origin is never entirely present to itself?
- The origin is also formulated as violence in the sense that metaphysics is violent. How could metaphysics be violent? There is also what Derrida calls a 'violence of the letter'. How is this possible? Can violence be equivalent to the trace (arche-writing as the play of différance)? These are questions that require close attention.

Actual murder: Oedipus and beyond

According to Girard, 'human culture is predisposed to the permanent concealment of its origin in collective violence' (1989: 100). But 'persecutory texts' evoke 'real violence' (9). A truly rigorous reading of such texts reveals the truth behind them. In short: 'all myths [to focus on these] must have their roots in real acts of violence against real victims' (25). Society is founded on an original murder – a murder that, historically, took place. Despite appearances, Girard's focus here is not on a search for the origin of society in documents, monuments and artefacts in the manner, for example, of the prehistorian; it is rather about detecting the origin in myths, rituals and practices that can be observed as these are currently enacted, or as they are described by anthropology.

For its part, the approach of deconstruction remains in touch with that of the prehistorian in the conceptualisation of arche-writing, as is confirmed by the following passage from *Of Grammatology*:

> Ever since phoneticization has allowed itself to be questioned in its origin, in its history and its adventures, one sees its movement merge with that of science, religion, politics, economy, technics, law, art. The origins of these movements and these historical regions do not dissociate themselves, as they must do for the rigorous delimitation of each science, except by an abstraction that one must remain aware of and must practice with vigilance. *This complicity of origins may be called arche-writing. What is lost in it is therefore the myth of the simplicity of origin.* This myth is linked to the very concept of origin; to speech reciting the origin, the myth of the origin and not only to myths of origin. (Derrida 2016: 100; emphasis added)[3]

The significance of this paragraph for Girard's approach to myth cannot be exaggerated. For it shows that however sceptical philosophy might be regarding the reality of an origin, the hypothetically dubious origin is not at all the result of the deciphering of myth, ritual or document in the present, but is rather the result of a journey back as far as it is possible to go – a journey beyond the point of departure of prehistory but one that perhaps is inaugurated by prehistory if Derrida's references to André Leroi-Gourhan's research in prehistory are any guide. In a sense, 'origin' in *Of Grammatology* has to be interpreted as a kind of 'a priori' that is the most original of all that is original. As such, it cannot be grasped through an engagement, confrontation or encounter with a current institutional practice, cultural ritual, or social or economic structure. The regional or ontic nature of the sciences or mode of thought that would make the origin explicit are too empirically focused for that.

Heidegger's conception of the primordial status of (pre-Socratic) Greek philosophy can serve to illuminate the basis of Derrida's philosophy. For, precisely, it is the invisibility or hiddenness to modern humanity of Being in the Greek philosophy of Being that should be revealed as the true beginning of Western thought. The Latinisation of culture (including Descartes's inaugural 'subjectivist' philosophy) in the West has, according to Heidegger, been a key contributor to the covering over of the question of Being, so that the true beginning is no longer detectable in current thought and action. It is because 'modern man' thinks as 'subject' that the beginning (the origin) becomes inaccessible.[4] For 'modern man' truth becomes *veritas* in contrast to truth as *aletheia* – as 'dis-closedness'. And we see that '[v]*eritas est adaequatio intellectus ad rem*' ('truth is the adequation of the intellect to the thing', also called the 'correspondence theory of truth' (cited by Heidegger 1992: 50)).

If the true beginning for Heidegger, or the origin (were it to exist) for Derrida, is unavailable via modern subjectivist thought and existing institutions (whether these be texts or practices), the same is not true for Girard. In a certain sense, it is being in the 'present' that gives access to the origin – indeed, that leads inexorably, whether one intends this or not, to a real origin, as the following passage from Girard makes clear:

> If sacrifice has a real origin, the memory of which myths keep alive in one way and rituals commemorate in another, then it seems clear that we are dealing with an event that initially made a very strong impression. Very strong, but not unforgettable – for in the end it is forgotten. But this impression, although subject to later modification, *lives on in the religious observances and perhaps in all the cultural manifestations of the society*. (1979: 92; emphasis added)

Compared to the Heideggerian 'primordial thought' which thinks Being, Girard would have to be located within modern thought that has subjectivist roots and thus thinks time as chronology because chronology is the form of 'objectivised history', the counterpart of the human as essentially subject. History is then events[5] in series as they are 'for me', 'for us', 'for society'. On the face of it Girard seems to fit in very well with Heidegger's characterisation of 'modern' thought. In order to refine and nuance this conclusion, and to situate it in relation to Derrida's thinking on the origin, it is first necessary to provide an insight into Girard's theory of violence.

*

In the conclusion to *Violence and the Sacred*, Girard reiterates that 'religious imitations' 'had their origin in a real event' (1979: 309), which was an actual murder, a murder that, although empirically inaccessible, can be detected in 'facts [...] drawn exclusively from texts that invariably offer distorted, fragmentary, or indirect testimony' (309). Thus through anthropologists' descriptions of rituals, festivals, sacrifices and rites of all kinds invoked to cope with change, through myths and literary forms such as Greek tragedy and the modern novel à la Dostoyevsky, plus a range of diverse literary and scientific sources, Girard patiently pieces together parts of the jigsaw that is the trials and tribulations of the surrogate victim. The latter constitutes the scapegoat mechanism that must necessarily come into play if generalised violence in 'primitive' societies is to be contained.[6]

But how do we know that myths from a multitude of different contexts actually allude to the surrogate victim and the containment of violence when, on the face of it, there is no explicit mention of the need for a victim? To be specific, how do we know that the Oedipus myth, as Girard claims, ultimately only makes sense if, in Sophocles's plays, Oedipus is equivalent to the surrogate victim? A response to this question will reveal much about Girard's *modus operandi*. Oedipus is evoked on numerous occasions throughout Girard's oeuvre, but the Oedipus myth is given particular attention in two chapters dedicated to this theme: one titled 'Oedipus and the Surrogate Victim' in *Violence and the Sacred* (1979: 68–88) and another titled 'What is Myth?' in *The Scapegoat* (1989: 24–44). Interest in the myth in question is compounded by the fact that Greek tragedy is an undeniable part of the literary canon of the West and a formative element in Freudian psychoanalysis. Thus, although it is one thing to speak of the killing of a sacrificial victim in the stories from non-Western 'archaic' societies, it is quite another to show that the surrogate victim or scapegoat mechanism might also be a founding moment of Western culture.

It is worth noting that in a chapter prior to his study of Oedipus in *Violence and the Sacred* Greek tragedy is evoked as a key domain that brings the notion of sacrificial crisis into sharp focus. That is, rather than bringing to bear a wide range of ethnographic sources in order to reveal the nature of sacrificial crisis, Girard chooses to focus in the first instance on ancient Greek culture as revealed by the genre of tragedy. There are a number of reasons as to why Girard places this genre in particular and literature in general at least on a par with the ethnographic accounts that he reports on in the second half of the chapter in question. Chief among these reasons is that literature is revelatory of cultural life despite itself; it is not inhibited by interpretative perspectives as is often the case with ethnography. For example, Frazer in *The Golden Bough* has a very jaundiced view of religion in general, a fact that impinges upon his interpretation of the cultural life of the societies he studies. In short, literature (of the nondidactic kind) is unselfconscious in its portrayal of reality. There is no ideological brake that would skew things in a certain direction. Even though Girard might not approve of the analogy, it seems clear that literature has about it the quality of a Surrealist practice where the writer, like the analysand, keeps writing or talking to the point where conscious attempts to censor discourse become clear indices of the very unconscious elements that were supposed to remain invisible and silent. More generally, it is well known that normally distasteful or unacceptable things can be presented and pass muster in the guise of fiction – much as someone who commits a serious faux pas might quickly say, 'but I was only joking'. This fact is particularly important because the theme that is obliquely present in tragedy is something that cannot be broached in normal discourse (whether scientific or critical) and is only indirectly alluded to in tragedy: namely, the loss of all distinctions in society which leads to violence. In Girard's words: 'Tragic drama addresses itself to a burning issue. The issue is never directly alluded to in the plays, and for good reason, since it has to do with the dissolution by reciprocal violence of those very values and distinctions around which the conflict of the plays supposedly revolves' (1979: 56). Tragic drama thus *shows* the eruption of violence when distinctions dissolve. It also shows how such violence must be dealt with if the dissolution of society is be avoided.

Broadly speaking, Girard says that, instead of being historical like the Jewish prophets, 'the Greek tragedians evoked their own sacrificial crisis in terms of legendary figures whose forms were fixed by tradition' (44). This point is crucial for understanding Girard's method, which imitates the tragedians in as far as it, too, is not strictly speaking historical. In the latter case, one would focus on specific events in the past in order to understand the present. However, Girard's method takes the present as ritual and myth, as performance, as art and literature, and these taken together as the enactment of cultural life become the indices of a past, a past that, while it may never be fully revealed, gives a profound insight into the fact that the preservation of society depends on the control of violence.[7] In this regard, we read that: 'Tragedy is the balancing of the scale, not of justice but of violence' (45).

Girard, then, chooses to initiate a discussion of the sacrificial crisis and the issue of violence through an analysis of Euripides play, *Heracles*. 'The real subject of the play', says Girard, 'is the failure of a sacrifice, the act of sacrificial violence that suddenly *goes wrong*' (40). Sacrificial violence is an act of violence that is intended to put a stop to violence. But in *Heracles* this does not happen. Heracles's wife and children are offered as a sacrifice to Lycus, whom Heracles kills. Heracles, accompanied by his wife and children, then seeks to purify himself by preparing a sacrifice of his own. Suddenly, he is gripped by madness and mistakes his wife and children for enemies and kills them. Violence, instead of being curbed is beginning to spread: 'The sacrificial rites were no longer able to accomplish their task; they swelled the surging tide of impure violence instead of channeling it. The mechanism of substitutions had gone astray, and those whom the sacrifice was designed to protect became its victims' (40).

Tragedy demonstrates that violence erases differences. Thus, whatever the status of a character might be in Greek tragedy 'violence invariably effaces the differences between antagonists' (47). All are cowed in a similar fashion by violence. Distinctions – identities – can thus be obliterated by violence, the result of such obliteration being the dissolution of social life. As observed in Greek tragedy as in ethnographic accounts of non-Western 'primitive' societies, violence is contained through the sacrifice of a scapegoat or 'surrogate victim'. The community unites against a single victim in order to ensure the containment of violence. It is time, now, to look at Oedipus as surrogate victim as presented by Girard.

Oedipus

To begin with, each of Oedipus's characteristics mark him out to be the surrogate victim: he is lame (victims often have a deformity, sometimes of monstrous proportions); he is subject to the 'fatal flaw' of anger, but in this he is similar to other characters in the play. As Girard observes: 'there would be no tragic debate if the other protagonists did not become angry in turn' (1979: 69). Anger, indeed, is a sign of the dissolution of differences that defines the sacrificial crisis. This is the crisis that Oedipus is destined to resolve, initially as redeemer, but ultimately as surrogate victim. This is one of the symmetries marking out the sacrificial crisis along with reciprocity. Thus, Oedipus accuses Tiresias of having a part in the murder of Laius, while Tiresias counters by accusing Oedipus. Of this, Girard concludes that: 'Reciprocity is busy aiding each party in his own destruction' (71).

Thebes is wracked by plague. What is its cause? Who is to blame? Such are the questions evoked by the crisis. The latter has arrived because patricide and incest have been committed. To make further progress in the analysis of the story of Oedipus, Girard argues that the mythical version needs to be brought into contact with the tragic version. For to keep 'literature' insulated from 'mythology' (73) means that the true significance of Oedipus's fall from grace will remain hidden. Frequently, myth can help explain a literary work and the obverse is also true: a literary work can bring insight to the meaning of a myth.

Sophocles, Girard points out, has inserted two replies into his text which bring myth and tragedy into contact with one other. The mythic element reveals that, in the end, Oedipus is not in fact guilty – for his true status is that of surrogate victim. Thus: 'Oedipus replies to the chorus which has pleaded with him to spare Creon: "What you are asking, if truth be told, is neither more nor less than my death or exile"' (73). Nevertheless, at least for a period, Oedipus's destiny is still in the thrall of patricide and incest – both of which constitute a violence that contributes to the loss of distinctions. How in the end is Oedipus not guilty of these crimes? He did, after all, kill his father, Laius, at the crossroads and then took his mother for a wife. How can he really be the innocent 'surrogate victim' that Girard claims Sophocles play shows him to be? The answer is that, certainly, Oedipus commits the acts that would be defined as patricide and incest. But it is the next step that does not hold – namely, that Thebes is subject to a plague because someone has committed patricide and incest. The guilty party brought the plague; he also failed to respect distinctions, and this gives rise to violence. As Girard indicates, '[t]he oracle itself explains matters: it is the infectious presence of a *murderer* that has brought on disaster' (76). And our author adds that: 'In tragedy, and outside it as well, plague is a symbol for the sacrificial crisis' (76); it is the latter which leads to the designation of a scapegoat or surrogate victim whose death will supposedly end the crisis. Patricide and incest are also symbols or indicators of the crisis, but while plague evokes the contagious nature of the sacrificial crisis, patricide and incest allow the ills of the community to be sheeted home to a single individual: thus, 'Oedipus becomes the repository of all the community's ills' (77). He is quoted as saying that: '"Believe me, you have nothing more to fear. My ills are mine alone, *no other mortal is fit to bear them*"' (77; emphasis added). Even so, from this it can be surmised that although Oedipus may well have committed the acts of which he is accused, the erasure of distinctions cannot have resulted in Oedipus's unique acts alone; the whole community is guilty to the extent that violence becomes contagious, but it cannot accept its guilt. Blame must be attributed to a single individual. When this is done and the resultant execution/sacrifice is accomplished, violence will come to an end for a time. With the surrogate victim, regardless of this victim's guilt or innocence, comes unanimity – the very mechanism that brings a halt to the violent contagion. Girard summarises his position thus: 'The general direction of the present hypothesis should now be abundantly clear; any community that has fallen prey to violence or has been stricken by some overwhelming catastrophe hurls itself blindly into the search for a scapegoat' (79).

Aspects of the myth of Oedipus find their way, Girard tells us, into Sophocles's drama, particularly the notion that Oedipus fulfils the roles of surrogate victim, so that, with his death, the community will free itself from reciprocal violence. At one point in the analysis, it is said that 'our modern way of thinking' finds it hard to accept that idea that a hero can be '"good" without ceasing to be evil' (86). But is this case?

Indeed, the literary theory of Mikhail Bakhtin (1981[8]) and Julia Kristeva (1979) tells a different story. There, it is said that myths, folktales and epics are peopled with morally homogenous protagonists, protagonists who are either 'good' *or* 'evil' (even if it is initially unclear in the story as to which side of the moral ledger a particular character might fall). Kristeva designates this situation as one of 'disjunctive symmetry', where opposites mirror each other without any mixing of positive and negative qualities.[9] The modern novel, by contrast, she argues (and here she follows Bakhtin), is 'non-disjunctive': a protagonist could, for example, be both good and evil, cruel and kind, intelligent and stupid. In this context, the position of the hero is always evolving. That is, with the modern novel, heterogeneity gives rise to a complex psychology and an openness to the world, which contrasts with the simplicity, homogeneity and closed nature of myth and folktale.

Does Oedipus, then, have the complex, 'dialogical' psychology of a protagonist of the novel, or is his psyche essentially 'monological'? This is the question. Noticeably, Kristeva as a literary theorist in the 1960s and early 1970s does not, in her interpretive work, consider the Oedipus myth in particular or Greek tragedy in general, while, as psychoanalyst from the mid-1970s, the Freudian Oedipus complex and its figure of the father becomes a central component, not only of analytic theory but also of the Kristevan approach to literature. When Girard claims that 'Oedipus [in both myth and tragedy] is initially an evil force and subsequently a beneficial one' (1979: 86), he is placing the Greek hero much closer to a modern way of thinking than he seems to realise. Oedipus, subject to the fatal flaw of anger accompanied by pride, which contributes to him killing his father, accepts responsibility for murder and incest and gives himself up as surrogate victim for the good of the community. So, against Kristeva, one can say that the Oedipus myth does not easily if at all fit with the idea of a protagonist as one component of a disjunctive opposition; and against Girard, we can say, à la Kristeva, that the hero in the modern novel, if not in the modern way of thinking, tends to have a complex psychology, where good and evil can reign simultaneously, if not in equal measure.

Against Girard, however, is that fact that as surrogate victim or scapegoat, Oedipus is deemed to be entirely to blame – the unique guilty party – for the woes of Thebes, whereas the community is entirely blameless. Oedipus is bad and the community is good. Such a dichotomy would conform to the Kristevan principle of disjunction as the impossible union of opposites and would fail to mirror the complexity of existence.

The further point to make, though, is that Girard's approach goes well beyond that of literary criticism, of whatever genre, and depicts something that is crucial to an understanding of the foundation of society – a foundation, it must be acknowledged, that has a decidedly religious ring to it. In short, myths tell us, claims Girard, that there is a murder at the origin. It is this claim that prompts us to return to the notion of origin in Derrida's philosophy of deconstruction.

The Deconstruction of the Origin

Derrida, as we have seen, sets out the key components of a deconstruction of the origin. If metaphysics is the source of presuppositions and assumptions, deconstruction can be defined as the effort to question – deconstruct – metaphysics. This is a challenging task to the extent that deconstruction itself may well be inhabited by metaphysics. Be this as it may, let us revisit the notion of origin. Points that can be adumbrated here the better to orient ourselves towards the issues at stake are as follows: (1) Origin has been understood as a past-present that would be retrievable in a representation; (2) To be present is to be an identity that does not brook difference; in the West, the system effaces difference (Derrida 2016: 25); (3) The past as a present evokes the 'meaning of being in general as *presence*' (2016: 13); (4) Truth, like being and presence is identical with itself; (5) Nature is often conceived (e.g., by Rousseau) as a full presence without remainder – a natural origin will, therefore, be fully present; (6) History and knowledge are geared to search for, if not to find, an empirical origin; (7) Time, in the colloquial, metaphysical sense, is constituted by the series of 'now' moments – durationless moments – that both Bergson and Heidegger criticised; Zeno's paradox depends on this notion of time; (8) To be identical with itself, to be a full presence, nothing else can exist but the origin; there can be no addition to the origin, for it is, like nature, a plenitude from which nothing can be added or subtracted; (9) When it comes to language, 'the formal essence of the signified is *presence*' (Derrida 2016: 19); the origin would be a signified; (10) For its part, and finally: 'The supplement is neither a presence nor an absence. No ontology can think its operation' (142).

Along with 'supplement', there are other terms in Derrida's quasi-conceptual arsenal that bring presence, plenitude, identity, etc., into question; namely: trace, erasure, difference, reserve, spacing, arche-writing. Specifically:

> The concept of the arche-trace must accede both to that necessity and that erasure. It is in fact contradictory and unacceptable within the logic of identity. The trace is not only the disappearance

of origin, it would say here [...] that the origin did not even disappear, that it was never constituted except as a back-formation by a nonorigin, the trace, which becomes the origin of the origin. (66)

In the end, 'there is no originary trace' (67). As we have seen, what is in play is 'the myth of the simplicity of origin' and to the myth of origin that would undermine the very notion of myths of origin.

*

Erasure of proper names is the beginning of arche-writing. So says Derrida in his chapter on Lévi-Strauss's study of the Nambikwara in *Tristes Tropiques* (Derrida 2016: 121). The erasure of the 'proper' (equivalent to spacing) evokes arche-writing, which opens up the possibility that no society is 'without writing'. Such at least is Derrida's argument (cf. 118). Moreover, arche-writing (or 'writing in general') can be brought into contact with writing in the colloquial, everyday, sense. Arche-writing is the 'first possibility of the spoken word' (76), just as the *'graphie'* is the visible form of writing.

Clearly, for Derrida, presence, identity, nature, plenitude, consciousness, as well as origin – that is, all the accoutrements of metaphysics[10] – together presuppose, as their condition of possibility, ache-writing, ache-trace, différance, supplement, etc. – whether or not this is acknowledged or recognised. There is, then, a 'difference in presence' (77) and in identity, and a lack in nature and plenitude (requiring a supplement). Again, in the essay on Freud and the scene of writing, it is said, as regards life, that: 'Life must be thought as trace before being is determined as presence' (Derrida 1967: 302). Thus, in every case where essence, substance, the primary or the 'first', the original or foundation, are at issue, trace is the condition of their possibility. 'It is', Derrida reiterates, 'the non-origin which is originary' (303).

Nevertheless, it would be illuminating to know precisely what the necessity is for the deconstruction of metaphysics. Is it always already inscribed within metaphysics itself, as has been suggested above (origin evokes the non-origin, etc.)? Or is the ground of deconstruction the fact that all thinking is essentially part of a discursive formation, so that the play of language is always to the fore? As an attempt to think through the problems here, consider the notion of a moment in history as a past present. Is this moment more 'past' than it is 'present'? Perhaps the historian tries to think the past as a non-present, so that what is written up is truly past, not an imagined present. The problem pertains to deriving a means of thinking and imagining outside, or beyond the moment as present. It is a matter of doing justice to the 'pastness' of the past, something which no doubt poses a threat to consciousness and its imaginary schemas.

The foregoing needs to be considered in relation to the famous statement: '*There is nothing outside the text* [there is no outside-text; *il n'y a pas de hors texte*]' (172). Often, it is not possible to be sure how things actually proceed here. Suffice it to say that Derrida rarely formulates ideas in and of themselves and instead forges his thinking through reading texts and addressing issues raised within a discursive domain. Is there no escape from this? Does it imply that there is no extra-discursive external referent? So, rather than considering in isolation the notion of origin (which is germane to understanding Girard on the surrogate victim), Derrida is to be found analysing the texts of Rousseau where origin and supplement are in play – where, because origin is in play, the notion of supplementarity reveals itself.

Derrida writes on the issues of the origin and history in Lévi-Strauss in *Writing and Difference* (1978: 351–370). Our attention to this reading is warranted given that Girard also reads Lévi-Strauss in order to discern the role therein of the surrogate victim. The aim here is to determine the status of origin in the thought of Derrida and Girard, respectively. On the face of it, Derrida's intensely philosophical approach seems incompatible with the apparently empirical approach to the origin of society taken by Girard. This, then, is the issue that guides the following discussion.

What initially interests us here is that Derrida points to a 'privileged' human science, one that might offer a way of shaking up the metaphysical notion origin: it is ethnology. Hence, the relevance of looking more closely at the work of Lévi-Strauss. As a preliminary point made prior to his analysis, Derrida recognises that any 'critique' of metaphysics is forced to use the resources of metaphysics. There is no way round this. Thus a critique of origin, like the critique of history and time will, at least to begin with, inevitably rely on these terms.

Ethnology is not only a science, it is noted, but is also a discourse (356). Of note as illustrative of deconstruction is the opposition, nature-culture, as discussed by Lévi-Strauss in a number of his works.

What pertains to nature are universal human traits (need for food, shelter, etc.), while what pertains to socio-cultural norms and prohibitions constitute culture. However, the incest taboo crosses the nature-culture boundary; for it is universal, being found in all societies (which would make it part of nature), and it is also the subject of prohibitions which play themselves out in various ways depending on the particular culture or society concerned. In this light, one wonders whether, with regard to the human, there is a sphere that is purely nature and one that is purely culture. For the deconstructionist, the opposition seems to be inherently metaphysical.

A similar point is made regarding the opposition proposed by Lévi-Struss between the bricoleur and the engineer as applied to language. If bricolage means gathering one's linguistic tools and concepts from wherever these might be found, the engineer equivalent would mean constructing language and concepts from scratch, so that '[i]n this sense the engineer is a myth' (360). In other words, there is inevitably some bricolage in the work of the engineer, just as there is an element of the engineer's rigour in the work of the bricoleur. The opposition, bricoleur-engineer, can thus never be absolute.

Key oppositions, Derrida proposes, fail to hold in an absolute sense. What are the consequences for the notion of origin and of history? In this regard, Derrida offers the following illuminating statement regarding Lévi-Strauss's approach to the notion of history:

> by reducing history, Lévi-Strauss has treated as it deserves a concept which has always been in complicity with a teleological and eschatological metaphysics, in other words, paradoxically, in complicity with that philosophy of presence to which it was believed history could be opposed. The thematic of historicity, although it seems to be a somewhat late arrival in philosophy, has always been required by the determination of Being as presence. (367)

Again, on the conception of history: 'History has always been conceived as the movement of a resumption of history, as a detour between two presences' (368). Ultimately, however, although 'origin', 'history' and time as 'now' moments (implied in the 'detour between two presences') are the product of metaphysics, it is impossible to dispense with these notions. And without history (and thus the origin?) there is the risk of lapsing into ahistoricism (368). Indeed, so few are the concepts without a metaphysical inflexion that it is not a matter of dispensing with them, but, for the deconstructionist, of 'inhabiting them in a new way'. On the one hand, it is impossible not to deal with *historia* (history) or the *ēpistēmē* (knowledge); but on the other hand, these domains, like the human sciences in general (Heidegger's ontic realm) are the plaything of metaphysics, which means that they are based on certain assumptions that are open to question; assumptions, for example, about the rigour and purity of oppositions such as those just examined of nature-culture and engineer-bricoleur. Similarly, while the origin (to refer to it) as presence might be accepted within historical discourse, we know that this is a metaphysical notion and that, deconstructively, a present origin is a myth (255) and that it is 'the non-origin' that is originary (255).

The question is – a question that can only be posed here without being definitively answered – does deconstruction depend on metaphysics to be what it is? For, presumably, without metaphysics there would be nothing to deconstruct. Here, in the context of an engagement with Girard's work, this question raises the prospect of the *necessity* of the empirical, even while the latter is cast as the epitome of philosophical naïveté. In a reading of Girard, the words of Philippe Lacoue-Labarthe do nothing if not confirm the point just made: 'Such an analysis [by Girard of Plato's relation to tragedy] could be indisputable, if it did not presuppose (and this is what hides behind the evident-and willful-"*empirical naivete*" of the appeal to the reality of the primitive collective murder) the idea that the scapegoat is necessarily arbitrary at the beginning' (Lacoue-Labarthe 1978: 14; emphasis added). Although Lacoue-Labarthe refers to 'empirical naivete', what he means is that there is a failure to recognise the philosophical import of what is being said, and in this sense, Girard is being *philosophically* naïve.

Lacoue-Labarthe does, however, pinpoint the way in which Girard's characterisation of desire and mimesis do seem to provide an opening for deconstruction, in as far as one can speak of the desire 'imitating desire' or of desire desiring desire (18). For if, as Girard says, desire does not have to do (directly) with an object, but, effectively, with desiring the other's (the model's) desire, there is as a result an evident vicariousness at the origin to the extent that the origin becomes a representation of the desire of the other. In this light, Lacoue-Labarthe pertinently asks:

Would mimesis, *in the sense in which Girard uses it*, not require a rethinking of representation? That is, prior to the classic 'theoretical' representation (to the dualism of the present and the represented), a conception of representation in which the *re-* of *repetition* would govern – and dispel – any presentational value (any sense of "objective" exhibition, derived or secondary externalization, spectacle for a subject, etc.)? (18)

Representation, which is supposedly secondary, suddenly becomes the origin as such, just as, in Derrida's reading of Rousseau in *Of Grammatology*, there is a supplement at the origin. For this reason, it calls out to be rethought. But of course, Girard does not think in terms of the *concept* of origin, but in terms of the *event* that occurred and thus gave rise to society. It is in this sense, that Girard justifies the historical reality of the original murder:

> Why in my system must the crisis – and victimage – be considered to have been historically actualized? Because the efficacy of unanimous victimage alone can account for the nature and organization of the mythemes and 'ritemes' in all of primitive religion. This nature and organization coincides too well with the foreseeable distortions of victimage in countless myths and with its reenactment in countless rituals to authorize the slightest doubt. (Girard 1978: 39)[11]

Arguably, the 'strength' of Girard's position derives from the way he counters the philosophical objections to his promotion of the 'extra-textual' referent. So, *pace* Derrida, there *is* something 'outside' the text. This, at least, is Girard's hypothesis – not his theory. For: 'A purely theoretical discussion is always a philosophical discussion in disguise' (Girard 1977: 936). As evidence for his position, Girard points to what he calls, 'texts of mystified persecution': 'Their interpretation does not provide a metaphor or a model. *It is the thing itself*' (939; emphasis added). As Girard explains:

> These texts range from the documents of medieval and modern anti-Semitism, including violent pogroms, to the records of the Spanish Inquisition and the trial of witches down to the primarily oral text of modern racism, the lynching of blacks, for instance, in the American South. (937)

When it comes to persecution, then, a formalist and philosophical approach to the text (structuralist, poststructuralist) is found to be seriously wanting. Such a position is of course naïve relative to Derrida's philosophical sophistication. Whether 'hors-texte' (the source of the scandal) makes impossible an engagement with persecution is no doubt debatable. Rather than saying that reality is a text, a different inflexion emerges when one says that reality (the material world) is a text – or is 'written' (as we shall see). In this case the drift to the origin has consequences unforeseen by the taken-for-granted attitude of common sense. The origin – or the originary in general – is central to the institution of history and is therefore, Derrida proposes, dependent on archewriting, as is the case of all institutions (Derrida 2016: 48). Materiality as such is writing, in as far as materiality always takes a specific form (cf. 'pro-gram' in biology, cybernetics and education). This would explain why it is that there can be 'language' as 'action, movement, thought, reflection, consciousness, the unconscious, experience, affectivity' (9). And this can be called 'writing', which would include,

> not only physical gestures of literal, pictographic, or ideographic inscription, but also the totality of what makes it possible; and further, beyond the signifying face, the signified face itself; and so for all that can make room for an inscription in general, whether it is literal or not and even if what it distributes in space is alien to the order of the voice: cinematography, choreography, of course, but also pictorial, musical, sculptural 'writing'. One might also speak of athletic writing, and with even greater certainty, if one pays attention to the techniques that govern those domains today, of military or political writing. All this to describe not only the system of notation secondarily connected with these activities but the essence and the content of these activities themselves. It is also in this sense that today the biologist speaks of writing and of *pro-gram* for the most elementary processes of information within the living cell, And, finally, whether it has essential limits or not, the entire field covered by the cybernetic *program* will be the field of writing. (9)

Moreover, 'what writing betrays in its nonphonetic moment, is *life*' (27; emphasis added). Can one get more concrete than this? Broadly speaking, then, writing encompasses the concrete; this is why there is no outside to the text. More remains to be said, though, about 'origin' and the 'trace'. For example, it has already been noted that the notion of trace implies that there never was an origin as full presence, so that origin becomes a kind of retrospective illusion – also described as a myth.

But, also, 'the thought of the trace will never be confused with a phenomenology of writing' (74). Again: 'the original absence of the subject of writing is also the absence of the thing or the referent' (74). When Derrida says that the origin is a 'myth', he means: it is false. Thus, the idea of a simple origin identical to itself is false. The origin is a myth because it is false rather than being false because it is a myth. But in any case, the deconstructionist gives up on the possibility of interpreting myths as a means of establishing what is true in the manner of Girard. Certainly, for Girard myth is oriented to conceal the innocence of the scapegoat and the actual role of the community in murder; but, if one pays attention, it also reveals that a murder took place. This, at least, is Girard's claim. Is it a philosophically naïve claim? Is Derrida's approach philosophical essentially because it is subtle and complex? In short: is it philosophical because it implicitly defines itself against non-philosophy? Or is it possible to work with a certain philosophical sophistication in order to strengthen Girard's case? Or is it the reverse that is true?

What seems self-evident is that Girard's thesis (murder at/as the origin of society) is a challenging one that unavoidably raises questions that need to be addressed and in that very endeavour prompts responses that can hardly avoid being philosophical – the philosophical question of questions: 'What is . . .?' And in this regard, the crucial question is: *what is* violence?

Violence in the socio-cultural realm presupposes a border to be transgressed, an object – a victim to be violated. In the context of Girard's work, this is murder. But the term (murder) is used very loosely; for it is, strictly speaking, homicide, and the latter presupposes 'law'. Consequently, the killing of the victim is murder from a modern perspective, not murder as such. Indeed, Girard's point is that the scapegoat mechanism operates *in the absence* of law understood as a judicial institution. Fantasies about how the scapegoat is the cause of all the woes of the community is the substitute for law, it being the case that only with the institution of the law in the modern sense does the scapegoat mechanism get fundamentally challenged, if not eliminated. That is, while it may be true that over the period of time since the existence of Sumerian culture and society (5500–4000 BC) laws, moral precepts and prohibitions against homicide might, from time to time, have been enacted, it can be argued that it is only in the modern era and the emergence of – in Weber's terms – 'legal-rational authority' that certainty regarding the law against murder can be guaranteed. Thus, with regard to Roman law, Judy Gaughan shows that while murder was a crime under the Monarchy (753–509 BC) (2010: 10), '[i]n republican Latin no words existed that can be literally translated as *murder, crime, criminal courts* or *criminal law*' (2010: 2). In effect: 'The Romans [during the Republic] not only had no legislation prohibiting murder, they had no word for murder' (3). Moreover, 'the word *crime* did not exist during the republic either' (3).

Consequently, to call the first, or original crime 'murder', as Girard does, seems to be another retrospective illusion unless, as Lévi-Strauss proposes in relation to *Totem and Taboo*, society was already constituted as society when the first murder (which is supposed to constitute society) took place. But given that the law against murder is only consolidated in the modern era, the basis of Girard's claim looks shaky.

*

Before the emergence of the institution of the law, the scapegoat is killed, as we have seen, in order to bring an end to violence. The latter is largely the result of mimetic rivalry, which, in its turn, is the result of mimetic desire. That is, human desire is essentially the desire of the other. Thus, I do not desire an object for its own sake, but desire what an other desires. While it seems reasonable, on this basis, to say that desire is social, rather than purely individual, Girard has a tendency to psychologise it; that is, to think of it in terms of the reciprocal desire and actions of two solitary individuals. For example, at one point he says that:

> As I imitate the desire of my neighbour, I reach for the object he is already reaching for, and we prevent each other from appropriating this object. His relation to my desire parallels my relation to his, and the more we cross each other, the more stubbornly we imitate each other. My interference intensifies his desire, just as his interference intensifies mine. This process of positive feedback can only lead to physical and other forms of violence. Violence is the continuation of mimetic desire by other means. Violence does not play a primordial role in my perspective; only mimesis does. (Girard 1987a: 123)

When it is recalled that, in other statements, Girard has claimed that murder is at the origin of society (Freud, it is said, was right about this, but wrong in his interpretation of it as being evidence of the psychological 'disposition of the subject'), it is difficult, if not impossible, to reconcile how mimetic desire, as essentially social (this, in the end, seems to be Girard's point), could constitute the foundation of society.[12] For, as Lévi-Strauss says, it is a vicious circle: society comes into existence via the auspices of mimetic desire, but mimetic desire only exists via the auspices of society. Let it be noted that it is the *thinking* here that is defective. Or, to put it slightly differently: philosophically speaking, Girard's propositions call to be more rigorously articulated. Such would be the way that a philosophical approach cannot be avoided in an engagement with Girard. It is, in particular, the *speculative* nature of Girard's claims about the origin (the idea of being able in some way to access evidence of the 'first' murder) that raises questions, and not just notion of the origin and time as pure presence.

Ultimately, the interested interlocutor wants to know just how, precisely, violence, original murder, the scapegoat and mimetic desire fit together. And in this regard, there is the further complicating question of Girard's account of hominisation, which I now want to discuss.

Hominisation

Not only is the victimage mechanism (i.e., the first murder) the origin of society and culture, but it is, for Girard, also the origin of hominisation (Girard 1987b: 97). Hominisation means, of course, 'the transition from animal to man' (84). To think of hominisation is to evoke the paradox I have raised elsewhere (Lechte 2018) of the animal as the origin of the human (as in the theory of evolution) but where the human *qua* human is what distinguishes itself from animality.[13] Be this as it may, the chief difficulty Girard encounters in his attempt to bring hominisation within the frame of the first murder is that it places his research within the auspices of prehistory and even of palaeontology – domains that have produced significant knowledge with regard to human evolution, both biological and cultural. One need only evoke here the work of Girard's compatriot André Leroi-Gourhan on the evolution of tool making and writing (more generally, technics) to be reminded of the gaping lacunae in Girard's foray into hominisation (cf. Leroi-Gourhan 1964a, 1964b, 1973). Consequently,

Girard, especially in *Things Hidden Since the Foundation of the World* (1987b), comes across as a thinker engaged in pure speculation, as the following passage confirms: 'We can conceive of hominization as a series of steps that allow the domestication of progressively increasing and intense mimetic effects, separated from one another by crises that would be catastrophic but also generative in that they would trigger the founding mechanism' (96). Despite claiming to be scientific and thus factual here, there are no factual details related to the evolution of the human (*Homo sapiens*) and society that would convince anyone of good faith that something profound is being stated. In another passage, Girard claims that:

> Between what can be strictly termed animal nature on the one hand and developing humanity on the other there is a true rupture, which is collective murder, and it alone is capable of providing for kinds of organization, no matter how embryonic, based on prohibition and ritual. It is therefore possible to inscribe the genesis of human culture in nature and to relate it to a natural mechanism without depriving culture of what is specifically, exclusively, human. (97)

Compare the above passage with that of Leroi-Gourhan on the same topic:

> In ethnology, the beginnings of these periods [of human evolution] are marked by the great discoveries in technics: sharp stone flakes, polished stone, agriculture, metals, mechanisation. These discoveries, taken at the highest level, seem to have been made by groups simultaneously, and punctuated by long periods of apparent stagnation: Neolithic-agriculture-breeding, semi-industrialised metallurgy-techniques, industrialised mechanised-techniques. (1973: 380)

Amongst other things, the complex evolution of technics, without which there would be no writing, language or art – and therefore no religious ritual – is completely absent from Girard's vision of hominisation.

The philosopher of technics, Bernard Stiegler, summarises Leroi-Gourhan's take on hominisation in the following terms:

> Hominization is for Leroi-Gourhan a rupture in the movement of freeing (or mobilization) characteristic of life. This rupture happens suddenly, in the form of a process of exteriorization which, from

the point of view of paleontology, means that the appearance of the human is the appearance of the technical. Leroi-Gourhan specifies this as the appearance of language. (Stiegler 1998: 141)

So, language and the technical (or technics) would for Leroi-Gourhan appear together. More broadly, the cultural and technics are indissolubly imbricated: there is no culture without technics, which does not mean that technics is bereft of a cultural overlay. It is not a matter of Girard agreeing with the prehistorian on this point, but one of *engagement*. No conclusions regarding hominisation can be drawn without an engagement with the prehistorical record.[14] Girard does not engage with this record. This is his weakness.[15]

Ironically – in light of Girard's effort to conceptualise hominisation – Leroi-Gourhan's *Le geste et la parole* is referred to by Derrida in *Of Grammatology* in the context of the relationship in the development of technics between the 'face' and the 'hand' (2016: 91). Thus, Derrida writes: 'Leroi-Gourhan describes the slow transformation of manual motricity which frees the audio-phonic system for speech and the look and the hand for writing' (91–92). Even though Leroi-Gourhan does not escape the traps of 'mechanist, technicist and teleological language' (92), his endeavours have raised key questions regarding the very notion of hominisation.

When it comes the formation of the human in prehistory, then, Derrida does not, as Girard claims, have a 'taboo on the search for an origin' (1987b: 62). Instead, we have two differing approaches to the process in question. On the one hand, there is the projected speculation that an original murder driven by mimetic desire led to the birth of the human (Girard); on the other, we have the painstaking research into the emergence and evolution of technics and writing as différance and writing, in the colloquial sense, as the mechanism that brings into question the notion of the human.

In attempting to tie the emergence of hominisation to an original murder Girard has played to his weaknesses, not to his strengths. The latter have to do with his insight that current practices in literature and rituals related to myths demonstrate the workings of mimetic desire and evoke historical acts of persecution. In short, it is the 'present' and not prehistory that is Girard's forte. A certain 'truth' thus emerges in myths, rituals and specific, modern literary texts, such as those by Shakespeare, Dostoyevsky, Stendhal and Proust. While modern literature is particularly rich in its evocation of mimetic desire, myths evoke the murder of the scapegoat. At any rate, it is through making the themes of the scapegoat and mimetic rivalry explicit in his readings of the texts in question that Girard has, as has already been noted, shown the positive fruits of his labours. All the more is this the case, perhaps, to the extent that an unconscious effort to conceal rather than to reveal the persecution or the rivalry constitutes the *raison d'être* of the texts in question. As we noted above, one of Girard's ways of putting this is to say that the text refers so something 'outside' itself.

Girard's approach here is not to be underestimated. For rather than revealing that the past is the secret of the present (to speak colloquially), he proposes that the present opens up the secrets of the past, which implies that the present is not entirely 'present' to itself: it is past and present, as it were. In astrophysics – to draw an analogy – the veracity of the Big Bang as the origin of the universe is not to be confirmed or refuted only by tracing the history of the 'death' of stars through the observation and study of supernova, which would be equivalent to going back in time to the origin. The Big Bang is now even primarily, confirmed (or denied) by the observation that the universe is expanding in the present, so to speak. Thus, as with Girard's method, the 'present' is giving access to the very distant past, rather than the reverse.

*

In his essay, 'Before the Law', Derrida says that the death – or 'murder' – of the father in *Totem and Taboo* 'is not an event in the ordinary sense of the word' (Derrida 1992: 199). And the philosopher elaborates:

> Event without event, pure event where nothing happens; the eventiality of an event which both demands and annuls the relation in its fiction. Nothing new happens and yet this nothing new would instate the law, the two fundamental prohibitions of totemism, namely murder and incest. However, this pure and purely presumed event nevertheless marks an invisible rent in history. It resembles a fiction, a myth, or a fable, and its relation is so structured that all questions as to Freud's intentions are at once inevitable and pointless. (199)

Notable here, is the way that, rather than analysing the logic of Freud's story (where a 'murder' founds the law), Derrida counsels caution as to the story's status (we do not know if Freud really believed it). In a sense, we can accept the story as a fact without accepting or denying the facts of the story. What for many might be a highly problematic part of Freud's theory becomes something about which it is impossible to come to a firm conclusion, even though the figure of the father is so central to psychanalysis.[16]

We are dealing, then, with Derrida's interpretation of Freud's apologue about the emergence, at the time of the primal horde, of the moral law in the wake of the killing of the father by the sons. The question is: is the story of the primal horde and the murder of the father really necessary for Freud's theory of the renunciation of anti-social instincts? To argue in the negative certainly seems plausible. If this were true, it would suggest that Freud had some sort of personal attachment to the story, a line of thinking that it is not possible to elaborate upon here. Girard, for his part, as we have seen, argues that myth always opens the way to a true state of affairs, even if, at the same time, it works to obscure this truth. Derrida, by contrast, seems to take an almost pragmatic approach to myth: the latter is something that, *qua* myth (i.e., *qua* content) is not true, even if, at the same time it can give rise to rigorous thinking.

No doubt one could claim that as the 'myth' of origin is also the myth of presence, all metaphysical notions are *mythical*: that is, they pass for being true (or: logical, rigorous, coherent, viable, scientific) when they are not true, or at least when they are susceptible to being deconstructed, which means that their status as metaphysical is revealed. Revelation here is a necessary act, for it is of the essence of metaphysics to be invisible where thought is concerned.[17]

A brief – and hopefully not too hasty – comparison between Girard and Derrida on myth and hominisation can be set out as follows: according to Girard an exhaustive study of myths from around the world will reveal a common thread, namely, the scapegoat mechanism and facts about the persecution of victims. Although this insight is not available at the manifest content of the myth, interpretation based on the analysis of many myths will show that the ultimate message of the myth is about the sacrifice of a surrogate as a means of limiting violence and of the actual persecution of victims, such as Girard demonstrates in relation to the Middle Ages in *The Scapegoat*.

Hominisation, Girard claims, is also founded on the scapegoat mechanism. So, in revealing this mechanism, myth – supposedly – gives access to the phylogenetic evolution of the human. Against this, however, is the fact that hominisation raises extremely complex issues in both prehistory and paleontology, issues that it is not within the province of myth to reveal.[18]

Given that myth in *Of Grammatology*, means 'untrue' or 'invalid', Derrida's response to *Totem and Taboo* is surprising. If what passes for truth (e.g., the simple origin) is mythical, does what passes for myth offer up something that can be called 'true'? Here, an answer in the affirmative will bring Derrida closer to Girard than might have been expected. But *can* one answer in the affirmative?

At one point in his reading, Derrida cites Freud's text on the consequences of the murder of the father as follows: 'They felt remorse [but how and why, if this is before morality, before law? J. D.] for the deed and decided that it should never he repeated and that its performance should bring no advantage' (Freud 2001: 159 cited in Derrida 1992: 198). Here, Derrida, rather than accepting the story as a myth or fiction, questions its logic, as Lévi-Strauss also does in asking how there can be a murder before the existence of the moral law that the murder inaugurates.

Again, questioning the story's logic, Derrida says that the crime 'inaugurates nothing since repentance and morality had to be possible *before* the crime' (198). Moreover, because the origin of the moral law is ultimately based in *psychical*, rather than historical reality (even if Freud himself was ambiguous on this) and because the search for its origin also provides part of the fuel for Freud's self-analysis, the myth of the primal horde and the killing of the father in fact gives, says Derrida, 'the history of that which never took place' (194). It thus 'resembles a fiction, a myth, or a fable' (199).

In light of Derrida's conception of 'myth', we can say that classifying Freud's account of the murder of the primeval father as a myth means that it is untrue in a real historical sense: the origin of myth is implicated in the myth of origin. For Girard, as we know, myth as such is no barrier to accessing historical truth. What Girard refuses to accept is the proposition – whether propounded by Lévi-Strauss or Derrida – that thinking reveals that the search for origins is at best paradoxical and at worst non-sensical. In this case, the understanding of what a crime is, what repentance is, what remorse is – or, indeed, what the law is can only happen *aposteriori* – after the fact. Thus, in Freud's story, for moral sentiments to be experienced in light of the 'original' crime, the moral law would have had to have been in force already. Similarly, for the original surrogate victim to be nominated, society would have had to exist already. Thus, the crime cannot be the *origin* of morality and the scapegoat cannot be the *origin* of the human as a social being. In sum: the first crime cannot be the origin of crime or the law, just as the first sacrifice of the surrogate victim cannot be the origin of the sacred or sacrifice. In this sense, as Derrida rightly intimates, it is necessary to consider a non-origin (supplement) as the origin of the origin – non-crime as the origin of the law; the non-victim as the origin of the sacred victim.

Nothing of this takes away from Girard's emphasis on the victim as opposed to the persecutor. The victim is innocent because the accusations made are entirely false at best and phantasmatic at worst, simply based on the community's fear and anxiety. Although, as we have seen, Girard rejects Freud's psychanalytic interpretation of the murder, he does not reject (what is for him) its historical reality. At some point in the past, there *was* an initial murder giving rise to society. By comparison, we saw, as might have been expected, that Derrida dubs Freud's account 'a fiction, a myth, or a fable', which means that the account does not give access to the knowledge of an actual murder.

Freud's apologue (and this is what Lacan confirms in his theory of the Symbolic) is about the birth of the Law (moral, religious, secular) and, in particular, the birth of the law against murder. Freud, then, signals the birth of the moral, religious or secular law (the judicial system) in contrast to Girard, for whom the birth of the social evokes a time when there was no law in this sense so that the only way to bring an end to a sacrificial crisis and its contagious violence was through the killing of an innocent scapegoat, For Freud, the 'name of the father' (the father as dead) gives rise to the moral law and to civilisation,[19] something which, for Girard, is destined to occur in the relatively distant future. In brief: for Girard there is a killing because there is no Law; for Freud, the killing gives rise to the birth of the moral Law: 'the dead father became stronger than the living one had been' (Freud 2001: 143). It is at this point in his otherwise well researched narrative that Freud throws caution to the wind and, like Girard, speculates on the origin of human guilt and morality.[20]

Killing of the surrogate victim; killing of the father – such is the difference between Girard and Freud. As Colin Davis says, the former is anonymous, while the latter is identifiable as being at the origin (whether real or psychic) of the family.[21] By emphasising the anonymity and innocence of the victim, Girard's approach can be construed as showing not what was lost with the dissolution of archaic societies, but what humanity has gained with the emergence of judicial institutions. In principle, law supports the victim, not the persecutor. It is no longer necessary to support the persecutor so that society might survive.

All this is very different from Walter Benjamin's or Agamben's approach to the Law. For Benjamin, 'law preserving violence' accompanies the Law, while, for Agamben, the founding violence remains present in sovereignty throughout Law's history. In both cases, Law is deemed to be interested rather than disinterested, committed rather than neutral, despite the icon of blind justice. Girard, as we shall see in the following chapter, not only points to the judicial institution as protector of the victim, but also sees the same institution as being founded on the Cross. In other words, Christianity is the harbinger of the modern notion of Law.

Notes

1. Girard differs from Freud to the extent that the founder of psychanalysis 'mistook parricide and incest for a great truth. This mistake produced the modern revival of the [Oedipus] myth, because Freud wrongly believed that Oedipus is psychologically, if not actually, guilty. Through Freud we relapsed into a mythical understanding of sociopsychological structures (Freud is a baffling combination of "blindness and insight")' (Girard 2017: 149).
2. Although presented in a peremptory style, Gianni Vattimo's claim is that the very notion of origin – given that it cannot fail to be metaphysical in character – implies violence. Cf.: 'the idea of *Grund*, of ultimate foundation, is an authoritarian idea. The notion of primeval evidence, of a *Eureka!*, of a moment in which I have reached bedrock, of a foundation at which no questions can or need be asked – that state, in which questions are lacking, is not the end product of violence, but its origin' (2019: 95). The origin, *qua* origin, would thus be violent.
3. The French text of the last two sentences reads: 'On peut appeler archi-écriture cette simplicité des origines. Ce qui se perd en elle, c'est donc *le myth* de la simplicité de l'origine. Ce *myth* est lié au concept d'origine lui-même: à la parole récitant l'origine, *au myth de l'origine* et non seulement aux mythes d'origine' (Derrida 1967: 140; emphasis added).
4. C.f.: 'Modern man has a "lived experience" of the world and thinks the world in those terms, i.e., in terms of himself as the being that, as ground, lies at the foundation of all explanation and ordering of beings as a whole. In the language of metaphysics what lies at the foundation

is *subjectum*. Modern man is by essence the "subject"' (Heidegger 1992: 165). Let it be added here that it is not necessary to follow Heidegger all the way to thinking history as destiny (*Geschichte*) or fate (*schichte*) to be prompted to ponder the implications of the dominance of 'subjectivism' in thinking, thus in thinking history as an object of thought. The question thus becomes: what does Girard's pursuit of the origin of human society presuppose?

5. As 'data', 'deeds' and 'facts' (Heidegger 1992: 55).
6. For example, Girard refers to the Dinka people in Africa, where the victim can be either animal or human – the animal being a 'stand-in' for 'the original victim', who is arbitrarily chosen (1979: 98). The victim can also be selected through games of chance, as with the Uitoto Indians of southeastern Columbia and the Kayans of Borneo (311).
7. Myths, similarly, keep alive the memory of sacrifice as the 'real origin' of society. Thus, the 'extraordinary number of commemorative rites that have to do with killing leads us to imagine that the original event must have been a murder' (Girard 1979: 92).
8. Bakhtin writes, for example, that: 'the hero of a novel should not be "heroic" in either the epic or the tragic sense of the word: he should combine in himself negative as well as positive features, low as well as lofty, ridiculous as well as serious' (1981: 10). Thus, by contrast, the hero in the epic or tragic sense is: either negative or positive, manifests low or lofty features, is ridiculous or serious.
9. See Kristeva (1979).
10. In this regard, Derrida adds: 'All dualisms, all theories of the immortality of the soul or of the spirit, as well as all monisms, spiritualist or materialist, dialectical or vulgar, are the unique theme of metaphysics whose entire history was compelled to strive toward the reduction of the trace' (2016: 77).
11. Just to recall where things stand between Girard and Agamben on the victim: for Girard, sacrifice founds the social system and sacrifice entails the killing of a scapegoat – even if this be a king. The scapegoat, therefore, is the sacrificial victim. Here, it is the arbitrariness of the choice that makes the victim. For Agamben, by contrast, the founding moment of modern political power is the capacity for *homo sacer* to be killed without this being a sacrifice (or murder). In this sense, the origin of power becomes power itself. There is no victim because there is no sacrifice.
12. For repeated references to the 'founding murder' see Girard (1987b: 40–41, 49, and *passim*). Girard writes, for example, that: 'There is an element of truth in *Totem and Taboo*, and it consists in tracing humanity's *origin* to a *collective murder*' (96; emphasis added).
13. Agamben recognises this, but at the same time implies that it is not a matter of a mistake on a theoretical level but is the basis of Western politics:

'In our culture, the decisive political conflict, which governs every other conflict, is that between the animality and the humanity of man. That is to say, in its origin Western politics is also biopolitics' (2004: 80). It has been argued that this implies that there is no victim at the origin of Western politics.
14. It is no doubt Girard's failure to engage here that has led to his flirtation with the much-disputed sociobiology (see Girard 2017: 70).
15. *Pace* Haw (2017: 192), it is, in this regard, anything *but* surprising that key researchers in human evolution and hominisation have failed to acknowledge Girard's work.
16. For an interesting and informative perspective on Derrida's interpretation of *Totem and Taboo*, see Ryder (2011).
17. Other instances of the appearance of the term, 'myth' in *Of Grammatology* (to remain with this seminal text for the moment) are: 'Immediacy is here the *myth* of consciousness' (Derrida 2016: 180; emphasis added). 'The concept of origin or nature is nothing but the *myth* of addition, of supplementarity annulled by being purely additive. It is the *myth* of the effacement of the trace' (181; emphasis added). Finally: 'If the space-time that we inhabit is *a priori* the space-time of the trace, there is neither pure activity nor pure passivity. This pair of concepts [...] belongs to the *myth of the origin* of an uninhabited world, of a world alien to the trace: pure presence for the pure present' (316; emphasis added to 'myth of the origin').
18. These issues include but are not limited to: (1) The emergence of bipedalism; (2) Hand manipulation and tool use; (3) Modification of the jaw and teeth; (4) The enlargement of the brain; (5) Changes in the vocal tract and the emergence of language and speech.
19. 'The totemic meal, which is perhaps mankind's earliest festival, would thus be a repetition and a commemoration of this memorable and *criminal* deed [the killing of the father], which was the beginning of so many things – of social organization, of moral restrictions and of religion' (Freud 2001: 142; emphasis added). Although this is Freud's conclusion, it should be acknowledged that his starting point (the primal horde) derives from Darwin's *The Descent of Man* (2004). Although Freud's use of the most recent ethnographic data of his day makes his approach far less simplistic than it is often presented as being, the killing of the father and the moral repercussions are ultimately the main focus of his thinking.
20. Richard Kearney questions Girard's own relation to persecution. He thus asks: '[I]s Girard's own critique of alienating ideologies of persecution not itself subject to critique?' (1999: 257). The validity and the implications of this question are not as great as Kearney thinks, for it is the sort of

question that inevitably leads to an infinite regress, where a claim about persecution would itself be infused with persecution – or rivalry. Another question Kearny poses is whether all non-biblical myths are inevitably persecutory, as Girard seems to suggest. Unless research as extensive as Girard's is carried out, an answer to this question cannot be forthcoming.

21. See Davis (2000).

6   Image, Violence, Victim and the Crucifixion: Girard's Version

WE HAVE SHOWN HOW Girard theorises violence as originarily linked to the sacred and the sacrificial crisis. Reference was made to his claim that in traditional societies, the sacrifice of a scapegoat was intended to end violence – at least for a time. In following on from this, the current chapter will address the way that Christ on the Cross (Crucifixion) becomes a revelation of the scandal of mimetic violence as the unjust killing of the scapegoat. Christ's Crucifixion also unites image and violence.

Girard argues that only Christian culture is 'non-sacrificial', which means that it favours the victim over the persecutor and that, as we have previously noted, Christianity is the basis of Western law. Girard is not alone in this view, one in which law and the defence of the victim go hand in hand. As a historian of law writes:

> [The] fundamental characteristics of the Western legal tradition were founded ultimately on Christian faith, first in its Roman Catholic form, later in its Lutheran and Calvinist forms. Deism, the religious faith of the French Enlightenment, substituted for the Christian belief in a divine law a belief in God-given reason. Nevertheless, in 1914 it continued to be widely believed, at least in the United States, that the ultimate sources of positive law are divine law, especially the Ten Commandments, and natural law as expressed in historical sources such as Magna Carta and the constitutional requirement of due process. (Berman 2000: 751)

For Girard, there is a fundamental relation between the history of law and his thesis that the Crucifixion signals a transformation from the rule of the persecutor to the law of the victim, as represented by the modern judicial system. Indeed, one could argue that the great strength of Girard's work is in its demonstration that the defence of the victim occurs through the auspices of Christianity. Other cultures and faiths have followed Christianity on this point so that the proportions reached of the defence of the victim are now global.

*

While Girard is highly critical of Nietzsche's attack on Christianity because it is based on the philosopher's defence of the persecutor over the victim,[1] the question arises as to the exact status of *ressentiment* in Nietzsche's text. In addressing the theme of Nietzsche's 'Dionysus versus the Crucified' (Girard 1984), Girard shows that while the philosopher is scathing about Christianity's defence of the victim (the weak), to the supposed detriment of the strong, and while the 'weak' are seen to be harbingers of *ressentiment,* what cannot be denied, Girard argues, is that Nietzsche – unlike the majority of anthropologists – clearly, albeit implicitly, distinguishes Christianity from sacrificial religions based on the scapegoat mechanism. That is, much as he decries the influence of Christianity, Nietzsche does not make the mistake of identifying it as just another (pagan) mythology. So, even though – as we have seen in Chapter 1 – Nietzsche is Christianity's virulent opponent he is also an astute interpreter of the nature of this religious orientation and its difference from other cults. The prevailing view of social scientists, by contrast, holds that:

> If the facts are the same in all these cults, it can be safely assumed, or so they [the anthropologists] thought, that these religions must be the same. And this element of sameness is obviously present in the Judaic religion with its ritual sacrifices, and even more spectacularly in the Christian religion. The passion of Jesus certainly constitutes the heart of the gospels, and what is it if not one more instance of these collective murders that are the daily bread of religions all over the world? (Girard 1984: 821)

Girard maintains, as was seen in the discussion of Chapter 2 (note 11), that Nietzsche – in opposition to social science – does not just say that 'God is dead', but that, 'We have killed him – you and I. All of us are his murderers' (Nietzsche 1974d: sect 125). Here, the inference is that, in being the murderers of God, sacrificial religion is evoked. The surrogate victim, often as not, becomes (equivalent to) a god. Indeed, murder is necessary for the god to become a god. So, ironically, Nietzsche's 'death of God', can equally give rise to a god: 'If God is always the product of his own collective murder, does not this text really say that the death of the gods is their life and that the life of the gods is their death?' (831).[2] As such, the 'death of God' does not necessarily give rise to atheism, as is commonly thought – not, at least, if the totality of religious experience across cultures is taken into account. And as Nietzsche's driving impulse is to undermine Christianity at every turn, it is unsurprising that he should be drawn in his thinking to the violence of sacrificial religion, of which the figure of Dionysus would be the prime representative.

Thus, in the wake of Girard's interpretation of Nietzsche's phrase, 'God is dead', the question arises as to how successful the Nietzschean enterprise is in opposing a religion that valorises the victim over the persecutor. Does Nietzsche's powerful rhetoric against *ressentiment*, against the 'despisers of life', and in favour of the 'tragic' view not run the risk of giving rise to more victims? Or does this really matter? The more victims, the merrier, as it were.

What Girard does not mention in relation to *Ecce Homo*, from which comes the phrase, 'Dionysus versus the Crucified' (Nietzsche 1989: 335), is Nietzsche's opposition to 'idols' [*Götzen*] or 'ideals' [*Ideal*] (218). If an idol for Nietzsche is an ideal, and ideals are a cover for *ressentiment*, the Dionysian or tragic view is, by contrast, about 'overthrowing' idols/ideals (218). In a circuitous way, therefore, opposing the religion of the victim entails the 'overthrowing' of idols. For the idols are essentially the moral ideals of Christianity.

Nietzsche's Dionysian vision gives him little time for Christ as the image because it means that Christ is divine. This, we will see, is the exact opposite of Girard for whom Christ – and not simply the historical Jesus – reveals the truth about the role of victimage. For Nietzsche, on the other hand, it is a question of the historical Jesus, Jesus as essentially mundane, not divine. Thus Nietzsche claims: 'He died for *his* guilt – all ground is lacking for the assertion, however often it is made, that he died for the guilt of others' (1974b: sect 27). Moreover, in a seemingly positive assessment that others have noted (see Williams 1998: 144), Nietzsche expresses the view that it is not the being of Jesus (His divinity), but Jesus's practice that is decisive: 'his *practice*: his bearing before the judges, before the guards, before the accusers and every kind of calumny and mockery – his bearing on the *Cross*' (Nietzsche 1974b: sect 35). Jesus, then, showed that 'it is through the *practice* of one's life that one feels "divine", "blessed", "evangelic", at all times a "child of God"' (sect 33). Thus, it would be that Nietzsche prefers the historical Jesus to the divine Christ as the '"Son of God", the *second person* of the Trinity' (sect 34) Nietzsche, then, rejects Christ as the image and the accompanying symbolism of the Cross in favour of Jesus as human, historical actor – an actor who, literally, was crucified. '*Not* a belief, but a doing' (sect 39) is the truth of Christianity as a historical movement. Christianity as faith and spirituality, on the other hand, is a '*crime against life*' (sect 47). Thus evoked is the key theme of Chapter 1 in the discussion of Bataille, where 'life', for Nietzsche, is seen to justify cruelty perpetrated on victims.

Let us, then, elaborate on the status of Christ as image, whether or not as *imagio dei* (image of God). It will be argued that Christ is image if, and only if, he is divine. In this regard Girard opposes Nietzsche's position that the Christian doctrine of the equality of souls (spirit) is merely part of the war against everything elevated (aristocratic) (sect 43). For Girard, it is Christ as divine, thus as image, that reveals the truth of the victimage mechanism, whereas Nietzsche, in denying Christ, as it were, gives this mechanism a modern boost.

A dilemma that arises for Girard in light of Nietzsche's claims regarding Jesus is as follows: Even though Girard refers to 'Christ' and 'Jesus' interchangeably, what is unclear is the extent to which the divinity of Christ – as opposed to the role of Jesus as historical figure – is crucial to the revelation of the 'falsity' of the sacrificial version of social life and the 'truth' of the non-violent biblical version. Certainly, Girard frequently pays homage to Christ's divinity and is a believer. But this is not the issue. Rather, the issue is about whether there is a necessary link between the divinity of Christ (Christ as image) and the *message* of non-violence that can be derived from the Crucifixion. In short, even though Girard says that 'Christ's divinity [...] is not dependent on the events of his earthly life' (1987b: 233), in terms of actions, is Girard's Christ really so different from Nietzsche's Jesus? Myths are false (they justify killing the innocent scapegoat), while the Bible is true: it reveals the injustice of scapegoating and the nature of human desire that plays a key role in it. Jesus, Girard claims, 'invites us to imitate his own *desire*' (1999: 31) – the goal being to 'resemble as closely as possible God the Father' (31).

When considering Girard's relation to Nietzsche on the question of the historical figure of Jesus versus the divine figure of Christ, what remains to be determined is whether Christ's divinity is a necessary correlate to the message of the Cross as interpreted by Girard; namely, that Jesus is innocent and his persecutors are culpable – that the crowd is wrong and the scapegoat victim is right, that sacrificial violence can never bring an end to violence. A number of commentators have pointed out that even though Girard has a great empathy for theology he in effect uses a 'pseudo-theological framework' (Farneti 2008: 30), which is nonetheless laced with theological terms such as 'Kingdom', 'Resurrection', 'Apocalypse' (33).[3] Along with Anthony Lusvardi (2017: 164), we can note that Girard himself acknowledges that his 'research is only indirectly theological' (1999: 249). Certainly, Girard believes in the Resurrection and Christ's divinity, but this, supposedly, does not impinge upon his 'anthropological analyses'. At certain points, Girard comes close to saying that it is His divinity that allows Christ to reveal the truth of the scapegoat mechanism. Thus, in conversation with Michel Treguer, Girard claims that: 'If the Passion were only something human, the voice of Christ would have been smothered, or he would have become a pagan divinity like the rest, a sacralised scapegoat, His real message would never have made it to us' (2014: 91). There is nothing here, however, that proves that Christ's divinity is integral to his message – namely, that the victim is innocent. No essential leap of faith is necessary for the message to be received and understood. In any event, Jesus's *kenosis* that Gianni Vattimo[4] considers to be so crucial would (at least for Vattimo)[5] render the divinity irrelevant in relation to the Cross.

The question, then, is: can Christ as image really play a role if Girard does not engage in theology? To respond to this question we first need to have an idea of Christ as image from a theological perspective. In this regard, the work of Jean-Luc Marion opens the way.

The Image and Victim for Girard

The incarnation of God in Christ: that is the image. If Christ is divine (i.e., is God incarnate), then Christ is the image of God. What we have to contemplate in reading Girard on Christ and/as the image is the argument that, in the words of Jean-Luc Marion,

> Christ on the Cross, holds no more than a typical relation, outside of similitude or dissimilitude, with himself. *Never the image as such*, he is only more radically disqualified when the absolute Face [...] submits to the violation not so much of his divine visage but more of his lesser human visage. (2013: 276; emphasis added)

Moreover:

> *Christ kills the image* on the Cross, because he crosses an abyss without measure between his appearance and his glory. He definitively *disqualifies the least pretension of an image* to produce or reproduce what it might of the glory of the original. (276; emphasis added)

If, indeed, 'Christ kills the image', what precisely is His status? In venerating Christ, is one venerating an idol? The theology involved – i.e., the sense in which Christ is the Son of God and is therefore divine – cannot be our focus here. Instead, what is of concern is the role of the Cross – understood as image in a non-theological sense – in Girard's thought. In 'The Triumph of the Cross' – the title of the key section and a key chapter of *Je vois Satan* (1999) (*I See Satan*) – the Cross becomes a synecdoche for the Crucifixion, which is the event and the revelation of the falsity of the sacrificial system.

Even though it does not seem to be essential to the theory of the innocence of the scapegoat, Girard constantly refers to the divinity of Christ.[6] For those observing from the outside (philosophers, scientists, even theologians) Christ's supposed divinity is a myth, much like the myths upon which 'primitive' religions are founded, if one is to believe the research of anthropologists. According to Girard, it is scepticism regarding Christ's divinity and the message of the Cross in favour of victims that has prompted the exit from Christianity of a vast number of adherents, those religiously trained included (1999: 163–164). Despite appearing to be on cusp of a theological orientation, it is no doubt Girard's claim to being scientific that most contributes to problematising any easy accommodation with theology.[7] In a manner that challenges the presuppositions of modern thought regarding Christianity, Girard claims that the fundamental difference between myth properly speaking and the Bible is that in myth the victim/scapegoat is always in the wrong – or at least is always expendable – whereas in the Bible the reverse is true: the victim is innocent (148). This, then, passes for a scientific not a theological claim. Myth is therefore false in claiming that the killing of scapegoat-victim is necessary to end violence, whereas in proclaiming the innocence of the victim, the Bible is true.[8] Perhaps most importantly for Girard's comparison of myth with the Bible is that myth stands for violence and the Bible stands for its elimination. More than this, in a continuing oscillation between theology and social science, we read that 'The most astonishing thing is that the Resurrection and the divinisation of Christ structurally correspond exactly to mythical divinisations, which they reveal to be false' (167). Moreover, it is the Resurrection of Christ that brings into view the truth that has always been hidden – 'the things hidden since the foundation of the world', the founding murder and the killing of the scapegoat. Let it be emphasised here that it is Christ's Resurrection, which presupposes His crucifixion, that guarantees the truth of the revelation of the innocence of the victims of sacrificial killing. Thus, Girard sums up by stating that: 'Christ's Resurrection consummates and completes the subversion and the revelation of mythology, of rites, of all that assures the foundation and the perpetuation of human cultures' (167). In a manner even more definite regarding the importance of Christ's divinity for his own work, Girard states that Christ's divinity rests 'on the full and complete revelation of the truth which illuminates mythology and it is this, I hope, which has nourished my own analyses from the beginning' (175). On this basis, one cannot avoid the impression that it is, for Girard, Christ's divinity that guarantees the truth of the revelation regarding mythology and that, therefore, theology as much as anthropology is here in play. Girard, in an interview, says at one point, 'Mine is a search for an anthropology of the Cross, which turns out to rehabilitate orthodox theology' (Girard 1996: 288).

'The Cross', Girard claims, 'gives rise to the triumph of the truth' (1999: 182) in the sense that it signals, in the writings of the Gospels, the falsity of the accusations made against Jesus. As such, in light of the Crucifixion, all victims 'are rehabilitated' (182). Based on the model of the victory parade of a Roman general – the triumph – Christ similarly is the 'victorious general' and the victory is the Cross (184). But unlike the Roman general who *inflicted* violence, the Cross stands for the one (and for those) who *suffered* (and who *suffer*) violence. The spectacle of the triumph in its grand but purely external visibility hides the 'invisible', 'unknown' 'violent and shameful origin' that is at the heart of the 'triumph', namely, the persecution of victims, of the 'many against one'. Thus, 'the Cross of Christ brings this reverse side of things to humanity for the first time' (187). Such a truth renders the strong of the world vulnerable to a collapse of their power. Power based on violence does not suspect the revelatory power of the Cross (187) – a power that overturns the existing state of things. The Cross becomes the light that illuminates the powers of darkness – of Satan, in Girard's language: 'Once this black sun becomes entirely illuminated by the Cross, it will no longer be able to limit its destructive capacity. Satan will destroy his kingdom and himself' (187).

Crucially, for the position advanced here regarding the image and what is imaged, Girard puts forward the argument that it is necessary to avoid 'confusing the representation with what is represented' (188). And so, against the commonly adopted approach, which expects to see the victimary mechanism represented in myths, Girard states that the said mechanism is not represented there because the genesis of myths is in the victimary mechanism itself. In brief: in a text dominated by the victimary mechanism, the latter will never be an explicit theme; by contrast, the same mechanism will be explicit in a text (the Gospels) where it appears explicitly (193). In effect, the victimary mechanism relies for its viability on the dissimulation of true nature: 'The essential characteristic of myth is to hide violence; that of Judeo-Christian scriptures is to reveal it and to suffer the consequences' (194).

If, for a moment, the principle just enunciated were applied to the image, what would be the result? Ostensibly, it would be that what appeared in the image might not be germane to its genesis, while, conversely, the image might be the result of what did not appear in it. Such a question is only pertinent, I suggest, if an image is to be equated with a text, or if it is equated with its mode of production, neither of which I would accept. Or, to put it another way: to argue that what is invisible in the image has an impact on the image's visibility takes us into another theological realm: that of Christ as image.

Christ as Image for Jean-Luc Marion

For Girard, then, the Gospels, as texts, render visible what persecutors want to remain invisible: the victimary mechanism and the injustice of the killing of the scapegoat. Jean-Luc Marion's question is: to what extent does Christ as image render the invisible (the Holy) visible. Christ's divinity, in other words, is essentially invisible; but Christ as image contradicts this.

According to Marion's commentary on the Second Council of Nicaea (AD 787), which attempted to resolve the iconoclastic debate, the image is not able to 'render visible the holiness of the Holy' (2013: 273). For the image, it is claimed, is concerned uniquely with visibility whereas the Holy is invisible. To the extent that it claims to make the Holy visible, it is an 'impostor' (274) and may well become an idol. Everything, then, is geared to avoid the worst of results: the dominance of the idol. By contrast, the icon, despite being a physical presence, evokes the Holy, or the prototype. It is in this sense transparent: it does not refer to itself but to something other than itself. They (icons) 'deserve and can demand the veneration of the faithful' (275).

But then again, Marion indicates, the icon 'like the Cross, is equivalent to a type' (275), meaning by this that a specific instance of *an* icon evokes *the* Icon, just as a specific instance of *a* cross is evokes the Cross without being identical to it. In other words, a specific manifestation of an icon or a cross evokes the prototype.

If an icon evokes Christ, what is the status of Christ Himself? The answer is that given 'the divine holiness of Christ' (277), Christ, it can be argued, now becomes an image in the sense that He is both God and Man, or, to put it another way: Christ is the medium connecting God and Man. At any rate, Christ is not simply an identity in a human sense but gives rise to something other ('the Father'), in the same way that an image gives rise to the imaged. An image is not simply itself. Or, as Marion says of the icon: 'The icon is ordered to holiness by never claiming it for itself' (280). In other words: 'The icon proclaims itself a useless servant of a veneration that it does not touch, but before which it effaces itself to the point of transparency' (281). Marion confirms that an image in itself (if there were such a thing) is an idol (284). The image becomes an idol because it ceases to be the medium that it essentially is. Christ, then, is image to the extent that '[i]n his person, human nature becomes, entirely, the type whose prototype consists of nothing less than divine nature' (285). Most significantly, the icon, in not being simply an object, 'leads us to question the objectification, production and consumption to which iconoclasm reduces the modern image' (287).

Christ as Image in Byzantium and Girard's View

It is as image that He is in the world. The Byzantine theology of Nicephorus as outlined by Marie-José Mondzain, extends Marion's understanding of (what amounts to) the image as medium of the epoch of the Second Council of Nicaea. Nicephorus proposes that Christ as image is not to be understood as in any way equivalent to the copy in relation to its prototype (*homeiosis*); nor is it equivalent to the visible as in perception but is invisible; it is the incarnation of the divine, but it is not a materialisation (Mondzain 1996: 110–124). In sum: 'The image is at the beginning, for at the beginning was the Verb and the Verb is the image of God' (106). Or again: 'the essence of the image [...] is in the divinity' (106). Christ is an image, therefore, to the extent that father and son are inseparable, if not indistinguishable. This is the situation evoked by the term, *skhesis*, where, according to Mondzain's rendering, the term implies that: '[t]o be the "image of" is to be in a living relation with; this is why the model of every relation is that of father to son' (105). In the end, the image gives access to the prototype – to the divine. Thus, the essence of the image is 'in the divinity' of Christ (106). Such is confirmed when Nicephorus states, in Mondzain's rendering, that: 'He who adores the image adores the prototype' (134). More than this, perhaps – with regard to Girard – is the view that 'the refusal of the image [by the iconolcasts] equates with a refusal of life itself' (149). To interpret this, we say that if the image is the incarnation of Christ's divinity, the latter is the overcoming of death made manifest in the Resurrection, and the negative in general, a negative that is underpinned by violence. In this sense the divinity of Christ as image is the overcoming of violence.

Despite acknowledging at various points that 'Jesus is both God and Man' (Girard 1987b: 216), Girard does not conceptualise this explicitly in terms of the image. That is, although Girard accepts Christ's divinity, he ignores the theology pertaining to Christ as equivalent to the image, where reflection centres on the notion that Christ encompasses immediately the divine and the human, as captured by *skhesis*.

Even as he says that a non-sacrificial reading brings out the divinity of Jesus, Girard's Christ is first and foremost the Christ of the Passion, of the Crucifixion, thus of the Cross. For this reason, the crucifixion of Christ is *not* a sacrifice;[9] nor will Jesus bring an end to violence as a scapegoat. Rather, to reiterate, Christ's death reveals the innocence of the scapegoat. He reveals that every society hitherto, where the scapegoat mechanism has been the mechanism used by the community to end violence, is based on a lie. Christ stands for putting an end to the violence that would supposedly end violence. 'Turn the other cheek', is the message. Alternatively, those who use violence will be used by violence (Girard).

It is true, then, that Girard argues that reading the Gospels from a non-sacrificial perspective reveals Christ's divinity and that it is this that enables Him to overcome sacrificial violence. Thus:

> To recognize Christ as God is to recognize him as the only being capable of rising above the violence that had, up to that point, absolutely transcended mankind. Violence is the controlling agent in every form of mythic or cultural structure, and Christ is the only agent who is capable of escaping from these structures and freeing us from their dominance. (1987b: 219)

And in 'rising above the violence' Christ, says Girard, 'brings to light all the victims buried by mankind' (235). 'These are the victims who have been assassinated since the foundation of the world, who begin to return upon this earth and make themselves known' (235). Again, it is Christ's divinity that enables victims to be brought into the light, as opposed to the lives of their persecutors.

Through Christ's divinity, which precedes His Crucifixion, but is confirmed by His Resurrection, Christ as image might well be inferred in light of mediaeval Christian theology. For the image, as we have seen, is the way 'Jesus is both God and Man' (216), even if Girard does not invoke the image to refer to this.

Jean-Luc Marion claims that the image detached from any prototype or original ceases to be an image, strictly speaking, and becomes an idol or, we could also say: a simulacrum.[10] The latter flourishes in contemporary theory (cf. Baudrillard) because, there, the represented is just another representation, the signified another signifier.

For his part, Girard, as we know, does not delve into the intricacies of the image *qua* image. He is more concerned with the Cross and what it signifies (it is not just a symbol). And there is a certain logic in this. The Cross becomes a sign of the Crucifixion which, in turn, evokes the fact that myths have hitherto (albeit unknowingly) presented the view of the persecutors, whereas the Cross stands for view of the victims.

Theology of the Cross

Theologians know well that Luther used the Cross to introduce a different theology in the early sixteenth century (1518), a theology of the cross (*theologia crucis*). According to Luther, what existed at the time was a theology of glory, where God was presented in the style of princes and warriors who accumulated a list of good works. The theology of the Cross, by contrast, 'was the doctrine of the satisfaction of our sins offered to God in the vicarious death of Jesus Christ. Because of his atoning death at the cross we become just and righteous by faith in him who offers us the forgiveness of our sins' (Pannenberg 1988: 163). Or, as John Caputo has put it, the cross in the Lutheran theology of the cross, 'stands for suffering flesh and for the solidarity of Jesus with everyone who suffers' (2010: 244). A 'theology of the cross' would then bring the victim into focus and thus the dimension of non-violence – or '*caritas*', as Vattimo would say.

Of course, Girard does not formally engage with such a theology. But the consequences of it open up the very issue of the recognition of the victim that is of most concern to him. Indeed, a criticism of Girard's approach to the Cross – or to 'Christology' – is that he pays little or no attention to 'the concrete "form" taken by Jesus's non-violent practice' (Milbank 2006: 398). The 'form' of non-violent practice, we could say, is implied by a 'theology of the cross' as Luther expounded it.

Nevertheless, for Jesus to be both God and Man, as Girard accepts, means that he is also the image – or 'Mediator, the one bridge between the Kingdom of violence and the Kingdom of God' (216). We know, too, that as Mediator – as medium – Jesus is also the image. From a secular perspective, Jesus as image shows the image as medium. *Qua* medium, the image as such does not die on the Cross; for it is not like an object that can be destroyed. The image, like Christ – and this is not at all a theological claim – lives eternally. And perhaps this is why it is always available to support a message of non-violence. The Cross, in short, because it is also image (medium), will never die.

But a theological perspective would seem (to the outsider) to show that only Christ *is* the image. He is not simply a symbol or part of a discourse. Indeed, the very reality or being of Christ is at stake here. Christ as image (as divine *and* human) puts an end to violence against the victim. Neither Agamben nor Bataille engage with Christ in this way. Agamben does not because he is so focused on Christ in the Trinity as the incarnation of glory. And even though glory comes to have a connection to the image in contemporary society through the media, the relation is nothing if not indirect. If Christ were an image in Agamben's sense, He could have no relation to the Father, as the image as a pure means can appear as such.

With Bataille, as was seen in Chapter 2, it is not Christ as image that is at issue because Bataille gives an '*a*theological' perspective to the Crucifixion, not a theological perspective that would highlight Christ's divinity. As a result, Christ becomes an instance of human sacrifice, the very instance that Girard argues Christianity is against.[11]

As already suggested, a theology of the Cross confirms this. Girard, in evoking the image (as Mediator) without acknowledging it also evokes an understanding of the image that would become the foundation of the Christian basis of the law as manifest in the judicial system, a system geared to the proper care of victims. And we will return to this.

Now, if Christ's divinity is the image as such, then it is also the image that intervenes in the revelation that society has been founded on injustice because founded on the scapegoat mechanism. In this sense, the image is against violence. Until violence is quenched, nothing else matters. Thus, the relation of human to human as founded on love can only be realised after violence against the victims has been eradicated. As Girard puts it:

> Not to love one's brother and to kill him are the same thing. Every negation of the other leads [...] toward expulsion and murder. The basis for all of this lies in the fundamental human situation of a mimetic rivalry that leads to a destructive escalation. This is the reason why killing and dying are one and the same thing. To kill is to die, to die is to kill – for both stay within the circle of evil reciprocity, in which reprisals inevitably take place. Not to love is to die, therefore, since it is to kill. (1987b: 214)

*

In a section of *Things Hidden*, Girard discusses the difference between the 'Logos of Heraclitus and the Logos of John' (1987b: 262–280). Perhaps, predictably, the Heraclitean Logos is seen to evoke violence and the scapegoat, while the opposite is the case for the Johannine Logos, which 'discloses the truth of violence by having itself expelled' (271). 'Having itself expelled' means not being recognised as different from the Logos of violence, or the Logos of the sacrificial reading. In short: 'The Logos of love [the Johannine Logos] puts up no resistance; it always allows itself to be expelled by the Logos of violence' (274). To put up resistance is not to end violence, but to have it continue.

The Johannine principle that in the beginning there was the Logos/Word/*Verbe* is certainly addressed by Girard with regard to violence. But what about the image? For the thinker of incarnation, Michel Henry, when the '*Verbe*' becomes flesh in the world, this also means that it becomes image: the Word 'shows itself to other men *as a man who is the image of God*, it shows them this through this man who was the original Image of the image of which man was made; it shows the Word (*Verbe*) in him' (Henry 2000: 370).

Clearly, if Christ is an image, meaning as we have said that He is both divine and human, a key aspect here has to be the invisibility (cf. the Holy) that is borne by the image.[12] This is why we read in Mondzain commenting on Nicephorus's philosophy of the image that 'the visible is not the sensible' (1996: 125). In other words, Christ's divinity as image cannot appear in any form of human perception.

It is with regard to visibility/materiality that a theology of the image seems to be opposed to a secular conception of the image as transparent. That is, from the latter perspective, if Christ is the image that gives access to the Father, then he (not the Father) should be the invisible entity – the medium – that would allow the Holy to shine through. Christ's material body should disappear into the Holy and maybe it does in light of the Resurrection and the Ascension. In this regard, one should take particular note of Marion's point that Christ became invisible/intangible after the Resurrection. As Marion asks: 'Just what does the Cross actually give to be seen? Does it offer the type of a prototype?' (2013: 277). When discussing Christ being invisible to the disciples after the Resurrection, Marion (2002) seems to err on the side not of Christ being actually invisible as a phenomenal entity and visible in His divinity, but as invisible to the disciples because they lacked the means to comprehend what was being presented to them. However, to a non-theologian, the situation seems clear: it is a matter of Christ being recognised in His invisibility. Thus the King James version says: 'And their eyes were opened and they knew him. And he vanished out of their sight' (Luke 23:31). The various and numerous renderings of this passage more than allow for the interpretation that the disciples recognised Christ in His invisibility.

Christ becomes image in the fullest sense when He is recognised not just as another body, but when he is recognised as the 'Son of God': '[the centurion] alone recognized there the visible trace of the invisible God; he interpreted this corpse as a sign of God – or better, as the one who is God' (Marion 2013: 277). Marion goes on to refer to the 'irremediable mark of the invisible in the visible [that] takes the shape of the Cross' (278). Again: 'the visible humanity gives to be recognized in the person of Christ the invisible divinity; this divinity, however, was not in any way directly visible in the humanity of Christ' (285). Despite appearance, perhaps, Marion recognises that the image is not 'merely an object' but becomes 'the instrument of communion' (= mediation) (286). It is the issue of the image as object in the modern age that needs to be subjected to analysis.

It is Christ's status as image that is of absolute significance as far as the revelation of the truth about sacrificial violence is concerned. Although Girard emphasises and makes violence explicit, it is the image – Christ as image – that is in fact at issue at the deepest level of this situation. While Girard engages with the theology relating to violence, he neglects the theology relating to the image.

The Cross, then, is the revelation of the truth of sacrifice as founded in the innocent surrogate victim. Christ on the Cross discloses the truth of sacrifice. He is thus not a sacrificial victim but endures the ordeal of Crucifixion in order to reveal that sacrifice can only end violence *with* violence, and only for a limited period. The Cross condenses of all this. In this sense it is evoked in Blake's 'Auguries of Innocence' poem, where a grain of sand reveals the world, a wild flower reveals 'a Heaven', infinity is held 'in the palm of your hand' and 'an hour contains eternity'. In each case, the very small, not to say tiny, element contains what is immense. An image, in short, contains what is immense. Similarly, in the words of Levinas, the image is the part that contains the whole – the whole as Being (Levinas 1998: 29). If, in this sense, Christ is the image, par excellence, it means that He is the part that is also the whole of the divine.

Law and the Cross

If Christ's Crucifixion signals the injustice of the scapegoat mechanism, it means that society is founded in injustice. As Girard's summary puts it: 'The Cross derives its dissolving capacity from the fact that it makes plain the workings of what can now only be seen – after the Crucifixion – as evil' (1987b: 193). Or again: 'The victorious general is [. . .] Christ and his victory is the Cross' (1999: 184). What, however, does the victory of the Cross entail as far as ending the scapegoat mechanism is concerned? That is to say: what does it take to bring about a just society? In the first instance, Girard takes a theologically informed position, where it is a matter of loving one's enemies and of submitting to violence rather than inflicting violence (184). But there is, as has been mentioned earlier, also the law in its secular guise that plays a part in controlling, if not eliminating, the temptation to find scapegoats. When writing in the context of the 'triumph of the Cross', Girard claims that: 'The perspicacity on the subject of scapegoats is a true mark of superiority of our society over all previous societies' (207). The road to justice, then, is through the law.

The law and the Cross thus form the basis of Girard's thesis that the surrogate victim is at the origin of society. The latter incorporates the idea that societies based on sacrifice gave way to societies based on the rule of law, which would include, amongst other things, the notion of due process and the presumption of innocence. Only after the Crucifixion – thus in light of the Cross – was it possible for law to be based on the defence of the victim rather than as a tool of the persecutor. This, one can very plausibly argue, is Girard's position. Modern law, then, exists in the shadow of the Cross. However, exactly how, when, and in which societies law, in this sense, becomes the dominant form of organisation for Girard, is difficult to determine. Would it be uniquely Western-style societies that gave rise to a legal tradition, while other societies remain inured in sacrificial crises and the killing of surrogate victims? Girard's own work, in this regard, implies that mediaeval Europe was still largely caught in the scapegoat mechanism, even if, at the same time, as one commentator has pointed out, 'law could be found in many cupboards: in nature, in the Bible (divine law), in customs of the people, in the law of nations (*ius gentium*), as well in the positive law of the prince' (Pennington 1993: 2). As this quote indicates, the situation is complicated by the fact that there are so many different genres of law to take into account. Just as his invocation of hominisation hardly addresses the prehistory scholarship on this topic, Girard, perhaps for good reason, also neglects the scholarship on the history of the emergence of Western judicial institutions, or of the emergence of legal forms in non-Western nations, while yet claiming that: 'We owe our good fortune to one of our social institutions above all: our judicial system, which serves to deflect the menace of vengeance' (1979: 15).

Because of the complexity of the history of law, it is, in all probability, necessary to begin with the current state of affairs as regards the presence or absence of the judicial system in its fully modern guise. The true basis for modern law of a Western hue is, for Girard, as we know, Christianity and the culture that it underpins. The event of this underpinning is the Crucifixion signified by the Cross. In a sense, the Western judicial system is equally a recognition of the need to contain vengeful violence and a recognition (albeit implicit) of the Christological basis of the law – a basis that refuses the scapegoat mechanism as a means for containing violence.

Conclusion

For Girard, we have shown, the Crucifixion is the form of violence that not only confirms the injustice of the scapegoat as victim, but also gives rise to the manifestation of Christ's (pre-existing) divinity in the Resurrection. The proof of divinity is also confirmation of the status of Christ as image. According to Girard, Jesus as an exceptional historical individual willing to sacrifice himself on the cross would not carry sufficient weight to undermine the scapegoat principle upon which societies hitherto had been founded. As the messenger of the injustice of the scapegoat system, Christ foreshadows the development of the judicial institutions that are needed to prevent the fall back into processes of injustice.

Clearly, now that the nature of the relation between violence and the image in Girard's work has been investigated, the question arises as to whether or not Girard's privileging of Christianity in human relations as mediated by the articulation of the law is justified. Powerful as Girard's thesis might appear to be (for who could deny the justice of defending the victim?), it remains to be seen whether such a position can bring unity rather than division, a division at least partly manifest in the clash of religions, a clash that might re-open wounds of scapegoating. Girard's claim is that all religions begin to converge when it is a matter of the victim. The extent to which this is so and the extent to which those of different faiths and ideologies can find this acceptable is what remains to be determined.

Perhaps, indeed, Vattimo's secularising and pragmatic approach to Christianity and his opposition to all foundational – that is, metaphysical – logics, thereby giving rise to a thorough-going nihilism that somehow still remains within a Christian orbit, needs to be closely analysed and brought alongside Girard's defence of the victim. This, then, would also need to be the basis of a future investigation. In the latter, consideration would have to be given as to just how Vattimo's adherence to Nietzsche's claim that there are no facts, or eternal truths, only interpretations, can be reconciled with Girard's defence of 'facts' and a scientific (as Girard sees it) approach to myth. Moreover, what would also remain to be shown is just how the 'death of God' leads, in Girard's case, to the *founding* of religion (every true god must die[13]), and in Vattimo's case to the dethroning of the God of metaphysics, which is (according to Vattimo) what God really wants for humanity; for the death of metaphysics brings, at the same time, the collapse of domination manifest in the concentration of power.

Such, then, is the way that Girard's thought on the relation between violence and the image might constitute the basis of future research into different 'ways of life' – ways of life that aim to bring justice to the world.

Notes

1. Girard says that not only does Nietzsche's opposition to Christianity centre on the latter's defence of the victim, but it is this that also offers succour to Nazism's attack on victims. See Girard (1999: 222–227).
2. The Father in Freud's myth of the primal horde, it should be recalled, becomes more powerful after his death than he was before it.
3. Farneti elaborates as follows: 'the construal of such issues as Kingdom, Resurrection and Apocalypse is inherently theological, as it would be difficult to articulate their meaning without taking into account God's agency in history. A discourse concerning the very nature of God's final Kingdom, or Christ's resurrection, or the Apocalypse, is theological in a deep sense, and any attempt to bring such notions to bear on a purely anthropological reading of the Gospels would inevitably dissolve them' (2008: 33).
4. As is known, with regard to the importance of Christianity in contemporary society, Vattimo is Girard's comrade in arms. Indeed, it was Girard's work that, Vattimo says, 'made it possible for me to grasp the historical-progressive essence of Christianity' (2010: 27). Christianity

reveals the violence inherent in all metaphysical structures – that is, in every unquestionable absolute, including an omnipotent and omniscient God. In this context, Vattimo finds the *kenosis* of Jesus fundamental to linking Christianity with secularisation. Thus: 'The key term that I began using after having read Girard is just that: secularization, which I take to mean the effective realization of Christianity as a nonsacrificial religion' (28).

5. The theology on this is divided, with some theologians (following Aquinas) arguing that *kenosis* still presupposes divinity, while others propose a separation between *kenosis* and divinity. For a summary of the issues here, see White (2011). For his part, Vattimo is not interested in exploring the theology on which the concept of *kenosis* is based.

6. See, for example, the section entitled 'Le Triomphe de la croix' ('The Triumph of the Cross') in *Je vois Satan tomber comme l'éclair* (Girard 1999: 141–235).

7. Cf. the following remark from the study of the 'Triumph of the Cross': 'As the present study wishes to be as objective and "scientific" as possible, there is no question of accepting with eyes closed the evangelical opposition between God and Satan' (Girard 1999: 144).

8. Cf.: It is a question of 'biblical truth and the lie of mythology' (Girard 1999: 153). Clearly, such a position lends itself as much to a theological as a social-scientific appropriation. Even more is this the case when it is a question of the biblical presentation of the divinity of Christ.

9. 'There is nothing in the Gospels to suggest that the death of Jesus is a sacrifice' (Girard 1987b: 180); 'the sacrificial interpretation of the Passion must be criticized and exposed as a most enormous and paradoxical misunderstanding' (180).

10. 'Being iconoclastic, metaphysics condemns the image to the rank of an idol' (Marion 2013: 282).

11. A future investigation might well pursue the implications of the difference between Christ as sacrificial victim, as Bataille suggests, and the Crucifixion as the revelation of the injustice of the scapegoat mechanism. If we are correct in seeing the victim for Bataille as the one with whom one suffers, to the extent that Christ is a victim is the extent to which Bataille would come to experience His suffering. With Girard, on the other hand, Christ comes to announce the truth of the victimage mechanism to the extent that He Himself is not a victim. This raises the question of how Christ's innocence is to be understood. In this regard, the following statement by Girard is significant: 'violence will find in Jesus the most perfect victim that can be imagined, the victim that, for every conceivable reason, violence has the most reasons

to pick on. Yet at the same time, this victim is also the most innocent' (1987b: 208–209).
12. Commentators have not failed to remark on this. See Henry (2000: 369), Mondzain (1996), and, as we have seen, Marion (2013: 286–287).
13. Cf.: 'All gods begin first of all by dying' (Girard 2017: 158–159).

Conclusion: Understanding Violence, Image and Victim

TO CONCLUDE THIS STUDY, I endeavour to address certain questions and issues that I see arising from the foregoing chapters. Indeed, in crystallising issues deriving from the thought of Bataille, Agamben and Girard on violence and the image the key differences between the thinkers will become evident. For instance, Bataille's dualism directly clashes with Agamben's total opposition to dualistic thought, an opposition that might be partly explained by the thinker's adherence to a modal ontology, given that with the latter the being of an entity is inseparable from its mode. In other words, there is no opposition between an entity and its mode of being in the world.[1]

For his part, Girard, like Bataille, is on the side of the victim and claims that in the wake of Christ's Crucifixion modern judicial institutions are, at least potentially, the victim's latter-day protectors.[2] This, however, is far from being adequately explained; nor is the history of the law brought into the picture. Indeed, our defender of the victim leaves much to be desired when it comes to documenting the evolution of jurisprudence and how the law might have, over two millennia, acted as a bulwark against the scapegoat mechanism. The task at hand is not easy here. For if society is effectively founded in injustice (killing of a scapegoat), the law, as a rectification of, and protection from, injustice, has been made to appear very much wanting. This is so in the work of the thinkers germane to this study, namely, in Agamben,

Benjamin and Derrida. However, law, rather than taking an explicitly 'victim' approach, aligns itself with justice. And it is the latter, Derrida has endeavoured to show, that is difficult, if not impossible to achieve. Or, indeed, as we shall see below, Derrida argues that justice and an experience of the impossible are inseparable (1990: 947).

From Girard's perspective, through the law the community takes responsibility for violence, whereas, with the societies based on the scapegoat mechanism, the community puts responsibility for the violence onto the surrogate victim. To a large extent, throughout the preceding chapters violence has been human violence, and, specifically, that of the killing, maiming or infliction of pain on one or more humans by other humans. Animal violence and the violence of nature have not been part of the story.

Even though violence and, to a lesser extent, the image, has been at centre stage in what has been illuminated and discussed, it is true that violence as such (violence as a theoretical concept) has only been thematised by Agamben as 'mediality'. Ditto for the image. But even with violence as a means, the very nature of violence is still not addressed. Violence as mediality does not tell us if violence is a violation, or a difference that destroys the integrity of identity, the death that dissolves all boundaries. While Girard sees Judeo-Christian culture giving rise to the law as the protector of the victim, Agamben proposes that law and political sovereignty are one, a sovereignty that derives from the (real or mythical) killing of *homo sacer*. Law is therefore inseparable from the play of violence and, in deciding on the exception, is complicit in its own suspension. In this way, despite Girard's positive announcements regarding the hegemony of the modern judicial system, for Agamben law opens the way to violence.[3] In other words, instead of bringing a halt to indiscriminate violence, Agamben clearly names law as its source, particularly since the second half of the nineteenth century. This explains why law will eventually become – presumably as the outcome of a progressive politics – something to be deactivated and abandoned, like a child's plaything.[4] In short, modern law begins in violence (as it does with Benjamin) and subsequently opens the way to violence by legitimating the nexus between sovereignty and the exception. From Agamben's perspective, then, the mistake that Girard makes is to think that, in being founded in Judeo-Christian culture, law's essential purpose is to be bring an end to persecutory violence.

Although Bataille speaks in an anthropological key that evokes the sacred and the profane, prohibition and transgression, the law, in the form of juridical institutions, would ultimately be part of the restricted economy. The law would keep at bay the inevitable violence wrought by the general economy. As we recall: the violence of the general economy is a feature of human existence, which, nevertheless, must be fought against. In this sense, Bataille's approach to law corresponds more to that of Girard than of Agamben.

Girard, Law and Christianity

As to its history, we have seen that there are diverse forms of the law (cf. Pennington 1993). Nevertheless, mythically, within the Judaeo-Christian tradition, the Father is the source of the law (not the Son). But this is moral rather than positive law.[5] There are, nevertheless, explicit substantive elements in positive law, such as: due process[6] that includes the presumption of innocence; the primacy of evidence; *habeas corpus*.[7] The point is that Girard only mentions the 'judicial system' in passing. Its history and mechanics are never addressed.[8] That is, it is never extensively thematised, and not at all problematised. The opposite is the case with Agamben where the law is entirely problematised because of its intimate link with sovereignty, and therefore with power. The latter derives from Agamben's appropriation of Schmitt's political theology, which, as we know, identifies sovereignty with the exception – that is, with the right to commit violence. The exception, indeed, almost covers what is essential about the law for Agamben.

Law of the Father, which psychoanalysis follows, evokes patriarchy. Andrew Benjamin has argued that the question of God is the question of law (2019: 2), whereas the question of the Son (Christ) is equivalent to the law's suspension.[9] If this were so, Girard's position becomes tenuous. For he argues, as we know, that it is only with Christ and Christian culture that the basis of modern judicial institutions – that bring an end to sacrificial violence – come into being. The history of the Western legal tradition shows that the values of the presumption of innocence, etc., mentioned earlier, as well as the resolution of disputes and prevention of violence by legal means, as opposed to family vendetta, monetary sanctions, or legal proof established through the ordeal, emerged at the beginning of the modern era, that is, progressively after the proclamation of Magna Carta in 1215.

Aspects of the History of the Western Legal Tradition

The evolution of the Western legal tradition from the eleventh century onward is a torturous and complex one, as the work of legal historian, Harold Berman demonstrates well.[10] While Magna Carta, which inaugurated the tradition of the lawful judgment by equals of those accused, along with the writ of *habeas corpus*,[11] underpins the values of the Western legal tradition, this tradition is in fact a synthesis of diverse sources,[12] beginning with Germanic[13] folklaw (*sic*). The latter was initially based in blood feud resulting from inter-clan and inter-familial rivalries – just as Girard would have predicted.[14] 'Germanic society in 1075 was dominated by primitive legal institutions. It was a predominantly tribal society, with very weak central authorities. Law was almost wholly embedded in the social, economic, political, and religious life of the society. Blood feud was a normal means of resolution and dispute' (Berman 1983: 11). In referring uniquely to England, William Duker paints a similar picture (see Duker 1978: 955–957).

In favour of Agamben's thesis of *homo sacer*, Berman mentions 'outlawry, involving forfeiture of all goods and liability to be *killed by anyone with impunity*' (Berman 1978: 565; emphasis added). Berman comments:

> Legal historians have given to this type of law the name Archaic Law. In its main outlines, it was characteristic not only of the Germanic peoples in the period prior to the eleventh and twelfth centuries, but also of all Indo-European peoples, from Kent to Kashmir, at one time or another in their development. (565)

It is obviously a big leap to say that, in some way, the one who can be 'killed by anyone with impunity' is the basis of modern legal sovereignty. What is ignored is the evolution of the law, fuelled by the impetus of Christianity and, after the Enlightenment, by the values of modernity.

Christianity did not initially overcome Germanic folklaw. In fact, it did not threaten the latter's existence at all, as Berman explains:

> One might suppose that the new religion that gradually spread through Europe between the fifth and tenth centuries would have threatened the very existence of the Germanic folklaw, which was founded in tribal myths of warring gods, in worship of rivers, woods,

and mountains, in concepts of the divine descent of the tribal kings, in absolute loyalty to kinship and lordship ties, and in an overriding belief in fate. Christianity replaced the old myths with the gospel of a universal Creator, Father of all men, who once appeared on earth in the form of His Son, Jesus Christ, worship of whom brings freedom from bondage to all earthly ties, freedom from fate, freedom from death itself. These new ideas must have seemed strange and abstract to Germanic men. (568)

Nor did Christianity pose a threat to 'Germanic social institutions', as can be seen from the fact that, 'the Church did not oppose blood-feud and ordeals; it only said they could not bring salvation, which came from faith and good works' (570). Moreover, the Church, as an institution, did not stand apart from social and cultural life (as would be the case in the modern era). Instead, '[e]cclesiastical and secular jurisdictions were intermingled' (570). Indeed: 'Christianity was Germanized at the same time that the Germanic peoples were Christianized' (570).

Again, seemingly in tacit support of Girard's view, Berman emphasises that folklaw, before Christianity, was concerned above all with the control of blood feud (582). Folklaw rested on honour and fate. 'the penitential law of the Church rested fundamentally on concepts of repentance and forgiveness' (582).

But before Christ's Crucifixion and the revelation of the truth of the scapegoat can be accepted as the dominant influence on modern Western judicial institutions, one is confronted by the far from simple evolution of the Christian Church – of the *institution* of the Church. Thus, the history of Christianity and the law is all about their, at times, troubled co-emergence. In 1075 Pope Gregory VII declared the absolute supremacy of the Pope and the Catholic Church and the subservience to spiritual power of the Emperor as the embodiment of temporal power. The culmination of the Pope's dominance leads eventually, as we know, to Luther and the Reformation, followed by the growing secularism of the modern era (1750 onward).

Rather than undivided support for the victim, Berman notes that, 'Luther also supported the adoption and strict enforcement of laws on vagrancy, begging, respectability, sumptuousness of dress, and the like' (1983: 18) and that 'both Lutheranism and the *Carolina*[15] share a revulsion against cruelty and arbitrariness; both place a high value on humaneness and consistency. Yet *both accept a certain amount of cruelty as inevitable – neither is willing to proclaim its complete abolition*' (22–23; emphasis added). As an institution, then, the Church, as opposed to Christ's death in support of all victims, partly aligns with the persecutors, something Girard fails to take into consideration, so concerned is he to put the case that Christ reveals the truth of the persecutory nature of pre-Christian social relations based on sacrificial violence.[16]

On the other hand, Berman points out that legal positivism (which dominates contemporary concepts of law and implies the separation of positive law from natural and customary law) was first proposed by the scholastic philosopher and theologian, Peter Abelard (1079–1142) (Berman 1983: 8n7) and that, subsequently, '[t]he Reformation laid the foundation for modern legal positivism' (18–19). More work would be required to show just what the implications of this influence of Christianity on law have been; suffice it say that explicit reference to the victim as such is unlikely, even if the implications might well favour victims over persecutors. But this is uncertain. All the more so if one takes Agamben's approach to law where the victim hardly counts, given that, for him, modern law is ultimately in the hands of sovereign power.

Agamben on Law and Image

But is the approach of Agamben to law a valid one? In this regard, we note that his focus (following Benveniste) on the text of the Roman grammarian, Sextus Pompeius Festus (*c.* 200 AD) on the origin of the term, *homo sacer*, is driven not by scholarship revealing the influence of Roman law in the history of Western politics, but by the influence of Schmitt's political theology and the latter's claims about the relation between sovereignty and the exception. The plausibility of Agamben's thesis that *homo sacer* is at the heart of sovereignty and the law is significantly reduced when it is recalled that a form of *homo sacer* is the basis of archaic societies, societies yet to take on the character of what could broadly be called 'European'. Berman's reference to Archaic folklaw – the law in operation prior to the eleventh and twelfth centuries – and to the killing of the outlaw by anyone with impunity does not occur in the context of a state apparatus.

For Magnus Fiskesjö, who takes a historical and ethnographic approach, *homo sacer* is anything but the basis of the modern judicial state:

Looking to history, we find punishments similar to homo sacer's [sic] exclusion from a home community noted from many places across Europe. However, they are everywhere firmly associated with *a situation in which judicial institutions guaranteed by state violence do not exist*; instead such banishments appear as the self-policing of nonstate communities without maintaining a police or military force commanded by a king or an emperor to enforce institutionalized law, and its judgments. (Fiskesjö 2012: 171; emphasis added)

This suggests that there is no historical, organic link between *homo sacer* and modern state power, or to the reality of sovereignty, but only to an image – *homo sacer* as an image – that acts, as has been said in Chapter 3, as the symmetrical other of sovereign power, and this is so because Agamben continually works with symmetries, whether or not these exist in reality. Up to a point, symmetries can be illuminating; after this point they begin to resemble a writer's 'tic'.

The image as mediality that appears as such, politics as mediality, pure violence as mediality – all of these domains presuppose that the medium becomes equivalent to the thing, or object, itself; or, rather, the medium becomes an *end* in itself, thus demonstrating that ends cannot easily be dispensed with. In order to subvert the idea and reality of ends (politics, for Agamben, is not about the realisation of a project, or an end), Agamben simply turns means into an end, the end becomes the drive for the open, the fragment, the incomplete, the technique, or style (the 'how'), rather than the result (the 'what'). But, then, what about law? Given our theorist's hostility to law, it is likely that it must fall into the category of ends, rather than means. Certainly, one is hard put to say that law is transparent (characteristic of means). But surely law is not an end in any simple sense.

Again, to take a leaf out of Girard's book, one can hope that a society founded in judicial institutions will be permanently established, but this is far from glorifying such institutions for their own sake. What is hoped for is that institutions will be the means of limiting, if not preventing, scapegoating and sacrificial violence. Ironically for Agamben, Weber, as is well known, characterised modern society as one of means, rather than ends – a society, as is known, of *zweckrationalität* – of means-ends rationality. On this basis, we would already be in a society of means, and this, for many, is the problem. Agamben's point (which is also Girard's) is, no doubt (and here he follows Benjamin), that there are, and always can be, bad laws, laws that are discriminatory and unjust (as was the case in Nazi Germany). Indeed, there can be laws that justify violence as much as inhibit it. On this basis, the law – or laws – must be embedded in values that give rise to the 'right' law – that law, as is the case on the Continent,[17] needs to be embedded in 'Right' (cf. German, *Recht*, French, *droit*, Italian, *diritto*, Latin, *ius*),[18] even if this 'Right' is historically determined.

Pennington observes that in the thirteenth century, the notion of 'bad' laws did not hold because all laws were deemed to be reflective of the will of the prince: 'The jurists had decided in the first half of the thirteenth century that the will of the prince was the key element that defined the validity of positive law. Therefore, if a statute of positive law was "bad", that is unreasonable or unjust, it was still valid law' (Pennington 1994: 211). Eventually, Pennington shows, such a position ceases to hold as the prince or other supposedly ultimate authority becomes subject to certain norms – such as being forbidden to 'expropriate property arbitrarily or to rule tyrannically' (212). The point is that a pragmatic position (the position of jurists in practice) on law is unable, or unwilling, to address the issue of 'bad' laws. Agamben does so, but only by dismissing – 'deactivating' – the law in relation to achieving laudable ends in its entirety.[19] This is a vast overreach. Sceptical as Agamben might be, then, law as such has to be understood as being, if not founded in justice, at least as being inseparable from it (that is as being inseparable from 'good' laws, laws as *Recht, doit, diritto*, etc).

Law and justice

As is known, Derrida, for his part, is apparently opposed to understanding law as the harbinger of justice. Indeed, he claims that justice, 'if such a thing exists, *outside or beyond law*, is not deconstructible. No more than desconstruction itself, if such a thing exists. Deconstruction is justice' (Derrida 1990: 945; emphasis added). Law here becomes separate and distinct from justice. Law does not equal justice because it is, or has largely functioned as, a calculus: 'Law is the element of calculation' (947), whereas 'justice is incalculable' (947). The problem here is that the 'purity'[20] of justice is such that existence (whether as act or law) tells against it ever being realised. Intuitively, Derrida seems to recognise the problem here and concedes that law does play a part in the manifestation of justice, but it is law that is not simply the application of a rule, a principle, a programme, a prescription or a precedent; it is not the law as a mechanical apparatus primed to spit out a ruling. This mode of the law exists, but it is not the mode that allows justice to be realised. The latter can only occur in the just *decision*, a decision made in all urgency, yet in freedom, a freedom that would radically separate the just decision from one that is entirely formulaic, one that did not endeavour to be in harmony with the *singularity* of the case at issue. This, Derrida claims, is a decision that is also undecidable: 'A decision that didn't go through the ordeal of the undecidable would not be a free decision, it would only be the programmable application or unfolding of a calculable process. It might be legal; it would not be just' (963). Ultimately, a decision must be made. Indeed, it must not be delayed! If it is not to be another idealist dead-end, justice has to appear; and it does this by way of the – or a – law. Derrida acknowledges this in as far as, according to him, the decision-maker must *claim* a law in which the decision is couched:

> this freedom or this decision of the just, if it is one, must follow a law or a prescription, a rule. In this sense, in its very autonomy, in its freedom to follow or to give itself laws, it must have the power to be of the calculable or programmable order, for example as an act of fairness. But if the act simply consists of applying a rule, of enacting a program or effecting a calculation, we might say that it is legal, that it conforms to law, and perhaps, by metaphor, that it is just, but we would be wrong to say that the decision was just. (961)

The law can render justice, then, as long as law is not simply reducible to a mechanical application. Significantly, Derrida's is an *internal* perspective on law – law as it is enacted in decisions made by judges. Historically, as Hunt indicates (1987: 10–13), an internal perspective is in keeping with a conservative conception of law. To be sure an internal approach is absolutely relevant, but it is not the end of the story. An *external* approach – such as is adopted by Girard – views law as such as a symbolic formation that stands for justice as the assurance of the rights of the victim. This is its deepest aspiration, whether or not this is realised in practice. In any event, I argue that not only is there no justice without law, but that a form of law – law as such – is the necessary face of justice. This is so even if, historically, the application of the law has been less than perfect.

On this basis, law becomes an end (justice) and is not simply a means (the everyday practice of law). Rather than giving up on the law in toto, as Agamben does, it is a matter of defending it in terms of its substantive, or essential aspect. If this is done, Girard's case in promoting the importance of judicial institutions assumes greater significance.

The Image and Object – The Image as Object

We have seen that the victim for Bataille is the victim in reality, the actual, suffering victim. Unlike both Agamben and Girard, Bataille does not take a speculative approach to the victim – the victim of violence. In the Chinese torture photos, the victim is there, suffering. But does an image really provide access to what is imaged? This was the question addressed in Chapter 2. Or is it a superficial presentation of an instance of the phenomenal world? In short, does an image give the illusion that access to the 'in itself' is possible? Again, the issue of mediality (to use Agamben's term) arises. Can mediality appear as such? If it did, would it be the mediality that it is?

In Object Oriented Ontology (OOO), as it is presented by Graham Harman (2018), the real object never appears to the human in its entirety, if at all. For along with the phenomenal domain, which appears to consciousness, there is also the noumenal realm, which does not. The world, in short, is more than its appearance to human consciousness. Such an approach is opposed to what Quentin Meillassoux calls 'correlationism'[21] – the idea derived from Kant that the world is the phenomenal, human world, that reality is human reality, as these are knowable through human consciousness, and as what can be experienced through the senses. For Harman, therefore, a sensual object (object of experience) can appear, but not a real object.[22] Consequently, in a manner that is analogous to the image as mediality (where the image is an object quite distinct from reality), Harman's sensual object is distinct from any real object, the latter being inaccessible.

Does the sensual object fall foul of Sartre's 'illusion of immanence'? – the illusion that the image is an object in its own right and is quite distinct from what is imaged? As Sartre explains, the illusion of immanence emerges when

> we [...] implicitly suppose that there exist two complementary worlds: one of things and one of images, and that, each time one

is obscured the other is thereby illuminated. This is putting images on the same plane as things, giving both the same type of existence. (Sartre 2004: 43)

If avoiding the illusion of immanence entails that the image not be conceived as an object or thing, is a privileging of consciousness not a problem, given that Sartre, follower of Husserl in the mid-1930s when his book on the imaginary was composed, also privileges consciousness? Perhaps it is but let us not rush to judgement just yet.

Harman's sensual object seems to correspond to Sartre's object of perception. But the latter has to do with knowledge, whereas the sensual object has to do with sensual qualities. The key point, however, is that while for Sartre knowledge via perception is cumulative, the image of the object is immediate. And it is precisely the category of the image that is absent from Harman's account. Perception and image are two relations that consciousness has with the object. Although the image is a relation of consciousness for Sartre, it is not a product of subjectivity, but is determined by the object. The image is the presence of the object in its absence, as can be demonstrated by the image in painting and especially in photography, where the image is not equivalent to the material of its incarnation (paint, canvas, frame, etc. – that is, it is not equivalent to a perception), but to what is imaged. This has been well covered in Chapter 2 in relation to Bataille above and elsewhere, and so does not require further elaboration here.

The question is: in what sense does a reading of key works by Bataille, Agamben and Girard show how the image, as the presence of the object in its absence, relates to violence? Although violence is almost impossible to define,[23] we assume that it is a form of disorder, if not of chaos. This raises the question as to whether violence can be an object, given that the latter is order, while violence is, at minimum, disorder. Could the image then be anything but a form of order in relation to violence? Does this mean – despite what has been discussed in relation to Bataille and Chinese torture – that violence can never be captured in an image because the image would be an amelioration of violence? If one wants to soften violence, just turn it into an image.

This, however, is to fall foul of the illusion of immanence because it is to assume that the image and the object have difference qualities – that the image is ordered, while violence as object is disordered, whereas the principle of the presence of the thing in its absence says that if what is imaged is violence then the image is the image of violence.

To be sure, Agamben's definition of the image as pure mediality cannot cope with the Sartrian principle. Through his interpretation of the work both written and filmic of Guy Debord, Agamben proposes that the image *is* an object. But this is to imply, in effect, that the image can never incarnate violence, that violence as such is unreachable, as though it descended on the world without the world being in the least in touch with what would be happening to it. Andy Warhol's car crash images would not be delivering the real thing to us.

What of the victim, violence and the image? Certainly, while victim and violence are quite explicit in the work of the three thinkers, the image marks a more problematic involvement. Or, at least this is the case outside of a religious or theological context; for in the latter, Christ suffers death as the image – that is, as being both human and divine. As an image, Christ can bring an end to sacrificial violence, or at least He can illuminate the truth that the sacrificial victim was/is innocent. Such indeed, as we have seen, is Girard's interpretation of the significance of the Cross.

Certainly, iconoclasm, as a movement, committed acts of violence against icons, if not against images. For violence against an image is in fact against the material icon, which implies an element of violence against Christ, violence against the thing in its absence, thus against what can make present what is absent, just as Christ can incarnate divine presence. Even though Girard's claim that the Crucifixion sets the scene for the whole of Western judicial culture is vastly in need of scholarly elaboration, it also opens the way for an understanding of the image in secular society that would be informed by Judaeo-Christian experience encapsulated in the notion of the simultaneity of the human and the divine in a single entity. Just as Christ at one level *is* God, so the image *is* what is imaged. Sartre's view of the image as the presence of the thing in its absence is perfectly in harmony with this, even if it is not popular today to say so.

Medium

In light of our study, it is worth considering medium as environment (or as absolute immanence), as Bataille implies[24] and the work of Mark Hansen has shown.[25] To be ensconced in a medium is to be in a state of immanence without the possibility of objectifying the medium.[26] With regard to the image, it is a matter of being ensconced in what is imaged, something that can perhaps be exemplified most strongly by cinema and photography.[27]

The critic's position with regard to the image is, of course, one where the image is objectified. This implies, however, that the critic will fail to appreciate the image *qua* image. This suits Agamben very well to the extent that mediality can be an object of study, while for Bataille, as was shown in Chapter 2, the image is not an object and least of all is it determined by its media specificity, which is ultimately McLuhan's position.

What is characteristic of many discussions of 'medium' (and the image as medium) is the failure to make distinctions, the first of these being to distinguish a medium from an object. But also – with particular reference to Agamben:

- Medium, as frequently noted (e.g., Krämer 2015), meant middle in Latin (also, middle in French is 'milieu').
- To be in the *middle* of the ocean or desert suggests being 'submerged in' to the extent of being unable to comprehend where one is. Compare: '*in medias res*' ('into the middle of things') as used in literature and cinema. Agamben fails to take this into account in his interpretation of Debord.
- Fenves (1998), as we saw in Chapter 3, noted that a 'pure middle' would have to be 'an immediate middle' that is essentially a medium and seems to evoke Benjamin's term, *reine Mittel* (pure means).

Comparatively speaking, then, the foregoing study reveals that Agamben's approach to medium as mediality is lacking in nuance.

Bataille and Nietzsche

It has also been shown that, unlike Bataille, Nietzsche focuses in on the suffering of the hero, and not on the suffering of any victim. The difference is that while the victim's suffering is caused by external sources, the hero's suffering is the result (whether witting or not) of his own actions. The hero copes through the outpouring of Dionysian anguish evocative of musical dissonance. And the victim? – how does a victim cope? Bataille's thinking offers a response to this, one revealed by the *lingchi* photos as analysed in Chapter 2. Rather than a psychoanalytically inflected approach, Bataille's relation to violence is to be at one with the victim of the torture, but not through identification, which is a self-conscious thus subjective act. Rather, as opposed to what would amount to a subjectivist ethic, the violence that constitutes the victim determines the form of the relation between victim and non-victim. In other words, we are dealing with an incarnation of Bataille's notion of communication, a notion of communication that is not reducible to a subject-to-subject encounter.

Is there a Truth about Violence?

In a vein similar to Agamben's, it was noted in the Introduction that the sociologist, Pierre Bourdieu, argues that there is symbolic violence. For Bourdieu, the state not only has a monopoly of the legitimate use of physical force (as Weber said), but also has a monopoly over the legitimate use of *symbolic* violence. Broadly speaking, symbolic violence includes intimidation, exemplified by, amongst other things, reputation as the basis of the ascendency of certain views and ideas in the play of *habitus* or acquired predispositions making one susceptible (or unsusceptible) to, 'reproachful looks' or 'tones', or to 'disapproving glances' (Bourdieu 1992: 51). Moreover, not only are intellectuals the wielders of symbolic violence but they are also its most notable victims. Here again, the foregoing description hardly proves to be very helpful in circumscribing the nature of violence.

References to symbolic violence – the forms of violence that would include Derrida's 'violence of the letter' – reinforce the impression that what is, in all seriousness, *called* violence *is* violence. Here, recall Heidegger's claim mentioned in the Introduction that interpretation can be violent. The problem with this wide-ranging notion of what violence can be is that it relates essentially to humans. That is, violence becomes that which *humans* call violence. Creatures other than humans are unable to speak of the violence done against them. They thus depend on humans to speak and act on their behalf. But it is still what humans call violence that counts as violence. Here, we are not dealing with a form of relativism but with the fact that violence is at the limit of thought and – to recall Bataille – perhaps at the limit of language.[28]

In this vein, and to underline how broad the notion of violence has become, we can in passing recall that Vattimo identifies violence with metaphysics (especially with metaphysics as the idea of an ultimate foundation, or origin[29]), in as far as the latter does not allow for further thought, for further questioning. Vattimo elaborates:

> Philosophically, violence can only be defined as the silencing of questions. That may happen in brutal forms, but also in philosophical forms, as when a philosopher concludes that he has reached the origin of all problematics: an example is Descartes's *cogito*. Obviously, metaphysics has not always been the origin of violence; but it is the case that the moments of greatest violence in history have always been justified by well-structured metaphysical pretenses. Burning heretics was a form of violence defended, in metaphysical terms, by a religion that professed an ultimate truth. (2019: 95)

Thus, for Vattimo and for Bataille (although from very different perspectives), violence is a form of silencing.

Derrida, as we have seen in Chapter 5, opts for a version of symbolic violence in his commentary on Lévi-Strauss's *Tristes Tropiques* in *Of Grammatology* (2016: 116–127). We recall that: 'The entire "Writing Lesson" is recited in the tones of violence contained or deferred, a violence sometimes deaf, but always oppressive and heavy' (116). Of course, he also refers to writing as *violating* presence, and to 'the violence of arche-writing, the violence of difference, of classification, and of the system of appellations' (119). How is this not to propose (a form of) violence at the origin? – we may well ask. In what sense is Derrida really at odds with Girard as far as the origin is concerned? And is he really at odds with Bataille, given that he refers to the presence of the anthropologist/spectator as a 'violation' of boundaries – a sort of empirical or literal violence? Is violence ultimately a violation of presence?

Presence as (a form of) identity is deconstructed to the extent that there is no identity without difference – that is to say, without identity being 'differed/deferred'. When the 'violation of presence' was mentioned, what should also have been mentioned was that as far as the deconstructionist is concerned it is the 'metaphysics of presence' that is at issue, not presence – not identity – as such. Full presence – complete identity – is always already violated, always a failed integrity.

Violence has always already taken place. And we cannot suppose that there was an original identity to be violated without privileging identity. Consequently, violence is more original than identity.

Nevertheless, it is clear on the other hand, that violence *qua* violence is never explicitly thematised by Derrida but is always assumed to be self-evident in its meaning and its functioning. This is but a further indication as to how difficult it is to define violence, Jean-Luc Nancy's attempt notwithstanding. In short, Derrida's approach to violence does not contradict the notion that violence is what is called violence.

*

It may be objected, however, that to adopt the position that what is *called* violence *is* violence opens the way for apparently cruel acts of torture and other violations not being called violent. Again, an apparently docile act might be called violent because, subjectively, it is experienced as violent, or there might be a pretence on the part of someone that an act was experienced as violent when, in fact, it was not. Thus, an objective basis for violence seems to be required. But is this issue of pretence – to focus on it for a moment – any different from that of illness as either genuine or simulated? In this situation it is a matter of being alert to objective symptoms, symptoms that the claimant would be unable to hide or control if it was a matter of a genuine illness. Let us say, then, that the notion of violence as what is called violence must also engage with what might be seen as objective criteria. In other words, the claim that violence has occurred must be justified.

What has not yet been addressed is the notion of 'acceptable violence'. If, as Bataille claims, there is always a degree of violence in eroticism, this suggests that there is a mode of violence that is not necessarily experienced negatively. We need to ask, though, whether what is *called* violence in eroticism *is* violence. To close the argument, some may believe that all one need do is evoke the name of the divine Marquis de Sade. For, surely, erotic pleasure in Sade is founded on real violence. It is no doubt impossible to give a definitive answer here, but two points can be made. The first is that the violence in question is largely, if not exclusively, perpetrated on the victim for the pleasure of the persecutor.[30] The victim does not experience such violence as pleasure. Secondly, Bataille's position, as was explained in Chapter 1, is that the Sadian universe, were it to be entirely replicated in 'normal' society, would bring about the latter's demise. Consequently, there can never be a generalised eroticism, just as transgression can never be generalised – can never become the norm – however much certain romantics might pine for this. From the position of the normal social being the violence of eroticism is therefore to be opposed.

It could be argued that Bataille's approach to violence and language should prevail (i.e., where violence is, there is no language) and that what is called 'symbolic violence' is in fact 'will to violence' – violence threatened, but not enacted. Actual violence, by contrast, is always traumatic (i.e., it bypasses the symbolic) and is a violation (it transgresses boundaries), while so-called symbolic violence, as a mediating force, is never entirely traumatic. So-called, symbolic violence is – to use Freud's term – a displacement of trauma.

Against this, it is known that certain victims are indeed *traumatised* by what is said, or gestured, or uttered in some form. Indeed, certain forms of sexual abuse, because they are committed on a victim prior to puberty, are repressed, and that what becomes traumatic can be a seemingly innocent memory after puberty. In this regard, the case Freud relates in *A Project for a Scientific Psychology* (1954) and analysed subsequently by Jeffrey Mehlman (1996), concerns a girl's phobia about going into shops alone. The victim had been abused in a shop at a time before puberty and was thus unaware of the significance of what had happened to her. After puberty the shop phobia presented itself, such that the memory of shop assistants laughing at her clothes became traumatic. Freud comments: 'Here we have an instance of a memory exciting an affect which it had not excited as an experience' (1954: 413).

The notion of violation does of course have a close connection to the law. As it is said, the moral law regarding the sanctity of human life is inviolate – that is, it should never be violated. Just laws should never be violated. To break the law is to commit an infringement – to encroach beyond a certain border, or boundary.[31] In this sense, it is notable that the law as such is subject to a certain violence; it does not simply mete out violence, as Agamben suggests. Every crime is a violation of the law, and every unauthorised violation of the person (to give just one example) is a crime.

However, the concept of violation with regard to law does not, of course, simply apply to the law in a legal or juridical context. It applies also to physical laws. One can, in an English context,[32] speak, for instance, of the violation of the second law of thermo-dynamics. The question – one that cannot be answered here – is whether the violation of law in any context presupposes violence and the violation of identity.

For Girard, as has been pointed out, the violence of the Crucifixion gives rise to support for the victim. In the most literal sense, the Crucifixion is a violation of the body of Christ. Nietzsche, who compares himself to Christ – Nietzsche who supports the persecutor – does not experience the violation of his body, nor is this body subject to traumatic violence, even if it is racked – violated – by illness.

Agamben's rejection of the law and his commitment to 'pure violence', leaves unanswered the question of the victim/object of this violence. In this context, it can be shown that, like Nietzsche, Agamben ultimately takes the side of the persecutor despite his rhetoric in favour of those, like refugees, who have become latter-day incarnations of *homo sacer*.

For Agamben, too, the image (to return to it) participates in the world of the human as sabbatical animal, where it has the function of acclamation. Ultimately, the activity called work will either no longer exist as such, or will exist only minimally. It is possible to read Agamben as the advocate of this position, a position that is supposedly in keeping with the true being of the human. As for the utopian Marx, so for Agamben: overcoming the lie that the human is reducible to work is what is at stake. Seen in this context, Agamben, clearly, does not wish to be a dualistic thinker. It must be *either* work *or* play. Bataille's thought, it has been shown, is the very opposite of this. Thus, in his reading of Sade and in his veneration of work, Bataille confirms that he is a dualistic thinker: yes, work can and does give way to play and all that that entails, but work is still an essential aspect of the human as a social being. In this light, we can speculate that a certain genre of radical thought believes that it is radical to the extent that it works to abolish all dualisms in the interest of promoting a single domain. In Agamben, the latter is 'play', the festival, nudity, the pornographic, action for its own sake (never for a particular end) and generalised profanation. The latter means never respecting existing dualisms, no matter how revered they might be. Thus, everything that has hitherto existed in the shadows of human life (Bataille's 'general economy') is to be brought to the fore, so that all dualisms, as the incarnation of inauthenticity, can be abolished.[33] With profanation, for instance, Agamben argues that what is profaned (the sacred, or unreachable object) can be returned to 'use' (2015b: 73).

Perhaps, more profoundly for Agamben, it can become the source of play (75).[34] It may be the sacred domain that serves as an example of what can be profaned, but the point is that profanation serves to bring everything under the same roof, as it were. There is no longer anything essentially 'outside' the profaned, no hidden, secret or concealed domain to which objects withdraw. But even if this is the case, it is necessary to profane *even* 'the unprofanable'.[35]

We have, then, an indication as to why mediality and therefore the image becomes entirely opaque and present for Agamben. For there can be no dualism of invisible means and opaque ends; mediality, in short, cannot withdraw into the object, but must appear in its own right, as it supposedly does in Debord's films. Similarly, violence as mediality would normally not appear in virtue of being mediality; it thus appears in Agamben's thinking because there is in principle nothing that does not appear. Here, there is indeed what could be called absolute appearing the purpose of which is to render meaningless the very notion of dualism.

*

Both Girard and Bataille agree that the realm of the sacred is essentially violent. Unlike Girard, who views the sacred as something to be overcome, Bataille sees it as part of what it means to be human – part of the general economy that needs, as far as possible, to be kept under wraps, even if this is a Sisyphean task. The general economy – the underbelly of human life – cannot ever be avoided. But, at the same time, it is imperative to fight against it overtaking the restricted economy – the latter being the economy of work and 'normal', non-violent social life. This is the basis of Bataille's dualism.

Girard, who, in the end, is not a dualist, holds out the prospect that the human underbelly can be overcome in light of the Crucifixion. The underbelly can be overcome because Christ reveals the truth of its existence. Judicial institutions, based in a Christianised culture without always recognising it, have the task, as has been seen, of overcoming sacrificial violence, a violence often originating in the rivalries that characterise human desire.

Three thinkers, then, raise questions about violence and the image that should prompt us – especially in the current climate of violence – to go in search of answers, even if this search proves to be an endless one.

Can the Victim Speak?

A key question implicit in this study has been: can the human victim – *qua* victim – of violence, speak? Could one imagine those designated as scapegoats being able to speak – that is, defend themselves – on their own behalf? Here, it is reasonable to say that being condemned to silence at the moment of persecution is part of being a victim, whatever might be said or done after the suffering has concluded, as current forms of speaking out would illustrate. Girard's work, in particular, opens a way to thinking the issues here. Even if it were possible for a scapegoat to utter words, such an utterance will never make any difference. This is the precise situation in the death camps. There, no words – no speech – uttered by the victims would make any difference. The persecutor, as interlocutor, is totally oblivious to the victim's words. Violence against the victims becomes a sign – if violence can be a sign – of this obliviousness. Agamben's study, *Remnants of Auschwitz* (2005c), with its focus on the issue of being a witness to what happened in the camps, opens up a parallel trajectory with regard to the speech of the inmates: 'Auschwitz is the radical refutation of every principle of obligatory communication' (65). This is so in particular because, as the '*Muselmann*' (the Muslim) shows, inmates are reduced to a state where the border between the human and the non-human becomes indistinct. Perhaps – if one were to accept Agamben's overall approach – the *Muselmann* would be the most radical incarnation of the victim.

Agamben proceeds to question whether there can be a witness to what happened at Auschwitz and other extermination camps – whether it is possible in such circumstances to 'speak of death' (73). The answer is that it is not possible, but also that it is not necessary because, controversially, the victim is the witness *as image* – as the *Muselmann*, as the one who cannot speak because the *Muselmann* embodies the non-human at the heart of the human (81–82).

Clearly, this is not the end of the story, but it is where we must leave it knowing that Agamben's approach brings to light issues that warrant being fully investigated in a separate study.

Notes

1. Thus, as an addendum to note 1 in Chapter 3, where reference is made to Being and existence, it can be observed that a modal ontology ceases to be dualistic (e.g., in the form of essence/accident). Thus, Agamben states

that: 'The mode in which something is, the being-thus of an entity is a category that belongs irreducibly to ontology' (2016: 174). As an illustration, Agamben refers to the Heideggerian categories, 'being' and 'existence', so that being is, ontologically, inseparable from its modes of existence: 'Dasein [existence] is the mode of a being that coincides completely with mode' (175).

However, the question still remains as to how a Hegelian style, monoview of the world does not result. And, we might ask, how do Agamben's categories of 'inoperativity' (Bataille's *'désoeuvrement'*) and 'work' not form an opposition, as they do in Bataille? Agamben writes, for example, 'if the fundamental ontological problem today is not work but inoperativity, and if this latter can nevertheless be attested only with respect to work, then access to a different figure of politics cannot take the form of a "constituent power" but rather that of something that we can provisionally call "destituent potential"' (266).

2. Girard does, however, acknowledge that 'like all modern technological advances [the judicial system] is a two-edged sword, which can be used to oppress as well as liberate' (1979: 23). As we have seen, for his part Agamben tends to play down the 'liberating' aspect of the law.

3. Those who might argue that Agamben does allow for the reform of the law – or at least, that there is an opening in Agamben's theory of law that could allow for reform – should be reminded of Benjamin's influence here and the fact that law is inseparable from violence, especially in the sense that the exception has become the rule. Thus, in invoking Benjamin, Agamben says that: 'Only a power that has been rendered inoperative and deposed by means of violence that does not aim to found a new law is fully neutralized' (2016: 268). The point is that for Agamben, law operates essentially in the interest of preserving sovereign or constituted power. In any case it is next to impossible to think of the reform of the law in isolation from an end, something quite distinct from the Benjaminian notion that Agamben supports of divine violence as a pure means.

4. The implication that the law can become analogous to a child's plaything is that Agamben's intended meaning is that law will be abandoned in toto. There is no avenue for reform. Catherine Mills (2008) has followed up this thread by arguing that when the fate of the law is to become like a child's plaything, the emphasis here should be on returning to the idea of play initially set out in Agamben's early work, *Infancy and History* (1993 [1978]). In abandoning the law, the human returns to the space of play first experienced in childhood. There is thus no question of 'saving' the law.

5. For his part, Weber distinguishes between substantive and formal, legal-rational law, moral law being substantive (i.e., concerned with

ends – with the 'substantively "right" decision' as Weber notes (1954: 228)), while the modern state is based in means-ends rationality (i.e., it is essentially concerned with means). In law, and no matter what type of authority is in place, 'all are confronted by the inevitable conflict between an abstract formalism of legal certainty and their desire to realize certain goals. Juridical formalism enables the legal system to operate like a technically rational machine' (226). Again: 'formal justice, due to its necessarily abstract character, infringes upon the ideals of substantive justice' (228). On the origin of law in vengeance, see Weber (1954: 50–51).
6. On due process, see Pennington (1993: 155–157), Pennington notes that: 'Torture undermines any idea of due process' (157).
7. Later, it will be suggested that law is even more firmly embedded in substantive elements, as is connoted by the notion of 'right'.
8. Combined with the neglect of the research of prehistorians in relation to hominisation – as was pointed out in Chapter 5 – the deficit is thus substantial.
9. Cf. 'Likewise, my brothers, you have died to the law through the body of Christ'. Romans 7:4 (English Standard Version).
10. See Berman (1977, 1978) and Berman and Reid (1994).
11. Arguably, first used in the centuries after Magna Carta to ensure the presence of the – often unwilling – accused before the King's bench (see Duker 1978: 995). As Duker observes in summary: 'an otherwise antilibertarian instrument (that is, one *compelling* appearance) was transformed into an instrument that safeguards individual freedom' (1054).
12. Thus, 'Roman law was continually "received" in Europe, in the same sense that Hebrew theology and Greek philosophy were continually received: each was assimilated, transformed, and given a new life, a new history, and each was repeatedly replenished by new approaches to its principal classical texts – the Bible, Plato and Aristotle, and the law books of Justinian' (Berman and Reid 1994: 2).
13. 'Germanic' refers to Northern European peoples generally (Berman 1978: 554n4).
14. Because Girard's continuing point of comparison with regard to law is 'non-Western' traditional societies, he entirely neglects the history of Western jurisprudence.
15. '[I]n 1532, Emperor Charles V promulgated a comprehensive criminal code for the Empire as a whole, the *Constitutio Criminalis Carolina*' (Berman 1983: 21).
16. While it is true that Girard might argue that his main concern is with a reading of the Gospels (see, for example, 1987b: 180–223) and not with the history of the Church, the claim that the Gospels are the basis of a

Christian culture (see 1987b: 224–262) inevitably brings the historical role of the Church into view.

17. Although, as Albert Kiralfy points out, the notion of 'right' in English law has a much more pragmatic resonance than is the case on the Continent, and, 'The English language has only one word for law, whereas most languages have several, and the word which English has retained is one which stresses the authority, or legality, of rules, rather than their inherent validity or justice' (Kiralfy 1985: 49). By contrast, 'German jurists like Radbruch have questioned the validity of unjust laws, rather as did the natural lawyers in former times' (53).
18. As Hans Kelsen acknowledges, 'If the idea of justice has any function at all, it is to be a model for making good law and a criterion for distinguishing good from bad law' (see Kelsen 1948: 383).
19. Here, to be noted is the fact that 'dismissal' or 'deactivation' of the law is not the total abolition of the law.
20. I say this even though Derrida would reject the term 'purity'.
21. Meillassoux (2009).
22. As Harman explains: 'Sensual objects would not even exist if they did not *exist for me*, or for some other agent that expends its energy in taking them seriously' (2011: 74; emphasis added).
23. Nancy's example of violence as extracting a screw with pliers only reinforces the impression that the range of instances that can count as violent is almost infinite. Moreover, as this example is also one of 'bricolage', it implies that a key aspect of the latter is that it is an incarnation of disorder and thus of violence (see Nancy 2005).
24. When Bataille says that the animal is in the world like 'water in water' (1994: 23), the world is the medium for the animal. Within the world, water is the medium for the fish.
25. See, for example, Hansen (2006a, 2006b).
26. Although to make this very statement seems to contradict the notion that medium as environment cannot be objectified, the qualification should be made that it cannot be *entirely* objectified, just as the object for OOO cannot be.
27. In this sense, we could say that 'immersive' artworks take the image to its logical conclusion, in as far as one is *in* the medium where objectification is impossible.
28. Bataille's claim is that violence does not speak and that there is no language of barbarity.
29. On this see above Chapter 5, note 2.
30. Earlier, it was said, with reference to the work of Lindsay Anne Hallam, that Sade's Justine is the quintessential victim – that is, victim for a persecutor (see Chapter 1, note 28).

31. Etymologically, infringement comes from the Latin: *infregere* in = into + *frangere* 'to break'.
32. Of course, with polities in which the English term, law, is translated as '*Recht*', '*doit*', '*diritto*', there ceases to be a connection with law as a physical phenomenon.
33. Sergei Prozorov claims that Agamben is hardly 'enchanted by the idea of pornography' and the 'liberatory function of sexual fulfillment' (2011: 77). This requires further investigation. Of course, Agamben does not admit to any mode of 'era '68'-style politics (where the difference between work and play, public and private, ethical and political, pornography and repressed sexuality supposedly disappears – or should disappear), but the question to be answered is whether the *logic* of his position inevitably leads to a dissolution of all forms of dualistic thought. In this sense, Agamben's lack of enthusiasm for Bataille's work becomes predictable.
34. Note also that: 'to return to play its purely profane vocation is a political task' (Agamben 2015b: 77).
35. Cf. 'The profanation of the unprofanable is the political task of the coming generation' (Agamben 2015b: 92).

References

Agamben, Giorgio (1991) *Language and Death: The Place of Negativity*, trans. Karen E. Pinkus. Minneapolis: University of Minnesota Press.
Agamben, Giorgio (1993 [1978]) *Infancy and History: On the Destruction of Experience*, trans. Liz Heron. London and New York: Verso.
Agamben, Giorgio (1995) *The Idea of Prose*, trans. Michael Sullivan and Sam Whitsitt. Albany: The State University of New York.
Agamben, Giorgio (1998) *Homo Sacer: Sovereign Power and Bare Life*, trans. Daniel Heller-Roazen. Stanford, CA: Stanford University Press.
Agamben, Giorgio (2000) *Means without End: Notes on Politics*, trans. Vincenzo Binetti and Cesare Casarino. Minneapolis: University of Minnesota Press.
Agamben, Giorgio (2002) 'Difference and Repetition: On Guy Debord's Films', trans. Brian Holmes. In Tom McDonough (ed.), *Guy Debord and the Situationist International: Texts and Documents*, 313–320. Cambridge: MA and Cambridge: The MIT Press.
Agamben, Giorgio (2004) *The Open: Man and Animal*, trans. Kevin Attell. Stanford, CA: Stanford University Press.
Agamben, Giorgio (2005a) *State of Exception*, trans. Kevin Attell. Chicago: University of Chicago Press.
Agamben, Giorgio (2005b) *The Coming Community*, trans. Patricia Dailey. Stanford, CA: Stanford University Press.
Agamben, Giorgio (2005c) *Remnants of Auschwitz: The Witness and the Archive*, trans. Daniel Heller-Roazen. New York: Zone Books. Third printing.

Agamben, Giorgio (2005d) *The Time that Remains: A Commentary on the Letter to the Romans*, trans. Patricia Dailey. Stanford, CA: Stanford University Press.

Agamben, Giorgio (2007) *Infancy and History: On the Destruction of Experience*, trans. Liz Heron. London and New York: Verso.

Agamben, Giorgio (2010) *The Signature of All Things*, trans. Luca D'Isanto with Kevin Attell. New York: Zone Books. Second printing.

Agamben, Giorgio (2011a) *The Kingdom and the Glory: For a Theological Genealogy of Economy and Government. Homo Sacer II, 2.* trans. Lorenzo Chiesa. Stanford, CA: Stanford University Press.

Agamben, Giorgio (2011b) *Nudities*, trans. David Kishik and Stefan Pedatella. Stanford, CA: Stanford University Press.

Agamben, Giorgio (2012) 'Image and Silence', trans. Leland de la Durantaye. *Diacritics*, 40 (2), ICONOGRAPHIES, 94–98.

Agamben, Giorgio (2014), 'Vocation and Voice', trans. Kalpana Seshadri. *Critical Inquiry*, 40 (Winter), 492–501.

Agamben, Giorgio (2015a) 'On the Limits of Violence (1970)', trans. Elisabeth Fay. In Brendan Moran and Carlo Salzani (eds), *Towards the Critique of Violence: Walter Benjamin and Giorgio Agamben*, 231–238. London and New York: Bloomsbury.

Agamben, Giorgio (2015b) *Profanations*, trans. Jeff Fort. New York: Zone Books.

Agamben, Giorgio (2016) *The Use of Bodies*, trans. Adam Kotsko. Stanford, CA: Stanford University Press.

Agamben, Giorgio (2018a) *Karman: A Brief Treatise on Action, Guilt, and Gesture*, trans. Adam Kotsko. Stanford, CA: Stanford University Press.

Agamben, Giorgio (2018b) *What is Philosophy?*, trans. Lorenzo Chieza. Stanford, CA: Stanford University Press.

Arendt, Hannah (1958) *The Human Condition*. Chicago and London: The University of Chicago Press.

Arendt, Hannah (1968 [1951]) *The Origins of Totalitarianism. Part Two*. San Diego, New York and London: Harvest HBJ.

Arnould, Elisabeth (1996) 'The Impossible Sacrifice of Poetry: Bataille and the Nancian Critique of Sacrifice'. *Diacritics*, 26 (2), 86–96.

Bachelard, Gaston (1995) *Le nouvel esprit scientifique*. Paris: Universitaires de France, "Quadridge".

Bakhtin, Mikhail (1981) 'Epic and Novel', in *The Dialogic Imagination: Four Essays*, 3–40, trans. Caryl Emerson and Michael Holquist. Austin: University of Texas Press.

Barthes, Roland (2010) *Camera Lucida*, trans. Richard Howard. New York: Hill and Wang.
Bataille, Georges (1970) *Œuvres complètes I*. Paris: Gallimard.
Bataille, Georges (1973) *Œuvres complètes V*. Paris: Gallimard.
Bataille, Georges (1979) *Œuvres complètes IX*. Paris: Gallimard.
Bataille, Georges (1986) *Visions of Excess: Selected Writings, 1927–1939*, trans. Allan Stoekl with Carl R. Lovitt and Donald M. Leslie, Jr. Minneapolis: University of Minnesota Press.
Bataille, Georges (1987) *Œuvres complètes, X*. Paris: Gallimard.
Bataille, Georges (1988a) *The Accursed Share: An Essay on General Economy, Vol I: Consumption*, trans. Robert Hurley. New York: Zone Books.
Bataille, Georges (1988b) *Œuvres complètes XI: Articles I, 1944–1949*, Paris Gallimard.
Bataille, Georges (1988c) *Inner Experience*, trans. Leslie Anne Boldt. Albany: State University of New York Press.
Bataille, Georges (1988d) *Guilty*, trans. Bruce Boone. Venice, CA: The Lapis Press.
Bataille, Georges (1990) *The Tears of Eros*, trans. Peter Connor. San Francisco, CA: City Lights.
Bataille, Georges (1991) *The Trial of Gilles de Rais*, trans. Richard Robinson. Los Angeles, CA: Amok Books.
Bataille, Georges (1992) *On Nietzsche*, trans. Bruce Boone. New York: Paragon House.
Bataille, Georges (1994) *Theory of Religion*, trans. Robert Hurley. New York: Zone Books. Reprinted.
Baudrillard, Jean (1993) *Symbolic Exchange and Death*, trans. Iain Hamilton Grant. London, Thousand Oaks, New Delhi: Sage Publications.
Belting, Hans (1996) *Likeness and Presence: A History of the Image Before the Era of Art*, trans. Edmund Jephcott. Chicago: University of Chicago Press. Paperback edition.
Belting, Hans (2005) 'Image, Medium, Body: A New Approach to Iconology'. *Critical Inquiry*, 31 (2), 302–319.
Benjamin, Andrew (2013) 'Towards a Critique of Violence', in *Working with Walter Benjamin*, 94–143. Edinburgh: Edinburgh University Press.
Benjamin, Andrew (2015) 'Responding'. *Philosophy Today*, 59 (1), 147–153.

Benjamin, Andrew (2019) 'Listening to God and the Founding of the Law: Notes on *Exodus*'. *Journal of the British Society for Phenomenology*, 32, 19–20.
Benjamin, Walter (1979) *Illuminations*, trans. Harry Zohn. Glasgow: Fontana/Collins.
Benjamin, Walter (1986) 'Critique of Violence', in *Reflections: Essays, Aphorisms, Autobiographical Writings*, trans. Edmund Jephcott, 277–300. New York: Shocken Books.
Benveniste, Émile (1969) *Le Vocabulaire des institutions indo-europeans 2: pouvoir, droit, religion*. Paris: Minuit.
Berger, Peter L. and Luckmann, Thomas (1966) *The Social Construction of Reality: A Treatise in the Sociology of Knowledge*. New York: Anchor Books.
Bergmann, Frithhof (1988) 'Nietzsche's Critique of Morality'. In Robert C. Solomon and Kathleen Higgins (eds), *Reading Nietzsche*, 29–45. New York and Oxford: Oxford University Press.
Bergson, Henri (2004) *Matter and Memory*, trans Margaret Paul and W. Scott Palmer. Mineola, NY: Dover Publications.
Berman, Harold J. (1977) 'The Origins of Western Legal Science'. *Harvard Law Review*, 90 (5), 894–943.
Berman, Harold J. (1978) 'The Background of the Western Legal Tradition in the Folklaw of the Peoples of Europe'. *The University of Chicago Law Review*, 45 (3), 553–597.
Berman, Harold J. (1983) 'Religious Foundations of Law in the West: An Historical Perspective'. *Journal of Law and Religion*, 1 (1), 3–43.
Berman, Harold J. (2000) 'The Western Legal Tradition in a Millennial Perspective: Past and Future'. *Louisiana Law Review*, 60 (3), 739–764.
Berman, Harold J. and Charles J. Reid, Jr (1994) 'Roman Law in Europe and the *Jus Commune*: A Historical Overview with Emphasis on the New Legal Science of the Sixteenth Century'. *Syracuse Journal of International Law and Commerce*, 20, 1–32.
Biles, Jeremy (2007) *Ecce Monstrum: Georges Bataille and the Sacrifice of Form*. New York: Fordham University Press.
Biles, Jeremy (2011) 'The Remains of God: Bataille/Sacrifice/Community'. *Culture, Theory and Critique*, 52 (2–3), 127–144.
Birmingham, Peg (2014) 'Law's Violent Judgment Does Agamben Have a Political Aesthetics?' *The New Centennial Review*, 14 (2), 99–110.
Blanchot, Maurice (2000) *The Instant of my Death*, trans. Elizabeth Rottenberg. Stanford, CA: Stanford University Press.

Bourdieu, Pierre (1992) *Language and Symbolic Power*, trans. Gino Raymond and Matthew Adamson. Cambridge: Polity Press.

Brook, Timothy, Bourgon, Jérôme and Bleu, Gregory (2008) *Death by a Thousand Cuts*. Cambridge, MA and London: Harvard University Press.

Bush, Stephen (2011) 'The Ethics of Ecstasy Georges Bataille and Amy Hollywood on Mysticism, Morality, and Violence'. *Journal of Religious Ethics*, 39 (2), 299–320.

Caputo, John (2010) 'Towards a Postmodern Theology of the Cross: Augustine, Heidegger, Derrida'. In Phillip Cary, John Doody and Kim Paffenroth (eds), *Augustine and Philosophy*, 243–267. Lanham, MD and Plymouth, UK: Lexington Books.

Cartledge, Paul (2000) 'Greek Political Thought: The Historical Context'. In Christopher Rowe and Malcom Schofield (eds), *The Cambridge History of Greek and Roman Political Thought*, 7–22. Cambridge: Cambridge University Press.

Connor, Peter (2000) *Georges Bataille and the Mysticism of Sin*. Baltimore, MD: Johns Hopkins University Press.

Danto, Arthur (1965) *Nietzsche as Philosopher*. New York: Macmillan.

Darwin, Charles (2004) *The Descent of Man*. London: Penguin.

Davis, Colin (2000) 'Fathers, Others: The Sacrificial Victim in Freud, Girard, and Levinas'. *Journal for Cultural Research*, 4 (2), 194–204.

Debord, Guy (2006) *The Society of the Spectacle* (no trans.). London: Rebel Press.

Debreuil, L. (2006) 'Leaving Politics: Bios, Zōē, Life'. *Diacritics* 36 (2), 83–96.

DeCaroli, Steven D. (2001) 'Visibility and History: Giorgio Agamben and the Exemplary'. *Philosophy Today*, 45, Issue Supplement, 9–17.

Deleuze, Gilles (1994) *Difference and Repetition*, trans. Paul Patton. New York: Columbia University Press.

Depootere, Frederiek (2012) 'Reading Giorgio Agamben's *Homo Sacer* with René Girard'. *Philosophy Today*, 56 (2), 154–163.

Derrida, Jacques (1967) *De la grammatologie*. Paris: Seuil.

Derrida, Jacques (1972) *Marges de la philosophie*. Paris: Minuit.

Derrida, Jacques (1978) *Writing and Difference*, trans. Alan Bass. Chicago: University of Chicago Press.

Derrida, Jacques (1988) 'Signature, Event, Context', in *Limited Inc*, trans. Samuel Weber and Jeffrey Mehlman, 1–23. Evanston, IL: Northwestern University Press.

Derrida, Jacques (1990) 'Force of Law: The Mystical Foundations of Authority', trans. Mary Quaintance. *Cardozo Law Review*, 11 (5), 919–1045.
Derrida, Jacques (1992) 'Before the Law'. In Derek Attridge (ed.), *Acts of Literature*, 181–220. New York and London: Routledge.
Derrida, Jacques (2000) *Demeure: Fiction and Testimony*, trans. Elizabeth Rottenberg. Stanford, CA: Stanford University Press.
Derrida, Jacques (2008) *Séminaire: La bête et le souverain, Volume I (2001–2002)*. Paris: Galilée.
Derrida, Jacques (2014) *The Death Penalty*, Volume I, trans. Peggy Kamuf, Chicago: Chicago University Press.
Derrida, Jacques (2016) *Of Grammatology*, trans. Gayatri Chakravorty Spivak. Baltimore, MD: Johns Hopkins University Press.
Direk, Zeynep (2004) 'Bataille on Immanent and Transcendent Violence'. *Bulletin de la Société Américaine de Philosophie de Langue Français*, 14, (2), 29–49.
Doane, Mary-Ann (2007) 'The Indexical and the Concept of Medium Specificity'. *D i f f e r e n c e s*, 18 (1), 128–152.
Duker, William (1978) 'The English Origins of the Writ of Habeas Corpus: A Peculiar Path to Fame'. *New York University Law Review*, 53 (5), 983–1054.
Eiland, Howard and Jennings, Michael William (2014) *Walter Benjamin: A Critical Life*. Cambridge, MA: Belknap Press, Harvard Imprint.
Elkins, James (2004) 'The Very Theory of Transgression: Bataille, Lingchi and Surrealism'. *Australian and New Zealand Journal of Art*, 5 (2), 5–19.
Elkins, James (2013) 'Introduction to Part I'. In Maria Pia Di Bella and James Elkins (eds), *Representations of Pain in Art and Visual Culture*, 3–11. New York and London: Routledge.
Farneti, Roberto (2008) 'A Political Theology of the Empty Tomb: Christianity and the Return of the Sacred'. *Theoria: A Journal of Social and Political Theory*, 116, 22–44.
Fenves, Peter (1998) '"Out of the Order of Number": Benjamin and Irigaray Toward a Politics of Pure Means'. *Diacritics*, 28 (1), 43–58.
Finlayson, J. G. (2010) '"Bare Life" and Politics in Agamben's Reading of Aristotle'. *The Review of Politics*, 72, 97–126.
Fiskesjö, Magnus (2012) 'Outlaws, Barbarians, Slaves. Critical Reflections on Agamben's *homo sacer*'. *HAU: Journal of Ethnographic Theory*, 2 (1), 161–180.

Fitzpatrick, Peter (2005) 'Bare Sovereignty: *Homo Sacer* and the Insistence of Law'. In Andrew Norris (ed.), *Politics. Metaphysics, and Death. Essays on Giorgio Agamben's* Homo Sacer, 49–73. Durham, NC and London: Duke University Press.
Freud, Sigmund (1954) *Project for a Scientific Psychology*, trans. James Strachey. In Marie Bonaparte, Anna Freud and Ernst Kris (eds), *The Origins of Psychoanalysis*. New York: Basic Books.
Freud, Sigmund (2001) *Totem and Taboo*, trans. James Strachey in *The Standard Edition of the Complete Psychological Works of Sigmund Freud, Volume XIII (1913–1914)*: Totem and Taboo *and other works*. London: Vintage Books.
Fried, Michael (1996) *Manet's Modernism: The Face of Painting in the 1860s*. Chicago: Chicago University Press.
Foucault, Michel (1974) *The Archaeology of Knowledge*, trans. A. M. Sheridan Smith. London: Tavistock Publications.
Foucault, Michel (1975) *Surveiller et punir: Naissance de la prison*. Paris: Gallimard.
Foucault, Michel (1979), 'The Life of Infamous Men', trans. Paul Foss and Meaghan Morris. In Paul Foss and Meaghan Morris (eds), *Power, Truth, Strategy*, 76–91. Sydney: Feral Publications.
Foucault, Michel (1984) 'Nietzsche, Genealogy, History', trans. Donald F. Bouchard and Sherry Simon. In Paul Rabinow (ed.), *The Foucault Reader*, 76–100. New York: Pantheon Books.
Gaughan, Judy (2010) *Murder was Not a Crime: Homicide and Power in the Roman Republic*. Austin: University of Texas Press.
Gerlac, Suzanne (1996) 'Bataille in Theory: Afterimages (Lascaux)'. *Diacritics*, 26 (2), 6–17.
Girard, René (1972) *La Violence et le sacré*. Paris: Grasset.
Girard, René (1977) 'Violence and Representation in the Mythical Text'. *MLN*, 92 (5), 922–944.
Girard, René (1978) 'Interview: René Girard'. *Diacritics*, 8 (1), 31–54.
Girard, René (1979) *Violence and the Sacred*, trans Patrick Gregory. Baltimore, MD: Johns Hopkins University Press. Paperback edition.
Girard, René (1984) 'Dionysus versus the Crucified'. *MLN*, 99 (4), 816–835.
Girard, René (1987a) 'Discussion' following a paper delivered entitled, 'Generative Scapegoating'. In Walter Burkert, René Girard and Jonathan Z. Smith, *Violent Origins: Ritual Killing and Cultural Formation*. Stanford, CA: Stanford University Press.

Girard, René (1987b) *Things Hidden Since the Foundation of the World*, trans. Stephen Bann and Michael Metteer. Stanford, CA: Stanford University Press.

Girard, René (1989) *The Scapegoat*, trans. Yvonne Freccero. Baltimore, MD: Johns Hopkins University Press.

Girard, René (1992) 'Origins: A View from the Literature'. In Francisco J. Varela and Jean-Pierre Dupuy (eds), *Understanding Origins: Contemporary Views on the Origin of Life*, 27–42, *Mind and Society*. Dordrecht, Boston and London: Kluwer Academic Publishers.

Girard, René (1999) *Je vois Satan tomber comme l'éclair*. Paris: Grasset.

Girard, René (2014) *When These Things Begin: Conversations with Michel Treguer*, trans. Trevor Cribben Merrill. East Lansing: Michigan State University Press.

Girard, René (with Pierpaolo Antonello and João Cezar de Castro Rocha) (2017) *Evolution and Conversion: Dialogues on the Origins of Culture*. London: Bloomsbury Academic.

Girard, René and Williams, James G. (1996) 'The Anthropology of the Cross: A Conversation with René Girard'. In James G. Williams (ed.), *The Girard Reader*, 262–288.

Gratton, Peter (2011) 'What More Is There to Say? Revisiting Agamben's Depiction of *Homo Sacer*'. *The European Legacy*, 16 (5), 599–613.

Hallam, Lindsay Anne (2012) *Screening the Marquis de Sade: Pleasure, Pain and the Transgressive Body in Film*. Jefferson, NC: McFarland Publications.

Hamacher, Werner (1994), 'Afformative, Strike: Benjamin's "Critique of Violence"', 110–138. In Andrew Benjamin and Peter Osborne (eds), *Walter Benjamin's Philosophy: Destruction and Experience*. London: Clinamen.

Hansen, Mark B. N. (2006a) 'Media Theory'. *Theory, Culture and Society*, 23 (2–3), 297–306.

Hansen, Mark B. N. (2006b) *Bodies in Code: Interfaces with Digital Media*. New York and Milton Park: Routledge.

Harbord, Janet (2016) *Ex-Centric Cinema: Giorgio Agamben and Film Archaeology*. New York and London: Bloomsbury.

Harman, Graham (2011) *The Quadruple Object*. Winchester, UK and Washington, USA: Zero Books.

Harman, Graham (2018) *Object Oriented Ontology*. London: Pelican Books.

Haw, Chris (2017) 'Human Evolution and the Single Victim Mechanism: Locating Girard's Hominization Hypothesis through Literature Survey'. *Contagion: Journal of Violence Mimesis and Culture*, 24, 191–216.

Heidegger, Martin (1978) *Being and Time*, trans. John Macquarie and Edward Robinson. Oxford: Basil Blackwell.

Heidegger, Martin (1982) *On the Way to Language*, trans. Peter D. Hertz. New York: Harper and Row.

Heidegger, Martin (1991a) *Nietzsche. Volumes One and Two*, trans. David Farrell Krell. New York: HarperSanFrancisco. Paperback edition.

Heidegger, Martin (1991b) *Nietzsche, Volumes Three and Four*, trans. Joan Stambaugh, David Farrell Krell, Frank A. Capuzzi, New York: HarperSanFrancisco. Paperback edition.

Heidegger, Martin (1992) *Parmenides*, trans. André Schuwer and Richard Rojcewicz. Bloomington and Indianapolis: Indiana University Press.

Heidegger, Martin (2014), *Introduction to Metaphysics*, second edition revised and expanded, trans. Gregory Fried and Richard Polt. New Haven, CT and London: Yale University Press.

Heinämäki, Elisa (2012) 'Nothing Distinguishes Us from God'. *Angelaki*, 17 (3), 113–122.

Henry, Michel (2000) *Incarnation: Une philosophie de la chair*. Paris: Seuil.

Hollier, Denis (1990) 'The Dualist Materialism of Georges Bataille'. *Yale French Studies*, 78, 'On Bataille'.

Hollywood, Amy (2002) *Sensible Ecstasy: Mysticism, Sexual Difference and the Demands of History*. Chicago: Chicago University Press.

Hubert, Henri and Mauss, Marcel (1981 [1898]) *Sacrifice: It's Nature and Function*, trans. W. D. Halls. Chicago: University of Chicago Press. Midway reprint.

Hunt, Alan (1987) 'The Critique of Law: What Is "Critical" about Critical Legal Theory?' *Journal of Law and Society*, 14, (1), 5–19.

Hunter, Ian (2017) 'Giorgio Agamben's *Form of Life*'. *Politics, Religion & Ideology*, 18 (2), 135–156.

Husserl, Edmund (1981) 'The Lectures on Internal Time Consciousness from the Year 1905', trans. James S. Churchill. In Peter McCormaick and Frederick A. Elliston (eds), *Husserl: Shorter Works*, 277–288. Notre Dame, IN: University of Notre Dame; Brighton, Sussex: The Harvester Press.

Jakobsson, Ármann (2011) 'Beast and Man: Realism and the Occult in "Egils saga"'. *Scandinavian Studies*, 83 (1) (Spring), 29–44.

Jhering, Rodolphe (1886) *L'Esprit du droit dans les divers phases de son développement*, Volume 5, trans. O. de Meulenaere. Paris: Marescq.

Joyce, Conor (2003) *Carl Einstein in Documents and his Collaboration with Georges Bataille*. Bloomington, IN: Xlibris.

Kaplan, Louis (2013) 'Sontag's *Regarding* and Bataille's *Unknowing*'. In Maria Pia Di Bella and James Elkins (eds), *Representations of Pain in Art and Visual Culture*, 52–63. New York and London: Routledge.

Kearney, Richard (1999) 'Aliens and Others: Between Girard and Derrida'. *The Journal of the Institute for Cultural Research, Lancaster University*, 3 (3), 251–262.

Keenan, Dennis (2003) 'Nietzsche and the Eternal Return of Sacrifice'. *Research in Phenomenology* 33, 167–185.

Kelsen, Hans (1948) 'Law, State and Justice in the Pure theory of Law'. *Yale Law Journal*, 57 (3), 377–390.

Kiralfy, Albert (1985) 'Law and Right in English Legal History'. *The Journal of Legal History*, 6 (1), 49–61.

Kracauer, Sigfried (1995) 'Photography'. In *The Mass Ornament: Weimar Essays*, 47–64, trans. Thomas Y Levin. Cambridge, MA and London: Harvard University Press.

Krämer, Sybille (2015) *Medium, Messenger, Transmission: An Approach to Media Philosophy*, trans. Anthony Enns. Amsterdam: Amsterdam University Press.

Kristeva, Julia (1979) *Le Texte du roman: Approche sémiologique d'une structure discursive transformationnelle*. The Hague: Mouton Publishers. Third printing.

Lacoue-Labarthe, Philippe (1978) 'Mimesis and Truth'. *Diacritics*, 8 (1), 10–23.

Lampert, Laurence (1974) 'Heidegger's Nietzsche Interpretation'. *Man and World*, 7 (4), 353–374.

Larrabee, Mary Jeanne (1989), 'Time and Spatial Models: Temporality in Husserl'. *Philosophy and Phenomenological Research*, 49 (3), 373–392.

Lechte, John (2012) *Genealogy and Ontology of the Western Image and its Digital Future*. New York: Routledge.

Lechte, John (2013) 'The Ontology of Photography: The Human and "Acheiropoietos"'. Paper given at the Birmingham City University,

School of Art, 'On the Verge of Photography' conference, 25 May. See: https://www.youtube.com/watch?v=_TDw7iYMOK0

Lechte, John (2018) *The Human: Bare Life and Ways of Life*. London: Bloomsbury.

Lemke, Thomas (2005) '"A Zone of Indistinction" – A Critique of Giorgio Agamben's Concept of Biopolitics'. *Outlines*, 1, 3–13.

Leroi-Gourhan, André (1964a) *Le geste et la parole I: Technique et langage*. Paris: Albin Michel.

Leroi-Gourhan, André (1964b) *Le geste et la parole II: La mémoire et les rythmes*. Paris: Albin Michel.

Leroi-Gourhan, André (1973) *Milieu et technique*. Paris: Albin Michel.

Levinas, Emanuel (1998) *Otherwise Than Being*, trans. Alphonso Lingis. Pittsburgh, PA: Duquesne University Press.

Livingston, Paul M. (2009) 'Agamben, Badiou, and Russell'. *Continental Philosophy Review*, 42, 297–325.

Lusvardi, Anthony R. (2017) 'Girard and the "Sacrifice of the Mass": Mimetic Theory and Eucharistic Theology'. *Contagion: Journal of Violence, Mimesis, and Culture*, 24, 159–190.

McLoughlin, Daniel (2015) 'On Political and Economic Theology: Agamben, Peterson and Aristotle'. *Angelaki*, 20 (4), 53–68.

McLoughlin, Daniel (2016) 'The Fiction of Sovereignty and the Real State of Exception: Giorgio Agamben's Critique of Carl Schmitt'. *Law, Culture and the Humanities*, 12 (3), 509–528.

McLuhan, Marshall (2008 [1964]) *Understanding Media*. London and New York: Routledge Classics.

Magnus, Bernd (1988) 'The Use and Abuse of *The Will to Power*'. In Robert C. Solomon and Kathleen Higgins (eds), *Reading Nietzsche*, 218–235. New York and Oxford: Oxford University Press.

Magnus, Bernd (1991) 'Deconstruction Site: The "Problem of Style" in Nietzsche's Philosophy'. *Philosophical Topics, Nineteenth-Century Philosophy*, 19 (2), 215–243.

Marion, Jean-Luc (2002) '"They Recognized Him; and He became invisible to them"'. *Modern Theology*, 18 (2), 145–152.

Marion, Jean-Luc (2013) 'The Prototype and the Image', trans. James K. A. Smith. In Kevin Hart (ed.), *Jean-Luc Marion, The Essential Writings*, 273–287. New York: Fordham University Press.

May, Simon (1999) *Nietzsche's Ethics and his War on Morality*. Oxford: Oxford University Press.

Megill, Allan (1987) 'The Reception of Foucault by Historians'. *Journal of the History of Ideas*, 48 (1), 117–141.

Mehlman, Jeffrey (1996) 'How to Read Freud on Jokes: The Critic as Shadchen'. In Lechte, John (ed.), *Writing and Psychoanalysis*, 41–60. London: Arnold.

Meillassoux, Quentin (2009) *After Finitude: An Essay on the Necessity of Contingency*, trans Ray Brassier. London and New York: Continuum. Paperback edition.

Melzter, Bernard N. and Musolf, Gil Richard (2002) 'Resentment and Ressentiment'. *Sociological Inquiry*, 72 (2), 240–255.

Mesnard, Philippe (2004) 'The Political Philosophy of Giorgio Agamben: A Critical Evaluation'. *Totalitarian Movements and Political Religions*, 5 (1), 139–157.

Milbank, John (1995) 'Stories of Sacrifice from Wellhausen to Girard'. *Theory, Culture and Society*, 12, 15–46.

Milbank, John (2006) *Theology and Social Theory Beyond Secular Reason*. Malden, MA: Blackwell, second edition.

Miller, James (1990) 'Carnivals of Atrocity: Foucault, Nietzsche, Cruelty'. *Political Theory*, 18 (3), 470–491.

Mills, Catherine (2008) 'Playing with Law: Agamben and Derrida on Postjuridical Justice'. *South Atlantic Quarterly* 107 (1), 15–36.

Mitchell, W. J. T. (1986) 'What is an Image?' In *Iconology: Image, Text, Ideology*, 7–46. Chicago: University of Chicago Press.

Mitchell, W. J. T. (2005) *What Do Pictures Want?* Chicago: University of Chicago Press.

Mondzain, Marie-José (1996) *Image, icône, économie: Les sources byzantine de l'imaginaire contemporain*. Paris: Seuil.

Mondzain, Marie-José (2005) *Image, Icon, Economy: The Byzantine Origins of the Contemporary Imaginary*, trans. Rico Frances. Stanford, CA: Stanford University Press.

Müller, Adalberto (2016) 'Orson Welles, Author of *Don Quixote*, Reconsidered'. *Cinema Journal* 56 (1), 43–62.

Nancy, Jean-Luc (1991) 'The Unsacrificeable'. *Yale French Studies*, 79, 20–38.

Nancy, Jean-Luc (2005), 'Image and Violence' in *The Ground of the Image*, 15–26, trans. Jeff Fort. New York: Fordham University Press.

Nietzsche, Friedrich (1968) *The Will to Power*, trans. Walter Kaufmann and R. J. Hollingdale. New York: Vintage Books.

Nietzsche, Friedrich (1974a) *Beyond Good and Evil*, trans. R. J. Hollingdale. Harmondsworth: Penguin Books.
Nietzsche, Friedrich (1974b) *The Anti-Christ*, trans. R. J. Hollingdale. Harmondsworth: Penguin Books.
Nietzsche, Friedrich (1974c) *Twilight of the Idols*, trans. R. J. Hollingdale. Harmondsworth: Penguin Books.
Nietzsche, Friedrich (1974d) *The Gay Science*, trans. Walter Kaufmann. New York: Vintage.
Nietzsche, Friedrich (1982 [1881]) *Daybreak: Thoughts on the Prejudices of Morality*, trans. R. J. Hollingdale. Cambridge: Cambridge University Press.
Nietzsche, Friedrich (1989) *Ecce Homo*, trans. Walter Kaufmann. In *On the Genealogy of Morals and Ecce Homo*. New York: Vintage.
Nietzsche, Friedrich (1996 [1887]), *On the Genealogy of Morality*, trans. Carol Diethe. Cambridge: Cambridge University Press. Reprinted.
Nietzsche, Friedrich (2008) *Thus Spoke Zarathustra. A Book for Everybody and Nobody*, trans Graham Parkes. Oxford: Oxford University Press.
Nolan, Carrie (2004) 'Bataille Looking'. *Modernism/modernity*, 11 (1), 125–160.
Noyes, Benjamin (2000) *Georges Bataille: A Critical Introduction*. London: Pluto Press.
Pannenberg, Wolfhart (1988) 'A Theology of the Cross'. *Word and World*, 8 (2), 162–172.
Parmer, Jared W. (2017) 'Nietzsche and the Art of Cruelty'. *The Journal of Nietzsche Studies*, 48 (3), 402–429.
Paul, Robert A. (2010) 'Yes, the Primal Crime Did Take Place: A Further Defense of Freud's *Totem and Taboo*'. *ETHOS*, 38 (2), 230–249.
Peirce, Charles Sanders (1955) *The Philosophical Writings of Peirce*. New York: Dover.
Pennington, Kenneth (1993), *Prince and the Law, 1200–1600: Sovereignty and Rights in the Western Legal Tradition*. Berkeley: University of California Press.
Pennington, Kenneth (1994) 'Learned Law, Droit Savant, Gelehrtes Recht: The Tyranny of a Concept'. *Syracuse Journal of International Law and Commerce*, 20, 205–215.
Prozorov, Sergei (2011) 'Pornography and Profanation in the Political Philosophy of Giorgio Agamben'. *Theory, Culture and Society*, 28 (4), 71–95.

Restuccia, Frances L. (2012) 'Profaning the Messiah – or Why Can't Dulcinea Love Us?' *Philosophy Today*, (Summer), 232–242.

Robert, William (2013) 'Nude, Glorious, Living'. *Political Theology*, 14 (1), 115–130.

Rosenbaum, Jonathan (2007) 'When Will – and How Can – We Finish Orson Welles's DON QUIXOTE?' In *Discovering Orson Welles*, 296–307. Berkeley, Los Angeles and London: California University Press.

Ross, Alison (2012) 'Agamben's Political Paradigm of the Camp: Its Features and Reasons'. *Constellations*, 19 (3), 421–434.

Ross, Alison (2014) 'The Distinction between Mythic and Divine Violence: Walter Benjamin's "Critique of Violence" from the Perspective of Goethe's *Elective Affinities*'. *New German Critique*, 121 (41), 93–120.

Ross, Alison (2015) 'The Ambiguity of Ambiguity in Benjamin's "Critique of Violence"'. In Brendan Moran and Carlo Salzani (eds), *Towards the Critique of Violence: Walter Benjamin and Giorgio Agamben*, 39–56. London and New York: Bloomsbury.

Rousseau, Jean-Jacques (1975 [1779]) *A Complete Dictionary of Music*, trans. William Waring. New York: AMS Press. Reprint of London 1779 edition.

Rousseau, Jean-Jacques (1982) *The Social Contract*, trans. G. D. H. Cole, in *The Social Contract and Discourses*. London: J. M. Dent and Sons, reprinted.

Ryder, Andrew (2011) 'Politics after the Death of the Father: Democracy in Freud and Derrida'. *Mosaic: An Interdisciplinary Critical Journal*, 44 (3), 115–131.

Sahlins, Marshall (1974) *Stone Age Economics*. London: Tavistock.

Salzani, Carlo (2016) 'Nudity: Agamben and Life'. *Pléyade*, 17, 45–64.

Sartre, Jean-Paul (1947) 'Un Nouveau mystique', in *Situations I*, 143–188. Paris: Gallimard.

Sartre, Jean-Paul (2004) *The Imaginary: A Phenomenological Psychology of the Imagination*. London and New York: Routledge.

Scheler, Max (1994) *Ressentiment*, trans. William W. Holdheim. Milwaukee, WI: Marquette University Press.

Schmitt, Carl (2005) *Political Theology: Four Chapters on the Concept of Sovereignty*, trans. George Schwab. Chicago: Chicago University Press.

Sheaffer-Jones, Caroline (2015) 'Georges Bataille's "Manet" and the "strange impression of an absence"'. In N. Edwards, B. McCann and P. Poiana (eds), *Framing French Culture*, 231–256. Adelaide: University of Adelaide Press.

Sontag, Susan (2003) *Regarding the Pain of Others*. London: Penguin.

Spivak, Gayatri (1988) 'Can the Subaltern Speak?'. In C. Nelson and L. Grossberg (eds), *Marxism and the Interpretation of Culture*, 271–313. Basingstoke: Macmillan Education.

Stiegler, Bernard (1998) *Technics and Time, 1. The Fault of Epimetheus*, trans. Richard Bosworth and George Collins. Stanford, CA: Stanford University Press.

Surya, Michel (2002), *Georges Bataille. An Intellectual Biography*, trans. Krysztof Fijalkowski and Michael Richardson. London and New York: Verso.

Toscano, Alberto (2011) 'Divine Management'. *Angelaki*, 16 (3), 125–136.

Tubbs, Robert (2009) *What is a Number? Mathematical Concepts and Their Origins*. Baltimore, MD: The Johns Hopkins University Press.

Ungar, Steven (1990) 'Phantom Lascaux: Origin of the work of Art'. *Yale French Studies* (On Bataille), 78, 246–262.

Varela, Francisco J. and Dupuy, Jean-Pierre (eds) (1992) *Understanding Origins*. Dordrecht: Springer Science and Business Media.

Vattimo, Gianni and Girard, René (2010) *Christianity, Truth, and Weakening Faith: A Dialogue*, trans William McCuaig. New York: Columbia University Press.

Vattimo, Gianni (with Santiago Zabala) (2019) '"Weak Thought" and the Reduction of Violence: A Dialogue with Gianni Vattimo', trans. Yaakov Mascetti. *Common Knowledge*, 25 (1–3), 92–103.

Veyne, Paul (1997) 'Foucault Revolutionises History'. In Arnold Ira Davidson (ed.), *Foucault and his Interlocutors*, 146–182. Chicago: Chicago University Press.

Watkin, William (2014) '*The Signature of All Things:* Agamben's Philosophical Archaeology'. *MLN*, 129 (1), 139–161.

Watkin, William (2015) 'Agamben, Benjamin and the Indifference of Violence'. In Brendan Moran and Carlo Salzani (eds), *Towards the Critique of Violence: Walter Benjamin and Giorgio Agamben*, 139–152. London and New York: Bloomsbury.

Weber, Max (1954) *On Law in Economy and Society*, trans. Edward Shils and Max Rheinstein. New York: Simon and Shuster, A Clarion Book.

White, Thomas Joseph (2011) 'Kenoticism and the Divinity of Christ Crucified'. *The Thomist: A Speculative Quarterly Review*, 75 (1), 1–41.

Williams, James G. (ed.) (1996) *The Girard Reader*. New York: Crossroads Press.

Williams, Stephen N. (1998) 'Dionysus Against the Crucified: Nietzsche *Contra* Christianity, Part II'. *Tyndale Bulletin* 49 (1), 131–153.

Wolf, Herta (2007) 'The Tears of Photography'. *Grey Room*, 29, 66–69.

Zhuo, Yue (2015) 'Alongside the Animals: Bataille's "Lascaux Project"'. *Yale French Studies*, 127, 19–33.

Index

Abelard, P., 188
acceptable violence, 198–9
acclamation, 1, 6, 108, 109, 110, 114, 120, 125, 126, 200
Agamben, G.
  homo sacer, vii, viii, 1, 3, 5, 16, 20–1, 126, 160n11: paradigm and history, 88–92, 94; and power, 9–10; and sovereignty, 79–85, 188–9
  image, viii, 108–32, 200–1: cinema image, 122–9; as glory, 109–10, 125–7; and language, 6, 110; and law, 188–90; as mediality, 7, 16, 50, 109, 194, 195; *oikonomia* as glory, 111–16; theology of the, 116–22; and time, 110–11; and violence, 5, 126
  language, 5, 6, 87, 92, 110, 124–5
  nudity, 75n21
  Remnants of Auschwitz, 202
  victim *see* Agamben, G.: *homo sacer*
  violence, 16, 78–101, 200: and image, 5, 126; and law/sovereignty, 6, 80, 82, 83, 84, 85, 87–8, 184; and mediality, 78–9, 85–7, 108; and origin, 93–5; paradigm and history, 88–92; paradigm of the camp, 97–9; and set theory, 95–7; and signatures, 92–3
  Western politics, viii–ix, 160–1n13
animals, 14, 58–62, 93, 125–6, 152, 200
arche-writing, 144
Arendt, H., 6, 68, 104n13, 112
Arnould, E., 27
art, 14, 58, 59; *see also* Lascaux Cave images; Manet, E.

astrophysics, 155
Aztecs, 29

Bacchae, The (Euripides), 100
Bakhtin, M., 141
barbarity, 4, 36, 42
bare life, vii, viii, 20, 68, 80–1, 89, 91–2, 98, 103n5; *see also homo sacer*
Barthes, R., 52, 57, 70
Bataille, G.
  as dualistic thinker, 200
  image, viii, 16: Crucifixion, 175; Lascaux Caves, 2, 13–14, 50, 58–62; *lingchi* photographs, 13, 27, 50, 51, 54–5, 56–7, 65–6, 67–73; Manet's paintings, 2, 14, 50, 62–5
  nudity, 75n21
  sacrifice, ix, 12, 26–8, 67: and the instant, 28–31
  victim, vii–viii, 10, 26–8, 54–8, 76n24, 192: animals as, 14, 58–62; and civil identity, 67–9; and context, 69–73; de Rais as, 11–12, 40–4; and the instant, 28–31; *lingchi* photographs, 13, 27, 54, 55, 56–7, 65–6, 67–73; Manet's paintings, 14, 64–5; and Sade, 12–13, 37–8; and violence, 1–2, 15–16, 20–3, 40, 196
  violence, 10: acceptable, 198–9; and language, 3–4, 199; and victim, 1–2, 15–16, 20–3, 40, 196
'Before the Law' (Derrida), 155
Belting, H., 9, 116, 117
Benjamin, A., 185

Benjamin, W., 5, 78, 80, 88, 98, 99, 101, 122, 159
Benveniste, É., 78, 90, 95, 96, 101, 124
Bergmann, F., 32–3
Bergson, H., vii, 30, 110, 143
Berman, H.J., 163, 186, 187, 188
Berserkir, 11, 18–19n18, 41
Bible, 9, 166, 169, 178
Big Bang, 155
Biles, J., 23
Birmingham, P., 86
Blanchot, M., 30
Borel, A., 54, 56, 67
Bourdieu, P., 196
bricoleur-engineer opposition, 146
Brontë, E., 43
Brook, T., 54
Bush, S., 71
Byzantine theology, 117, 118, 172

Camera Lucida (Barthes), 57, 70
camp, paradigm of the, 97–9
Caputo, J., 174
Catholic Church, 187
childhood, 42–3
Christ, 3, 57
  in Agamben, 109
  in Bataille, 28
  and economy, 130–1n9
  as image, 165–73, 194: in Byzantium, 172; in Girard, 165–70, 172–3; in Marion, 170–1, 177; and theology of the Cross, 174–7
  in Nietzsche, 39
  see also Crucifixion
Christianity, 163–4, 164–7, 180, 185, 186–8
cinema, 101, 122
cinema image, 122–9
civil identity, 67–9
civilisation, 4
communication, 12, 27, 28, 54, 56, 64, 65, 69, 196
concentration camps *see* camp, paradigm of the; *Remnants of Auschwitz* (Agamben)
correlationism, 192
Cross, 167, 168, 169–70, 173
  and law, 177–9
  theology of the, 174–7
Crucifixion
  in Bataille, 175
  in Girard, viii, ix, 2, 8–9, 16, 164, 178, 200, 201
  see also Christ: as image
cruelty, 11, 23, 33–5, 37, 46–7n22, 66; *see also* violence

Davis, C., 158
de Rais, G., 11–12, 40–4
death
  in Bataille, 12, 27, 28, 29–30, 54, 65–7: and Lascaux Caves, 61; *lingchi* photographs, 69–73; and Manet's paintings, 62, 64–5
  of God, 165, 180
  in Nietzsche, 33
  Oedipus, 141
Death by a Thousand Cuts (Brooks et al.), 67, 68
Debord, G., 1, 109, 110, 116, 121, 123–4, 129, 194
DeCaroli, S., 95
deconstruction of the origin, 143–52
Deleuze, G., vii, 122
Depoortere, F., 79, 91
Derrida, J.
  context, 70
  hominisation, 154: on *Totem and Taboo* (Freud), 155–6, 157
  inner experience, 56
  language, 143
  law and justice, 184, 190–2
  origin, 14–15, 133–4, 135: deconstruction of, 143–5, 146, 148, 149, 150
  trace, 7
  violence, 197–8
desire, 147, 151–2, 154, 167, 201
Difference and Repetition (Deleuze), vii
discourse, 95
divine violence, 5, 78, 98, 99, 101, 122
Don Quixote (Welles), 127–8
Douglas, M., 79
Duker, W., 186

economic trinity, 114
economy, ix, 109, 111–12, 120, 130–1n9, 201
Elkins, J., 51, 55
eroticism, 13, 198–9
eternal return, 33, 35
Euripides, 100, 139
evil, 42–3
examples, 95
Execution of Maximilian, The (Manet), 62
expression, 123

Fenves, P., 99, 195
festival, 64
Fiskesjö, M., 188–9
Fitzpatrick, P., 81, 84, 89–90, 91
folklaw, 186–7, 188
Foucault, M., 90, 91, 92, 93–4, 95, 102n2, 119–20

Freud, S., 155–6, 157, 158, 199
fusion, 55, 71

Gamin aux cerises (Manet), 64–5
Gaughan, J., 151
genealogy, 93–4
Germanic folklaw, 186–7
gesture, 5, 61–2, 86, 101, 122, 124
gift, 28–9
Girard, R.
  critique of Nietzsche, 164–7
  image: Christ as, 165–70, 172–7; and Crucifixion, viii, ix, 2, 8–10, 16
  victim, vii, viii, 9, 16, 133, 160n11, 183, 202: and Christianity, 164–5, 177–9; and hominisation, 152–9; Oedipus, 141; and violence, 1–2, 14, 15, 137, 150, 184 (*see also* scapegoat)
  violence: and Christianity, 201; and Crucifixion, ix, 8–10, 163, 179, 200; and Heraclitean Logos, 175–6; and origin of society, 133–43, 145, 147–8, 150–2; and victim, 1–2, 14, 15, 184
glory, 109–10, 111–16, 120, 125, 126
God, death of, 165, 180
Gratton, P., 91
Greek tragedy, 138–9, 140
Gregory VII, 187
Guillaume, G., 111
Guilty (Bataille), 71

Hamacher, W., 99
Harbord, J., 128
Harman, G., 192, 193
Hegel, G.W.F., 28, 30
Heidegger, M., 11, 38, 136–7, 143, 196
Henry, M., 176
Heracles (Euripides), 139
Heraclitean Logos, 175
herd individuals, 13, 38
Hiroshima, 29
historical research, 93, 94–5
historical time, 93–4
history, 88–92, 119–20, 146
Hitler, A., 98
Hölderlin, F., 124
Hollywood, A., 69–70, 71, 74n9
homeiosis, 172
hominisation, 152–9
homo sacer, vii, viii, 1, 3, 5, 16, 20–1, 126, 160n11
  paradigm and history, 88–92, 94
  and power, 9–10
  and sovereignty, 79–85, 188–9
Homo Sacer (Agamben), 98
Hubert, H., 5, 23–6

Hunt, A., 191
Hunter, I., 102n1, 105n20, 125
Husserl, E., 30
hypermorality, 43

iconoclasm, 57, 118, 121, 194
iconoclasts, 118
iconophiles, 118
icons, 171
identity, 197
illusion of immanence, 192–3
image, vi–vii, viii–ix, 6–7
  in Agamben, viii, 108–32, 200–1; cinema image, 122–9; as glory, 109–10, 125–7; and language, 6, 110; and law, 188–90; as mediality, 7, 16, 50, 109, 194, 195; *oikonomia* as glory, 111–16; theology of the, 116–22; and time, 110–11; and violence, 5, 126
  in Bataille, viii, 16: Crucifixion, 175; Lascaux Caves, 2, 13–14, 50, 58–62; *lingchi* photographs, 13, 27, 50, 51, 54–5, 56–7, 65–6, 67–73; Manet's paintings, 2, 14, 50, 62–5
  in Girard: Christ as, 165–70, 172–7; and Crucifixion, viii, ix, 2, 8–10, 16
  in Marion, 170–1, 177
  media specificity, 51–4
  in Nancy, 2–3, 17n3
  in Nietzsche, 10–11, 118–19, 120
  as object, 192–4
immanent trinity, 114
immanent violence, 22
inner experience, 55–6
Inner Experience (Bataille), 20, 28, 66, 67
inoperativity, 87, 105n16, 111, 113, 120, 126
instant, 28–31
isonomia, 39–40

Jakobson, Á., 95, 96
Jhering, R., 84
Johannine Logos, 175–6
John the Baptist, 8
justice, 184, 190–2

Kant, I., 192
Kingdom and the Glory, The (Agamben), 108–9, 110, 111–16, 125
Kracauer, S., 52
Kristeva, J., 79, 141–2

La corde (Baudelaire), 64–5
Lacou-Labarthe, P., 147–8

language
  in Agamben, 5, 6, 87, 92, 110, 124–5
  in Bataille, 3–4, 199
  in Derrida, 143
  and historical research, 94–5
  in Sade, 36
Lascaux Cave images, 2, 13–14, 50, 58–62
law, ix
  in Arendt, 104n13
  and Christianity, 163–4, 185, 186–8
  and the Cross, 177–9
  and image, 188–90
  and justice, 184, 190–2
  against murder, 150–1, 157–8
  origin of, 93
  and paradigm of the camp, 97–9
  and set theory, 96
  and state of nature, 89
  violation of, 199–200
  and violence, 6, 80, 82, 83, 84, 85, 86, 87–8, 159, 183–5
  see also sovereignty; Western legal tradition
Le Déjeuner sur l'herbe (Manet), 62, 63
legal positivism, 188
Lemke, T., 90
Leroi-Gourhan, L., 135, 152, 153–4
Lévi-Strauss, C., 85, 92, 145–6, 151, 152, 157, 197
Levinas, 177
life, 32–4, 144
lingchi photographs, 13, 27, 50, 51, 54–5, 56–7, 65–6
  context of victim's death, 69–73
  victims and civil identity, 67–9
literary theory, 141–2
literature, 42, 43, 138, 154; *see also* texts
Livingston, P., 95–6
Lot-Falck, É., 61
Lusvardi, A., 167
Luther, M., 174, 187

McLoughlin, D., 87
McLuhan, M., vii, 121
Magna Carta, 185, 186
Magnus, B., 32, 45–6n17
Manet, E., 2, 14, 50, 62–5
Marcel, G., 29
Marion, J.-L., 57, 116, 117–18, 119, 168, 170–1, 173, 176–7
Mauss, M., 5, 23–6, 28
Means without End (Agamben), 101, 122
mediality, 1, 121–2, 125
  in Debord's films, 123
  image as, 5, 7, 16, 50, 99, 109, 189, 194, 195

violence as, 5, 78–9, 85–7, 96, 98, 101, 108, 184, 201
medium, 194–5
medium specificity/media specificity, vii, 51–4
Mehlman, J., 199
Meillassoux, Q., 192
metaphysics, 143, 144, 145, 147, 197
mimesis/mimetic desire, 147–8, 151–2, 154
Mitchell, W.J.T., 51–2
modal ontology, 78, 92, 102n1, 105–6n20, 125, 183, 202n1
modernity, 97, 120, 121
Mondzain, M.-J., 116–17, 118, 130–1n9, 172, 176
murder, 154, 165
  and law, 150–1, 155–6, 157
  as origin of society, 83, 134–43, 152
myths, 135, 137, 160n7
  disjunctive symmetry in, 141–2
  and hominisation, 154.155, 156–7
  origin as, 150
  and tragedy, 140
  v. the Bible, 166, 168–9

Nancy, J.-L., 2–3, 4–5, 17n3, 27–8, 31
nature-culture opposition, 145–6
Newton, I., 33
Nicephorus, 117, 172, 176
Nietzsche, F.
  Christianity, 164–7
  cruelty, 33–5
  genealogy, 93–4
  herd individuals, 13, 38
  image, 10–11, 118–19, 120
  interpretations, 180
  life, 1, 9, 11, 18n14, 21, 23, 31–5, 39, 46–7n22, 49n35, 49n37, 72, 77n34, 166
  power, 32, 34
  suffering, 195
  v. Bataille, 22–3
  victim, 1, 10, 11, 21, 31–2, 35, 38–40, 55, 72–3
  violence, 11, 22, 32, 200
  will to power, 11, 18n14, 21, 24–5, 32, 45–6n17, 46n18, 46–7n22, 48n26, 72–3, 77n34
nihilism, 118, 180
Nolan, C., 59–60, 61–2
normal man, 12–13, 38, 42
normality, 12–13, 36–7
novels, 142
Noyes, B., 43–4
nudity, 63, 75n21

object, image as, 192–4
Object Oriented Ontology (OOO), 192

Oedipus, 137, 140–3
Of Grammatology (Derrida), 134, 135, 148, 154, 157, 197
oikonomia, 6, 109, 111–13, 119, 120
Olympia (Manet), 62, 63
'On the Limits of Violence' (Agamben), 100
operational time, 111
origin, 14–15, 93–5
  of society, 133–43, 178: deconstruction of, 143–52; murder as, 83, 134–43

paintings, 52, 193; *see also* Manet, E.
paradigm of the camp, 97–9
paradigms, 88–92, 94, 95
Peirce, C.S., 53
Pennington, K., 190
perception, 193
photography, 52–4, 193; *see also* lingchi photographs
Plato, 89
play, 41, 58, 126, 200, 201
poetry, 124
political economy, 112
political theology, 6, 21, 125, 185, 188
politics, viii–ix, 86, 99, 101, 110, 120, 122, 160–1n13
power, viii–ix, 32, 34, 102n2, 126
  will to, 11, 18n14, 21, 24–5, 32, 34, 45–6n17, 46n18, 46–7n22, 48n26, 72–3, 77n34
  see also sovereignty
prototype, 57, 117–18, 171, 172, 173
pure means, 5, 86, 87
pure violence, 6, 98, 99, 100, 101

realism, 63
religion *see* Christianity
religious experience, ix
Remnants of Auschwitz (Agamben), 202
ressentiment, 38–9, 47–8n25, 164, 165
Resurrection, 167, 169, 172, 173, 176
revolutionary violence, 101
Ross, A., 80, 90, 99
Rousseau, J.-J., 14–15, 80
ruin, 41
Russell's paradox, 95–6

sacralisation, 26
the sacred, 79, 81–5, 201
sacrifice, viii, ix, 21, 59
  in Bataille, 12, 26–8, 67: and the instant, 28–31
  in Girard, 8, 9
  Hubert and Mauss, 23–6
  Manet's paintings, 64
sacrificial victim, vii–viii
Sade, Marquis de, 4, 12–13, 36–8, 198

Sartre, J.-P., 51, 56, 70, 192–3
scapegoat, vii, viii, ix, 2, 8, 9, 16, 141, 151, 158, 160n11, 202
scapegoat mechanism, 133, 137, 150, 156, 164, 167, 173, 175, 177–9, 184
Schmitt, C., 88–9, 96, 185, 188
Second Council of Nicaea, 117–18, 171, 172
sensual object, 192, 193
set theory, 95–7
Sheaffer-Jones, C., 62
shifters, 95, 96
sign, 7
signatures, 92–3, 101
skhesis, 172
'social construction of reality' thesis, vii
society of the spectacle, viii, 1, 5, 6, 109, 116, 121, 126–7
society, origin of, 133–43, 178
  deconstruction of, 143–52
  murder as, 83, 134–43
Socrates, 11
Sontag, S., 52–3, 54–5
sovereign power, viii–ix
sovereignty, 126, 184
  and *homo sacer*, 79–85, 188–9
  and state of exception, 95–7
  and state of nature, 89
  see also law
Spinoza, B., 78
state of exception, 89, 95–7
State of Exception (Agamben), 83, 86, 98, 101
state of nature, 89
statements, 92
Stiegler, B., 153–4
suicide, 64–5
Surya, M., 54
symbolic violence, vi, 196, 197, 199

Tears of Eros (Bataille), 31, 50, 54, 59, 65, 67–9
technics, 153–4
texts, 135, 145, 148–9
theology, 108–9, 112–16
  Byzantine, 117, 118, 172
  of the Cross, 174–7
  of the image, 116–22
  political, 6, 21, 125, 185, 188
thermodynamics, 33
Things Hidden (Girard), 175–6
Third Man, The (Goya), 62
Thus Spoke Zarathustra, 33
time, 30, 33, 110–11, 143
  historical, 93–4
  operational, 111

Titian, 63
torture, 2; see also lingchi photographs
Toscano, A., 119
Totem and Taboo (Freud), 151, 155–6, 157
trace, 7, 17–18n10, 143–4, 149–50
tragedy, 41, 138–9, 140
transcendence, 61, 113
transcendent violence, 22
transgression, 43, 59
transparency of the image, viii, 13–14, 50, 63, 73, 111, 120–1, 128–9
trauma, 199
Tubbs, R., 30
Twilight of the Idols (Nietzsche), 119

utility, 6

Varela, F.J., 134
Vattimo, G., 167, 174, 180, 197
Venus of Urbino (Titian), 63
victim, vi, 202
  in Agamben *see homo sacer*
  in Bataille, vii–viii, 10, 26–8, 54–8, 76n24, 192: animal as, 14, 58–62; and civil identity, 67–9; and context, 69–73; de Rais as, 11–12, 40–4; and the instant, 28–31
  lingchi photographs, 13, 27, 54, 55, 56–7, 65–6, 67–73; Manet's paintings, 14, 64–5; and Sade, 12–13, 37–8; and violence, 1–2, 15–16, 20–3, 40, 196
  in the Bible, 169
  in Girard, vii, viii, 9, 16, 133, 160n11, 183, 202: and Christianity, 164–5, 177–9; and hominisation, 152–9; Oedipus, 141; and violence, 1–2, 14, 15, 137, 150, 184 (*see also* scapegoat)
  Hubert and Mauss, 24–6
  in Nietzsche, 1, 10, 11, 21, 31–2, 35, 38–40, 55, 72–3
  and trauma, 199
victimary mechanism, 176

violence, vi, viii–ix, 2–6, 139, 193, 196–201
  acceptable, 198–9
  in Agamben, 16, 78–101, 200; and image, 5, 126; and law/sovereignty, 6, 80, 82, 83, 84, 85, 87–8, 184; and mediality, 78–9, 85–7, 108; and origin, 93–5; paradigm and history, 88–92; paradigm of the camp, 97–9; and set theory, 95–7; and signatures, 92–3
  in Bataille, 10: acceptable, 198–9; and language, 3–4, 199; and victim, 1–2, 15–16, 20–3, 40, 196
  divine, 5, 78, 98, 99, 101, 122
  in Girard: and Christianity, 201; Crucifixion, ix, 8–10, 163, 179, 200; Heraclitean Logos, 175–6; and origin of society, 133–43, 145, 147–8, 150–2; and victim, 1–2, 14, 15, 184
  and the law, 183–5
  in Nietzsche, 11, 22, 32, 200
  revolutionary, 101
  in Sade, 36–8
  symbolic, vi, 196, 197, 199
  see also cruelty
Violence and the Sacred (Girard), 137, 138

war, 41
Watkin, W., 92, 101
Weber, M., 119
Welles, O., 127
Western culture, viii–ix, 9, 55, 137
Western legal tradition, 186–8
Western politics, viii–ix, 160–1n13
will to power, 11, 18n14, 21, 24–5, 32, 34, 45–6n17, 46n18, 46–7n22, 48n26, 72–3, 77n34
Wolf, H., 52
writing, 149
Wuthering Heights (Brontë), 43

Zhuo, Y., 58, 59, 61